From
the
Earth

Other books by Eileen Yin-Fei Lo

The Dim Sum Book: Classic Recipes from the Chinese Teahouse

The Chinese Banquet Cookbook: Authentic Feasts from China's Regions

China's Food (co-author)

Eileen Yin-Fei Lo's New Cantonese Cooking

從地球大自然

中國蔬菜食譜

From the Earth

Chinese Vegetarian Cooking

Eileen Yin-Fei Lo

Calligraphy by San Yan Wong

Illustrations by Claudia Karabaic Sargent

Instructive diagrams by Jackie Aher

Macmillan • USA

MACMILLAN
A Prentice Hall Macmillan Company
15 Columbus Circle
New York, NY 10023

Library of Congress Cataloging-in-Publication Data

Lo, Eileen Yin-Fei.
From the Earth: Chinese vegetarian cooking / Eileen Yin-Fei Lo.
p.   cm.
Includes index.
ISBN 0-02-632985-9
1. Vegetarian cookery.   2. Cookery, Chinese.   3. Cookery
(Vegetables)   I. Title.
TX837.L54   1995
641.5'636'0951—dc20   94-22664
                                    CIP

Manufactured in the United States of America

10   9   8   7   6   5   4   3   2   1

This book is for Fred, Christopher, Elena, and Stephen,
faithful loving tasters all

Acknowledgments

This book I share with my husband, Fred, who cared about it as deeply as I; and with my children, Christopher, Elena, and Stephen, who tasted, ate, critiqued, and often complained, but never failed to return to the table.

And I thank Carla Glasser, my agent, and my editor, Justin Schwartz, for believing in my book.

Contents

大地食譜

Foods of the Earth

Two days of every month, the first and the fifteenth, were special in the Cantonese household of my grandmother, the small and autocratic woman I always knew as Ah Paw, which means "my mother's mother." She was a Buddhist, and on those days she would eat only vegetables, then retire to the couch in her salon to finger her wooden beads and pray to her ancestors, the names of whom were etched into a series of sticks standing atop a tiny cabinet near the sofa.

This was not only a monthly ritual. In the time of the Lunar New Year she would follow her practice of not eating meat, not consuming anything that had lived, for the first fifteen days of the New Year. And she would honor all of the birthdays in our family the same way.

This was my introduction to vegetarian cooking as a very young girl growing up in China. We were not vegetarians in the strictest interpretation of that word; it was just that on those special days my grandmother observed her Buddhist upbringing. She might take a soup, aromatic with herbs and Chinese parsley, which she liked, and steamed vegetables such as black mushrooms, tiger lily buds, and cloud-ear fungus, seasoned with ginger and often with spring onions, garlic, and black beans. But not too many black beans, not too much garlic, because she believed they imparted too much heat to her system.

I would go to the food markets with my aunt, the one I called Dai Kom Me, which means "mother's brother's first wife." This was something I loved to do, because the food vendors would give me sweets, candied lotus seeds or pieces of candied watermelon rind. We would bring back the foods, and Ah Paw would instruct the servants, and occasionally my uncle's second wife, who was a fine cook, in what to prepare, and how.

1

I never saw my grandmother go into the huge kitchen of her house, with its red-brick wood-burning stoves, but she always knew exactly how everything should be prepared to taste good, and I recall everyone always asking Ah Paw how to make this, how to cook that.

When I asked her about her special days she told me she was observing the laws of Buddha as she chose, according to her beliefs, beliefs that also extended to her absolute abstinence from beef, for that was forbidden by Buddha. On other days she would occasionally eat a bit of poultry, perhaps a small piece of fish. But never on the first or the fifteenth.

The tradition of eating only vegetables has its roots not only in Buddhism but in Taoism as well. Buddhist monks will never eat meat; Taoists may, if they choose, but few do. Eating vegetables became a sometime tradition in China, but as the tradition spread so did interpretations of it. Vegetables, and fruits, are part of the weave of China's fabric, not simply as foods but as part of customary observances. Vegetables are eaten for health and for nourishment, to be sure, but just as important is what is eaten, when, how often, in what season, or in what order, often dictated by the writings of Confucius, by Buddhism, by Taoism, or by mythological beliefs. In China, it is often said, we eat not the food but rather the symbol.

In China the people are surrounded by the earth's abundance, vegetables and fruits from the earth. Particularly in southern China, in the region around Canton, there are two crops of most vegetables each year, as well as the abiding presence of rice. I remember glorying in the seasons and their products—in spring we had papayas, mangoes, all variety of squashes, watercress, and bok choy; in summer there were lettuce, cabbage, carrots, turnips, cucumbers, and peppers; in fall came oranges, lemons, grapefruit, and our second helpings of squashes, gourds, and taro roots; and in winter came lotus and arrowhead roots, winter melon, water chestnuts, and pomegranates.

Because I began cooking, with my father as my teacher, at the age of four, I cannot recall a time when I was not interested in food and its preparation, in what happened to foods when they were cooked. As my aunt did, my father would take me from our home in Sun Tak, a suburb of Canton, into Canton's markets, and as we went about he would tell me to look at vegetables carefully. "Look for green," he would say. "Look to see that there is no yellow in the leaves, no touch of blackness. That happens to vegetables that are old. Look for leaves that are not broken or snapped. Look for roots that still have some dirt on them from the fields." I grew up with a reverence for fresh vegetables and fruits that I cling to to this day.

I remember, as clearly as if it were only yesterday, my grandmother, my aunt, my father, telling me that I must respect those foods that grew in the earth because they had meaning beyond the nourishment they provided.

Scallions were *chung*, and they were to be considered wise because the character for "wise" translates as *chung ming*. And why were they wise? Because scallions are long and hollow, and their hollowness connotes an open mind, open to knowledge, receptive to thought.

Noodles, which we made from wheat flour, meant long life, I always knew, because of their length. Always they were, and are, served on birthdays.

Lettuce—*sahng choi*, words that together mean not only "lettuce" but "lively" and "healthy"—was also a birthday vegetable. Chinese lettuce, quite different from the lettuces that we know in the West, are tiny bundles, much like miniature romaines, and we would serve them with their roots on special days, often hanging a whole lettuce, its root wrapped in lucky red paper, over the entrance to a house before preparing them to eat.

The words for lotus root, *lin ngau*, sound almost like *lin yau*, which means "abundance" or "plenty," and so when we served this vegetable we were wishing prosperity upon our guests.

When we set out fresh squares of bean curd, *daufu*, we hoped that the eater would become a landowner, for the shape of a cake of fresh bean curd represents a square plot of land.

Broccoli always signified jade, because of its color, and jade is the stone of youth. So broccoli is always a vegetable of the young, of youth.

This eating of vegetables for their meaning reached its peak each year at the Lunar New Year, when certain vegetables and fruits simply had to be prepared and served. It is always a day of friendship, good feelings, forgiveness, and renewal, and in our house we set out oranges, honey, sugar cane, and sugar-filled dumplings for their sweetness. Oranges in particular connoted not only sweetness but a continuation of good feelings. Tangerines were for good luck, and grapefruit, with their seeds, stood for abundance and a house full of children.

The same meaning was given to pomegranates, which we cut open not only to eat but also to look at the hundreds of seeds in them. "Many, many seeds mean many, many children, many, many boys," my mother and aunts would say. When my grandfather came to our house, each of his thirteen grandchildren would hold a cup of tea in readiness for him, and he would sip from each cup in turn before giving us each a tangerine, a red paper envelope containing "lucky money" coins, and sprigs of evergreen to help us grow.

At the New Year we would put up calligraphic signs in our house, none larger than that over the large container that held the rice we would eat. The sign would read *seong moon*, "always full." From this stock of rice would come our New Year cake, our *lin goh*, made of rice steamed with sugar-cane sugar, the cake a symbol that the coming year would be better than the last.

Our New Year meal was filled with meaning. We would be certain to have lotus root, with its holes, reminding us to take the time to think things through; and mushrooms, because to us they symbolized opportunities that should be taken. There were, in addition to our good-luck dumplings, vegetable spring rolls, sesame seed dumplings, and cakes made from turnips.

Other observances were not specifically related to particular dates but to occasions, as when a woman was expecting a child. It was a proper and kind gesture for her friends and neighbors to bring to her stalks of ripe wheat, or other grains. This indicated that the friends would share the pain of her childbirth. And when a new baby was to receive her or his first bath, various fruits and garlic were placed in the bath water to sweeten and protect the infant. It was also good luck for those invited to reach down into the water for a piece of fruit or garlic, for they were said to be seeking sons.

After a woman had given birth, it was, and is, customary to boil ginger with black rice vinegar and to eat it, this to build up one's blood.

Special cakes—*hung bau*, or red buns—were steamed for the births of baby girls. The dough was dyed red, and the buns were filled with sweet red bean paste. It was the custom of the time when I was young for the parents of the girl to give these buns to friends and neighbors. I know that my parents followed this custom when I was born.

At Chinese weddings there are no huge, tiered wedding cakes. Instead, small, round, flat cakes of dough, filled with either sweetened lotus seed paste, black bean paste, or red bean paste, were presented by the groom's family to that of the bride. These cakes, called *lo paw bang*, which translates as "wife's cakes," may also be filled with sweet nut paste.

This custom of eating buns to commemorate important occasions also extends to later times in life. Small steamed buns filled with sweet black bean paste and shaped like peaches are customarily given to people observing their sixty-fifth birthdays. Once this custom was only for the elderly. However, these peach buns now are given to birthday celebrants of all ages.

Most Chinese believed in the medicinal properties of vegetables and fruits as well, since they were traditionally associated with elements of the universe and with parts of the body. Many continue to do so today. The five flavors of food are sweet, sour, bitter, pungent, and salty. These relate, respectively, to earth, wood, fire, metal, and water, and to the stomach, liver, heart, lungs, and kidneys.

It is also believed that foods have innate characters, ranging from hot to very cold. Soybeans are considered sweet, with a warm character, but when cooked they are said to become hot. Leeks, though pungent, are warm; spinach, though sweet, has a cold character, it is believed; and vinegar, acidic and sweet, is nevertheless considered to be warm. Many people to this day in China eat foods that they believe balance their bodily systems between heat and cold, dryness and moisture, sweetness and sourness.

Early in the Ming dynasty, in the fourteenth century, a Confucian scholar, Chia Ming, wrote a treatise on the properties of various foods called *Yin Shih Hsu Chih*, the "Essential Knowledge of Eating and Drinking." In it he delineated the characters of fifty different grains, beans, and seeds; eighty-seven vegetables; sixty-three fruits and nuts; and thirty-three flavorings such as vinegars, oils, and sauces. An excellent account of this work appears in *Food in Chinese Culture*, edited by K. C. Chang and published by Yale University Press.

The presence of a wide variety of vegetables through the ages in China has been documented by many. It is known that in ancient China millet, wheat, and barley were important cultivated grains to be cooked—not to the extent of *fon*, rice, to be sure, but they were nevertheless grown widely. Of ancient lineage as well are soybeans, taro, and broad beans, and it is known that China abounded in vegetables and fruit that grew wild—melons, gourds, turnips, leeks, spring onions, bamboo shoots, lettuce, beans, lotus root, Chinese cabbage, mustard greens, garlic, and water chestnuts.

Two decades ago archaeologists uncovered a Han dynasty tomb in Hunan, and much was learned from it about vegetables and fruits in China, two hundred years before Christ. This tomb held within it the remains of a wealthy woman who was buried with forty-eight bamboo boxes and fifty-one pottery containers filled with various foods including rice, mustard, pears, plums, strawberries, ginger, lotus root, cinnamon bark, and that variety of ginger known as sand ginger or *galangal*. Not only were these vessels found, but there were slips of paper that mentioned other vegetables and fruits as being cultivated and eaten in China in 200 B.C.—bamboo shoots, melons, taro, ginger, sugar, salt, honey, soy sauce, fermented black beans. All of these are today part of the modern Chinese kitchen.

The Chinese way with vegetables is, then, not new. It is, however, constantly changing, being reaffirmed, renewed, and altered slightly with new foods. Its techniques have not changed. Vegetables are still steamed, stir-fried, deep-fried, blanched, and occasionally slow-cooked. The Chinese way is inherently healthful. Do not think of those masses of vegetables swimming in thickened cornstarch, for years the norm in the most mediocre of restaurants calling themselves Chinese. Think instead of the true, the traditional, methods the Chinese employ when cooking vegetables, a tradition wedded to the land.

What for years was thought of as Chinese cooking in the West was a cuisine of expediency. When Chinese men first immigrated to the United States and headed to the California gold fields or to the transcontinental railroad work gangs, they came without women; they cooked with whatever was at hand, whatever could be prepared quickly. It was this adaptive cuisine that came to be confused with true Chinese cooking, the more so when it became the food served in restaurants that called themselves Chinese.

True Chinese cooking is what I remember from the kitchen in my grandmother's house. We ate vegetables cooked so that they came to our table firm and crisp. We pickled vegetables and fruits for snacks or as additions to our meals. We made vegetable salads. We reveled in the diverse ways *daufu* could be prepared. We waited expectantly for the seasons so we could eat those fruits and vegetables that came at special times of the year.

Today I cook no differently from how I did as a young girl in Sun Tak, later in Hong Kong. I still steam vegetables carefully so that they are subjected to moist heat for just the right amount of time so they can be served with their characters intact, their fabric not destroyed. I stir-fry now as I did then, utilizing the principle of *wok hei,* which means "great flame," in which foods are whisked through a bit of oil at great speeds so that they cook quickly yet retain their youth. And how do I season? With a bit of salt, perhaps a pinch of white pepper, with a touch of soy, some drops of the oils and sauces I have created, with stock.

The differences today are in the varieties of vegetables and fruits. As is done in China and Hong Kong today, I cook with foods that have come lately to China—tomatoes, potatoes, yams, and peanuts, among others. I use curries that have come to China from India and Southeast Asia along with other spices and flavorings. These, however, do not change the basics, nor do they alter the fact that Chinese cooking is perhaps the most healthful in the world. In the Chinese kitchen nothing comes between fruits and vegetables in their natural state and the person who consumes them. How else to define healthful eating? I think Ah Paw would agree with that.

中
廚

The Chinese Kitchen

The wide variety of foods of the Chinese kitchen have become ever more familiar to Western tastes. With familiarity and recognition has come wider use, and these days more and more people, including chefs, shop in Chinese and other Asian groceries with confidence. It seems that every market, no matter its size, carries Chinese ingredients. This is to the good. Only a very few of the special foods and ingredients in this book are not available everywhere. The rest you will find in your local market or in Chinese and Asian shops. Most of the spices, oils, and condiments, as well as the bottled, jarred, and tinned foods and the soys, are of Chinese origin and are imported from the People's Republic of China, Hong Kong, Singapore, and Taiwan. Of late they have been joined by imports from Southeast Asia, the Philippines, Indonesia, Malaysia, Korea, and Japan.

Most are available by mail order as well, particularly those ingredients that are prepared, preserved, or dried, and advertisements for them can be found in the better cookery magazines. Brands have also proliferated. I have refrained from recommending brands except in instances where I believe a particular one is far superior to its counterparts and thus, in my opinion, essential to the recipe.

Bamboo leaves. See "Lotus leaves and bamboo leaves," page 13.

竹
筍

Bamboo shoots. These pale yellow shoots are the young beginnings of bamboo trees. They are spear shaped. Rarely, except on the West Coast, are fresh bamboo shoots available, and the few that reach other markets are often discolored and dried out. Use those that have been cooked and canned in water. Winter bamboo shoots are considered to be more desirable because they are generally more tender and of better quality. Cans will read "winter bamboo shoots" or "bamboo shoots, tips." The latter are as good as those labeled

7

"winter" and are less expensive. I prefer those that come in larger chunks, so that they can be cut to my particular specification. Once the can is open, shoots must be removed to another container. They will keep for 2 to 3 weeks in water, in a closed container, if the water is changed daily.

Bean curd, fresh. Called *daufu* by the Chinese and *tofu* by the Japanese, fresh bean curd comes in square cakes, 2½ to 3 inches on a side. Made from soybean liquid, or milk, the cakes are custardlike. I prefer the individual cakes rather than those that come several to the package or in large blocks, as the latter are sometimes old. Bean curd has little taste of its own, and its versatility lies in its ability to absorb the tastes of the foods with which it is combined. It may be kept refrigerated in a container of water, tightly closed, with the water changed daily. So treated, it will keep for 2 to 3 weeks.

Bean curd, dried. When bean curd is being prepared, a film forms on top of the soybean liquid. This is dried and cut into rectangular pieces about 1½ by 5 inches and about 1⁄8 inch thick. Ideally it is sun-dried, but more commonly the drying is done in factories under heat. It is then packaged in paper wrap labeled "dried bean curd, slice type." It is brittle and should be handled carefully. Kept in a closed container in a cool, dry place, dried bean curd will keep for at least a year.

Bean curd cakes. These begin as fresh bean curd formed into smaller cakes. They are pressed to remove almost all moisture, then cooked in water flavored with five-spice seasoning and soy sauce. They are dried and then packaged, six to an 8-ounce pack. They are brown in color and are usually labeled "soybean cake." They also come loosely bundled in a smaller size, about two dozen to the pack, and in larger sizes in bags of 10 ounces or 1 pound. The larger cakes tend to be white inside and have a milder taste. The smaller ones are spicier, with an added taste of chili. I recommend those that come six to a package, with the faint taste of anise imparted by the five-spice seasoning.

Bean curd skins, fresh. Like dried bean curd, this is a by-product of the cooking of soybean milk. Though it is made of the same film that forms in the cooking, it is thinner than dried bean curd, more flexible, and a bit moist. Usually it comes in round sheets, about 2 feet in diameter, folded in a plastic package and stored in the refrigerated sections of markets. These sheets usually come to the stores frozen, eight to a package. Often a retailer will separate them and create four packages of two skins each, which is often how they are sold. If you ask for them frozen you may receive a package of eight. Bean curd skins should be used as quickly as possible because they tend to become dry. They must be kept refrigerated. Take care to keep unused portions in a closed bag, because exposure to air, even for only a few minutes, will make them brittle. Refrigerated they will keep at least 2 weeks.

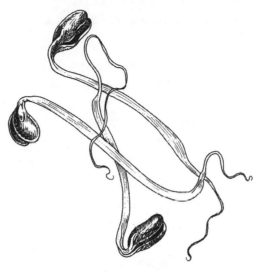

Soybean Sprouts

芽

菜

Bean sprouts. There are two varieties. The first, mung bean sprouts, are white and plump, with a decided crunch, and are grown from mung beans. They are sold by weight in Chinese groceries and can be stored in plastic bags in which holes have been punched. They must be stored in the refrigerator, and they will keep no more than 4 days, after which they become less firm and colorless.

The second variety, soybean sprouts, are also white, but longer than mung bean sprouts, with a yellow soybean at the tip. Storage is exactly the same as for mung bean sprouts.

粉

絲

Bean thread noodles. These are often called simply bean threads, or vermicelli bean threads, or cellophane noodles. They are made when mung beans are moistened, mashed, strained, and formed into very thin, white noodles. They come in ½-pound packages, or in 1-pound packages divided into eight 2-ounce bundles. Avoid other large packs of irregularly shaped sheets and long, thick, rough sticks, both of which are labeled "dried bean thread" and are sandy brown in color. They are made with soybeans and should not be confused with bean thread noodles. (Note: These latter are not used in this book. I note them in order to avoid any confusion.) There are also mung bean noodles, which are used in this book. See the section on noodles.

豉
鼓

Black beans, fermented. These fragrant beans are preserved in salt. They come either in plastic-wrapped packs or in cans. I prefer the packages, lightly flavored with ginger and orange peel. Before the beans are used, the salt must be rinsed off. They will keep for as long as a year, without refrigeration, as long as they are kept in a tightly sealed container. I do not recommend jarred black beans, nor are they used in any of the recipes in this book.

白
菜

Bok choy. This is surely China's most popular vegetable. The white-stalked, green-leafed vegetable, known as the "white vegetable" in Canton, is quite versatile because of its crispness and sweetness. It is sold by weight. It is often referred to as Chinese cabbage, but that is an error because it bears no resemblance to cabbage. It will keep for about a week in the vegetable drawer of a refrigerator, but it tends to lose its sweetness quickly, so I recommend using it when fresh.

上
海
白
菜

Bok choy, Shanghai. Smaller than the usual bok choy, it is bulb-shaped at bottom and its stalks come together at the top, rather than flowering. The stalks are pale green and the leaves are darker green. If you ask for Shanghai bok choy, you may be looked at strangely. In that case, simply ask for *tong choi*; you will receive it and will be rewarded with its sweetness.

原
鼓

Brown bean sauce. Also called yellow or ground bean sauce. It is made from fermented soybeans and wheat flour with sugar and soy sauce added.

Chinese Chives (dried and soaked)

蕹菜 **Chives, Chinese.** These are also known as garlic chives. They are more pungent than the American chive and are wider and flatter, though of the same deep green color. Yellow chives are the same vegetable, but they are deprived of sun and thus take on a lighter color. They are more delicate than green chives and milder, with more of the taste of onion than garlic.

菜心 *Choi sum.* This is a green, leafy vegetable with thin, tender stalks. It is all green, from its large outside leaves to the smaller inside leaves to the light green stalks, which are crisp and sweet. *Choi sum*, like other leafy vegetables, tends to lose its sweetness and so should be eaten as soon as possible.

雲茸 **Cloud ears.** Also called tree ears. They are fungi that when dried look a bit like round chips, either brown or brown-black. When they are soaked in water they soften and resemble flower petals. They may be kept indefinitely in a closed jar in a cool, dry place.

芫茜 **Coriander, fresh.** Also called cilantro and Chinese parsley. This is similar in appearance to parsley. It has a strong aroma and imparts a distinctive taste when used as a flavoring agent or a garnish. Often it is suggested that Italian parsley be used as a substitute. Do not follow that suggestion. There is no substitute for coriander. It should be used fresh so that its bouquet will be appreciated, but it may be kept refrigerated for a week to 10 days.

咖喱粉 **Curry powder.** A blend of spices, such as turmeric, cumin, fennel, and coriander seeds, plus others added. There are many brands of curry powder on the market. I prefer the stronger, more pungent brands from India, in particular the Madras brand.

茄子 **Eggplant, Chinese.** This bright purple eggplant is shaped somewhat like a cucumber and is about the same size. Its taste is like that of the eggplant most of us are used to, but its skin is quite tender and need not be removed before cooking.

五香調味 **Five-spice seasoning.** This is often used to flavor prepared foods like soybean cakes. The five spices of any combination can be of the following: star anise, fennel seeds, cinnamon, cloves, ginger root, licorice, nutmeg, and Szechuan peppercorns. Different makers prefer different mixtures, though anise and cinnamon predominate. You may devise your own five-spice seasoning by asking for a ready-mixed packet at a Chinese herbal shop. The herbalist will be only too happy to oblige. Often the spices are ground into a powder that is quite pungent and used only sparingly in dishes that demand strong flavors.

Garlic chives. See "Chives, Chinese," page 11.

生薑 **Ginger, fresh.** Also known as ginger root. This is one ingredient that you cannot do without in the Chinese kitchen. When selecting ginger roots look for those with smooth outer skins, because ginger begins to wrinkle and roughen with age. It flavors well, and the Chinese believe that it greatly reduces stomach acidity. It is used sparingly and should be sliced, and often peeled, before use. Its strength is often dictated by its preparation. In this book I use large chunks of ginger, I slice it, I peel it and leave it unpeeled, I often smash it lightly, and I julienne it, mince it, and shred it. When placed in a heavy brown paper bag and refrigerated, it will keep for 4 to 6 weeks. I do not recommend trying to preserve it in wine, or freezing it, because it loses strength. Nor do I recommend ground ginger or bottled ginger juice as cooking substitutes, because for fresh ginger there is no substitute. There is also young ginger, which is very smooth, slightly pink in color, and without the tough skin of older ginger. It is quite crisp. It is often called spring ginger, but that is a misnomer; it grows not in the spring but twice each year, late in the summer and in January and February. I use this young ginger to make my own Ginger Pickle (page 295). Pickled ginger is also available in jars and is a passable substitute.

白菜 **Gingko nuts.** Hard-shelled nuts shaped like tiny footballs, these are the seeds of the gingko tree, a common shade tree in China. The fruit is not edible, but the nuts are, when cooked. Pale green when raw, they become translucent when cooked. They are available fresh or canned. When fresh they require cooking (page 100). Those in cans are already cooked. Raw nuts will keep, refrigerated, in a plastic bag, for 4 to 6 weeks. Cooked, they will keep only 4 to 5 days. Canned nuts, when opened, should be used within a week. Both raw and canned nuts should be refrigerated.

 Hair seaweed. Dried seaweed called "hair" because of its black strands. It comes in packages of various sizes. It will keep indefinitely, in a closed jar in a cool, dry place.

 Hairy melon. This is a gourd-shaped green melon, generally larger than a cucumber, with fine fuzz covering its exterior. It is a cousin to the winter melon, and like the winter melon it tends to take on the flavors of the foods with which it is cooked.

海
鮮
醬 **Hoisin sauce.** A thick, chocolate-brown sauce made from soybeans, garlic, sugar, and chilies. Some brands add a little vinegar to the mix; others thicken the sauce with flour. Hoisin comes in large cans or jars, as well as in bottles. If purchased in a can, it should be transferred to jars and refrigerated. It will keep for many months.

豆
瓣
醬 **Horse beans preserved with chili.** The horse bean is the lima bean. To make this sauce, the beans are cooked, mashed, and mixed with ground chilies. It is a very spicy sauce and adds good heat to many dishes. It comes in jars that, once opened, must be refrigerated. It will keep for months.

辣
油 **Hot oil.** There are many brands of hot oil on market shelves. Only too often, however, they are based on inferior oils. It is preferable that you make your own. It is not difficult (page 36) and will be ultimately more satisfying. Also, you will be left with hot pepper flakes at the bottom of your oil, a bonus with many uses.

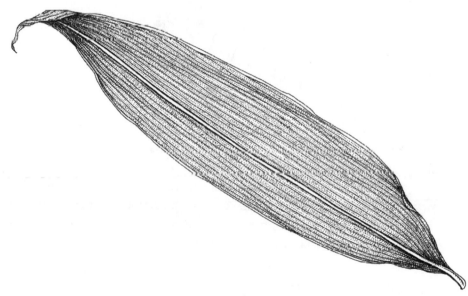

Bamboo Leaf

蓮 竹
葉 葉 **Lotus leaves and bamboo leaves.** Dried leaves used as wrappings for various steamed preparations. Lotus leaves impart a distinctive, somewhat sweet taste to the food they are wrapped around, and they are preferable to bamboo leaves. However, lotus leaves are usually sold commercially only to restaurants in

50-pound boxes. Bamboo leaves can easily be bought in smaller quantities and are quite good substitutes, but their taste and smell are different. Kept in a plastic bag in a dry place, the dried leaves will keep for 6 months to a year. If you are able to obtain fresh lotus leaves, then by all means use them fresh, or sun-dry them yourself for future use.

蓮
藕

Lotus root. This is the gourd-shaped root of the lotus. The roots often grow four or five together, connected like a string of sausages, each about 3 inches in diameter and 4 to 5 inches long. When the root is cut across, there is a pattern of holes not unlike the holes found in Swiss cheese. The texture is light, a bit dry, and crisp. Lotus root should be kept refrigerated in a brown paper bag and used within a few days of purchase, since it tends to lose both flavor and texture quickly.

Lotus Seeds

蓮
子

Lotus seeds. The olive-shaped seeds from the lotus pod. These are regarded as a delicacy by the Chinese and are priced accordingly, by weight. They may be kept for as long as a month at room temperature in a tightly sealed jar. I do not recommend keeping them that long, however, for their flavor weakens and their texture becomes tough over time.

冬
菇

Mushrooms, Chinese black. These dried mushrooms come in boxes or cellophane packs. They are black, dark gray, or speckled in color, and their caps range from about the size of a nickel to 3 inches in diameter. Those in boxes are the choicest, both in size and color, and are more expensive. Chinese black mushrooms must always be soaked in hot water for at least ½ hour before use, their stems removed and discarded, and they should be thoroughly cleaned on the underside of the cap and squeezed dry. In their dried form they will keep indefinitely in a tightly closed container. If you live in an especially damp or humid climate they should be stored in the freezer.

草
菰
菇 **Mushrooms, straw.** Small mushrooms with elongated, domelike caps. They are common in southern China and highly prized by the Cantonese. Occasionally to be found fresh, they are most often canned. Even when used from the can, they are regarded as a special food given to a favored guest.

Mustard pickle. See "Szechuan mustard pickle," page 18.

生
麵 **Noodles.** There are many variations on the noodle in China. There are wheat-flour noodles, fresh and dried, of various widths, made from flour sometimes mixed with eggs, often simply of flour and water. There are rice noodles, also fresh and dried, of various widths. Very fine rice noodles are often called rice sticks. (There is another food called rice noodle which is not a noodle. See "Rice noodle," page 16.) And there are mung bean noodles, in addition to the bean threads listed above. These are usually shaped like linguine and need only be soaked in hot water before use.

For most of the noodle dishes in this book, most types of noodle will be quite suitable. (Even fine vermicelli or cappellini pastas, fresh or dried, will substitute quite well, if you wish.) I have, however, given my preferences with the individual recipes.

油
類 **Oils.** Peanut oil is the preferred oil of the Chinese kitchen, not only for its healthful attributes but for the fine nutty flavor it imparts. I have used peanut oil, and sesame oil, to create a series of flavored and spiced oils and sauces to use in preparing various recipes in this book, to accompany dishes, and to use as dips. They are detailed in the portion of the book devoted to oils and condiments, pages 36–44.

蠔
油 **Oyster sauce.** A thick sauce, the base of which is ground dried oysters. It is a highly prized seasoning in China, not only for the flavor it imparts but for its richness of color. It is highly regarded by Buddhists, because the oyster is an allowed food in their vegetarian diet. Once opened, a bottle of oyster sauce must be refrigerated. It will keep indefinitely. It will also keep for a good period unrefrigerated, if used often and quickly, but I prefer to refrigerate it.

紅
豆 **Red beans.** These small, deep-red beans are used generally in sweet preparations, although occasionally they are combined with other foods in casseroles. The beans are sold in plastic sacks by weight and will keep indefinitely. Red beans are most often used in their paste form, made by mashing cooked beans and sweetening them with sugar. Red bean paste comes in cans and is used as a filling in pastries and in sweet desserts. Once a can is opened, the bean paste must be kept refrigerated in a closed container. It will keep for 4 to 6 weeks.

Rice. An entire portion of this book is devoted to rice in all of its forms. It begins on page 125.

Rice noodle. Known as *sah hor fun*, or "sand river noodle," this is not strictly a noodle. It does not come in strands or bunches but rather in sheets, occasionally round, usually square. It is snowy white with a glistening shiny surface when bought fresh—as it should be—and is usually oiled and folded before packing. Before using rice noodle you must carefully unfold it and cut the pieces you need from it. It cannot be stored at room temperature but must be refrigerated (it will keep 3 days) or frozen (it will keep 1 to 2 months). After refrigeration or freezing, it must be brought to room temperature and steamed to restore its pliability. Rice noodle is sold in noodle factories in cities' Chinese neighborhoods, and some food shops will get it for you upon request.

Rock sugar or rock candy. This is a compound of white sugar, raw brown sugar, and honey. It comes in 1-pound sacks and looks like a collection of small amber rocks.

Sah Gut. Commonly known in the West as jícama, this bulbous root is sweet and crisp, with a sand-colored exterior and white interior. It can be eaten raw or cooked. In Mexico and the Southwest, it is known as jícama, reflecting its origin. Jícama has been adopted widely and cultivated in Asia. Stored in a brown paper bag and refrigerated, it will keep 3 to 4 days.

Sesame oil. This is an aromatic oil with a strong, nutlike smell, used both as a cooking oil and as an additive or dressing. It is made from sesame seeds. Adding a bit of this oil to an already prepared dish imparts fine flavor, particularly in the case of some soups. It is thick and brown in versions from China and Japan, thinner and lighter from the Middle East. I recommend the former. Stored in a tightly closed bottle at room temperature, it will keep at least 4 months.

Sesame seeds, black and white. Black seeds, either roasted or not, are customarily used as a decoration or as an ingredient in the preparation of sweet fillings. Roasted white seeds are generally used in dumpling fillings or as garnishes and occasionally in the making of sweets as well.

Sesame seed paste. Also called tahini, this is a paste made by mixing ground white sesame seeds with soybean oil. It comes in jars. It is smooth, with the consistency of peanut butter, and its sesame taste is quite pronounced. After opening, the jar should be refrigerated. It will keep for 6 months.

紹
興
酒

Shao-Hsing wine. This is a sherrylike wine made and bottled in the People's Republic of China and in Taiwan. There are several grades. I use not only the basic wine, but also the best refined grade of Shao-Hsing, which is labeled *hua tiao chiew*. You may simply ask for *Far Jiu*, which is a generic term, like "burgundy." Take care not to buy something called "Shao-Hsing Wine for Cooking." I use Shao-Hsing widely in this book, as you will note, for it adds a great deal to individual dishes. Dry sherry is an acceptable substitute.

絲
瓜

Silk squash. A somewhat odd, thin, cucumber-shaped gourd, with pronounced ridges running along its length. It is deep green, but its flesh is white and faintly sweet with a soft texture. It is very good in soups.

酸
菜

Sour mustard pickle. This leafy, cabbagelike vegetable is called *kai choy* by the Chinese, or "leaf-mustard cabbage." Its taste is strong and distinctive. It is used fresh but more commonly in its preserved form, water-blanched and cured with salt and vinegar. It is best in stir-fried dishes and soups. It is sold loose by weight, or in cans. The cans will read "sour mustard pickle" or "sour mustard greens" or simply "mustard greens." If bought loose, place in a tightly sealed plastic container and keep refrigerated, for not more than 2 weeks. Once cans are opened, the greens should be stored in the same manner, and they have the same storage life.

鼓
油

Soy sauce. This comes in light and dark varieties. The light soys are usually taken from the top of the batches being prepared, the darker soys from the bottom. Both are made from soybeans, flour, salt, and water. There are many brands from many countries, but I believe the best-quality soy sauce is a Hong Kong brand called *Yuet Heung Yuen*. The light soy from this manufacturer is labeled "pure soybean sauce"; the dark soy (it is often called "double dark") is marked "C soy sauce." Dark soys are best for imparting a rich color to a dish; light soys are used for their somewhat sweeter taste. There is even a soy sauce flavored with mushrooms, and it is so labeled. The Chinese believe soys give body and richness to cooking. I often combine the various soys for different tastes and colorings, as you will see. Some soys come in cans, though most are bottled. If in a can, transfer to a bottle. Soy can be kept indefinitely in a tightly capped bottle at room temperature.

Star anise. Often called eight-star anise, this is the tiny, eight-pointed dried fruit of the Chinese anise tree. The flavor of this spice is more pronounced than that of aniseed. It should be kept in a tightly sealed jar in a cool, dry place. It will keep for a year but will gradually lose its fragrance.

Szechuan mustard pickle. Also called mustard pickle, it is made from Chinese radishes cooked with chili powder and salt. It can be added to soups and stir-fried with vegetables. It is never used fresh, only in preserved form. It can be bought loose, by weight, but more often can be found in cans labeled "Szechuan preserved vegetables" or "Szechuan mustard pickle." As you can see, the labeling is not always precise, so be careful when you shop so that you obtain the correct vegetable. Szechuan mustard pickle should not be confused with "Sour mustard pickle" (page 17).

Szechuan peppercorn. Quite different from the usual peppercorn, this is reddish in color and not solid but open. In Canton it is called flower peppercorn because of its shape. It is not hot or peppery, but rather mild. Store these peppercorns in a tightly capped jar as you would ordinary peppercorns. Several recipes call for ground Szechuan peppercorns. These cannot be bought; you must grind them yourself. To do so, use a mortar and pestle, or smash with the broad side of a cleaver blade, then strain through a sieve. Store in a tightly closed jar. Once ground, Szechuan pepper can be used as a base for a flavored oil (page 38).

Tapioca starch. Also called tapioca flour, it is made from the starch of the cassava root. Much of it comes packaged from Thailand. It is used as a basic ingredient in some doughs, as a thickener for sauces, or as a coating. Store as you would any flour.

Taro Root

芋
頭

Taro root. This is a starchy root of the taro plant. It is called *poi* in Hawaii and is somewhat like a potato but is more fibrous and is tinged throughout its interior with fine purple threads. It must be eaten cooked, usually steamed or boiled. When the taro root steams, it emits a pleasant chestnutlike aroma. After cooking it can be mashed. When stir-fried, it can be cooked in the raw state.

天
津
白
菜

Tientsin bok choy. Often called Tientsin cabbage, celery cabbage, or Napa cabbage, it comes in two varieties, a long-stalked type and a rounder sort that is much leafier. It is the latter variety that is most often labeled with the city of its origin (or Tianjin, the new spelling). It is also the sweeter of the two, and I prefer it. It is at its best in spring. It may be kept refrigerated in a plastic bag for about a week, but like bok choy, it tends to lose its sweetness, so I suggest using it early.

冬
菜

Tientsin (Tianjin) preserved vegetable. This is a mixture of Tientsin bok choy, garlic, and salt. It comes either in crocks from the the People's Republic of China or in plastic bags from Hong Kong. The crocks are labeled "Tientsin Preserved Vegetable" or "Tianjin Preserved Vegetable."

金
針
菜

Tiger lily buds. Elongated, reddish brown lily buds that have been dried. They are also known as golden needles. The best are those that have a softness to them and are not dry and brittle. Sold in packages, they will keep indefinitely in a tightly covered jar stored in a cool place.

Tree ears. See "Cloud ears," page 11.

蘿
蔔

Turnips, Chinese. These large, white vegetables are 8 inches long (or longer) and 2 to 3 inches across at their thickest point. They have an admirable crispness and can be nearly as hot as radishes. They will keep for a week in a refrigerator vegetable drawer but are best used promptly.

浙
红
醋

Vinegar, Chinkiang. This very strong, aromatic red vinegar made from rice is used widely in the kitchens of Chiu Chow and Hakka. It has a distinctive taste. Red wine vinegar may be used in its place, but it is not a true substitute.

Water chestnuts. These are not actually nuts. Rather, they are bulbs, deep purplish brown in color, that grow in muddy water. To peel fresh water chestnuts is time-consuming, but once done the rewards are great. The meat of the water chestnut is sweet, juicy, crisp, and utterly delicious. Canned water chestnuts are a barely adequate, though serviceable, substitute. In fact, if you cannot find fresh water chestnuts I would rather you use fresh jícama instead of the canned chestnuts. Quite versatile, water chestnuts can be eaten raw, or stir-fried, or used in soups. They are even ground into a flour that is used to make pastries. They should be eaten fresh for the greatest enjoyment. As they age they become less firm, more starchy, and less sweet. If you keep their skins on, with the mud remnants, and refrigerate them in brown paper bags, they will keep 4 to 5 weeks. Peeled and placed in a container with cold water and refrigerated, they will keep 4 or 5 days, provided the water is changed daily. Canned water chestnuts may be stored similarly.

馬蹄粉 **Water chestnut powder.** Used to make cakes or to thicken sauces. Sauces containing this powder will give the foods over which they are poured a shiny, glazed appearance.

澄麵粉 **Wheat starch.** The remains of wheat flour when the wheat's protein is removed to make gluten. This starch is the basis for some dumpling wrappers and has other uses, as a flour, as well. The starch will keep for at least a year if stored in a tightly sealed container and kept in a cool, dry place.

冬瓜 **Winter melon.** This looks a bit like a watermelon and has the same oblong-round shape. Its skin is dark green and occasionally mottled, while its interior is greenish white with white seeds. Winter melon has the characteristic of absorbing the flavors of whatever it is cooked with. When it is cooked, usually in soups, or steamed, the melon becomes translucent. Often the whole melon is used as a tureen, with other ingredients steamed inside of it after it has been hollowed out. It should be used almost immediately, for it tends to dry quickly, particularly after it has been cut. It is usually sold by weight.

包皮類 **Wrappers.** Various wrappers are used in this book and are discussed at length in the individual recipes. There are won ton wrappers, spring roll skins, egg roll skins, Shanghai spring roll skins, water dumpling skins, and rice paper.

Chui Ngai
Kitchen Techniques

Chui Ngai. These two words say it all. Kitchen techniques. The very special techniques of the Chinese kitchen, its implements, its basics. Chinese cooking utensils differ from those of the chefs of France and of Italy, and its classic techniques are so different. There is no battery of knives; there is the cleaver. There is no collection of pots; there is the wok, perhaps the world's finest all-purpose cookpot.

And the skills needed to use those tools, while simple, are different. Stir-frying in the wok. Using it to deep-fry and to steam, to blanch vegetables and to boil noodles. The use of aromatic leaves to wrap foods and to impart flavor to them. These processes may seem daunting initially. Often people will say that they lack the ability to cook in the Chinese manner. Do not believe it.

Learning to cook the Chinese way is not in the least difficult. I have taught many, many people to cook everything from perfectly boiled rice to vegetable preparations of many steps and many ingredients. While it is true that representations of the foods of all regions of China can be eaten in restaurants these days, that should not be an excuse for not learning how to prepare what I and others consider the most creative and varied cuisine in the world. Not to learn is to cheat yourself out of the satisfaction and well-being that come with accomplishment.

Chinese cooking, perhaps more than any other, is an art that changes constantly. It is added to, altered by the talents of its practitioners. It is a living cuisine. But it is not mysterious. Really. It has only to be learned, and learning the techniques of Chinese cooking is anything but tedious. Rather, it is a delight. Nor should you be awed by the idea of preparing a meal of several courses. Many dishes can be prepared ahead, or those that require less preparation can be paired with those needing more. The fun is in the challenge. The

21

reward is in the eating. It seems to me that a few hours spent to prepare something that will be both beautiful to contemplate and delicious to taste is time well spent. I remember my grandmother telling me, when I was a little girl and my father was teaching me to cook, that the most important asset you could bring to learning to cook was patience. Then you could create something that brings happiness and smiles of satisfaction to the faces of those who are enjoying your efforts. Is that not a fine reward? It is to me.

That is the sort of thinking I have tried to transmit to my students through the years, that the process itself is delicious.

The key to this enjoyment is to do things correctly and with economy. Ingredients and utensils must be prepared. Any cookery can be overpowering and frustrating if you are ill prepared, and Chinese cuisine, with its disciplines, is no different. Yet it can be relatively free of most concerns if you attend to basics. Basics means not only familiarizing yourself with the different vegetables, sauces, oils, and spices, but learning their properties and the techniques that enhance them. It also means learning the capacities of the tools necessary to work with these foods.

中
式
鑊

Wok. The range of woks these days is wide, though unfortunately most of them are inadequate. The best to use is one made of carbon steel, with a diameter of about 14 inches. It is the all-purpose Chinese cooking utensil, used for stir-frying, deep-frying, dry-roasting, and sauce making. With the addition of bamboo steamers it is also perfect for steaming food.

A carbon-steel wok, available in Chinese or Asian markets, will cost only about six dollars and will be perfect when properly seasoned. There are many other kinds of woks available—made of stainless steel, aluminum, and various thicknesses of iron. I do not recommend any of these for general use, particularly stir-frying, although the stainless steel wok is fine for steaming. In most cases these woks are more expensive than the best carbon-steel ones. Nor do I favor any of the Teflon-coated woks. Chinese stir-frying requires intense, direct heat, and such heat can damage, or loosen, this coating.

If the wok is to be used several times in the course of one cooking session, then it should be wiped with a towel, over heat, before each use. The wok is best used with a wok ring that steadies it over the flame.

鑊
蓋

Wok cover. Usually of aluminum, this cover, about 12 to 13 inches in diameter with a top handle, sits firmly in the wok. It enables the wok to be used for stews, for steaming, and for boiling. Years ago in China it was made of wood.

Wok brush. This is a slightly oversized, oar-shaped wooden brush with long, very stiff bristles. It is used, with exceedingly hot water, to clean all of the cooking residue from the wok without any detergents.

Wok ring. This is a hollow steel base that nestles over a single stove burner. The round base of the wok settles into it firmly, thus ensuring that the wok is steady on the stove and that the flames of the burner will surround it.

 Bamboo steamers. Circular frames of bamboo with woven bamboo mesh bases and covers, these come in various sizes, but those 12 to 13 inches in diameter are preferred because they sit quite nicely in the wok. Foods rest on the woven bamboo, and steam passes up through the spaces. The steamers can be stacked two or three high so that different foods can be steamed simultaneously. Steamers are also made of aluminum and of wood with bamboo mesh bases. There are also small steamers, usually of bamboo or stainless steel, that are often used for individual servings. Also useful for steaming are the steel insets that fit into pots, usually used for such items as asparagus, corn, or pasta. For the recipes in this book, two bamboo steamers and one cover should be sufficient.

Chinese spatula. This is a shovel-shaped tool available in either carbon steel or stainless steel, and in different sizes. The carbon steel spatula has become rare in recent years. For the recipes in this book, a stainless steel spatula is recommended. If a carbon steel spatula is to be used several times in the course of one cooking session, then it should be wiped with a towel, over heat, before each use.

Chinese cleaver. This is another all-purpose tool. It cuts and dices. It minces, and its flat blade and its handle can mash. It can be used as a dough scraper. Usually of carbon steel with a wood handle, it is also available in stainless steel, either with a wood handle or with blade and handle of one piece of steel. There are different sizes. I prefer, for the recipes in this book, a stainless steel cleaver with a wood handle, the blade of which is 8 inches long and 3½ inches wide. Try to find a professional tool made by Dexter in the United States.

 Bamboo chopsticks. In addition to being what the Chinese eat with, these are marvelous cooking tools. They make fine stirrers, mixers, and serving pieces and are available usually in packages of ten. Avoid plastic chopsticks. They cannot be used for cooking and are more difficult to manipulate than those of bamboo.

Chinese strainer. This is a circular steel-mesh strainer attached to a long split-bamboo handle. Strainers come in many sizes, from as small as a person's palm to as large as 14 inches in diameter. For all-purpose use I prefer one 10 inches in diameter. As an option, there are rather large all-stainless-steel strainers made by piercing holes in a circle of steel. They may either have wood handles or be of one piece of steel, their handles hollow steel tubes. Both of these come in a 10-inch-diameter size.

The following will complete your Chinese kitchen:

> Frying pan, cast-iron, 10 inches in diameter
>
> Round cake pan
>
> Selection of steamproof dishes
>
> Strainer, fine all-purpose
>
> Large ladle
>
> Small hand grater
>
> Garlic press
>
> Kitchen shears
>
> Cooking thermometer, for deep-frying

These days most kitchens are equipped with electric mixers and food processors. Slicing and chopping can be done with a food processor, if desired, but I prefer the control I can exert with my hand and a cleaver. It is the traditional way, the way of the finest chefs, and I recommend it. Once you become adept with the cleaver, I think you will prefer it too.

Cooking with the Wok

There is nothing more traditional in Chinese cookery than that thousand-year-old Chinese creation, the wok. First made of iron, later of carbon steel, still later of stainless steel and aluminum, it was, and is, shaped like an oversized soup plate. Its concave shape places its belly right into the flame or heat source of a stove and makes it the ideal cooker.

In carbon steel it is as perfect as a cooking utensil can be. It conducts heat almost instantaneously. Though it is not a pot or a pan, it functions as both. Its shape permits food to be stir-fried, tossed quickly through tiny amounts of oil so that the food cooks yet does not retain oil. The shape of the wok permits one to make it a steamer simply by placing bamboo steamers in its well. Wok cooking, more than any other sort these days, is natural cooking.

If you buy only one wok, it should be of carbon steel. Avoid those with nonstick finishes because they cannot be properly coated with oil. Avoid plug-in electric woks, because you cannot control their heat as precisely as you must. Stainless steel and aluminum woks are fine for steaming but cannot compare in versatility with the carbon steel wok.

A wok of carbon steel is not pretty when it is new, because of its coating of sticky oil. Once cleaned and seasoned, however, it is ideal and will last for years. A new wok should be immersed in extremely hot water with a little liquid detergent. The interior should be cleaned with a sponge, the outside with steel wool and cleanser; then the wok should be rinsed and, while wet, placed over a flame and dried with a paper towel to prevent instant rust. Discard the paper towel, and with the wok still over a burner, 1 teaspoon of oil should be tipped into its bowl and rubbed around with another paper towel. This oiling should be repeated until the paper towel is free of any traces of black residue. The wok is then ready for use.

What I usually do with a new wok is make a batch of French fried potatoes in it. That is the perfect way to season it. I pour in 4 cups of peanut oil, heat the wok until I see wisps of white smoke rising, then put in the potatoes.

After the first washing, detergents should *never* be used in the bowl of the wok. It should be scrubbed with extremely hot water and a stiff-bristled wok brush. After rinsing, it should be wiped quickly with a paper towel, then placed over a flame for a thorough drying. If you have finished cooking in it for a day, then it should be reseasoned with a bit of peanut oil rubbed around inside with a paper towel. Do this for the first fifteen to twenty uses, until it becomes shiny and dark colored, which indicates it is completely seasoned.

Techniques

Stir-Frying

This is surely the most dramatic of all Chinese cooking techniques. It is fascinating to watch finely sliced and chopped foods being whisked through a bit of oil and tossed with a spatula. The hands and arms move as the wok is often tipped back and forth. Stir-frying is all movement, all rhythm. What leads to it is all preparation.

The object of stir-frying is to cook vegetables precisely to the point at which they retain their flavor, color, crispness, and nutritive value. All vegetables, thinly and evenly cut, must be next to the wok, ready to be tipped into the hot oil. This is simply organization, so that as you cook you will have everything within reach and the rhythm of stir-frying will not be interrupted. The best stir-fried foods are those that retain their natural characteristics while at the same time absorbing and retaining the heat from the wok.

When I am to stir-fry I usually heat the wok for a specific time, usually from 30 seconds to 1 minute. I pour oil into the wok and coat the sides by spreading the oil with a spatula. I drop a slice of ginger into the oil; when it becomes light brown, the oil is ready. When cooking vegetables I usually add a bit of salt to the oil. I place the food in the wok and begin tossing it through the oil, 1 to 2 minutes for such soft vegetables as bok choy and scallions, about a minute longer for firmer vegetables such as cabbage, carrots, and broccoli. I scoop out the vegetables with a spatula, and they are ready to be served.

If vegetables are too wet they will not stir-fry well, so they should be patted dry with paper towels (a bit of moisture will remain). If they are too dry, however, you may have to sprinkle a few drops of water into the wok while cooking. When water is sprinkled in this manner, steam is created, which aids the cooking process.

Stir-frying may appear initially as a rather frenzied activity, but it is not. The more you do it, the more you will realize that it is simply establishing a cooking rhythm.

Deep-Frying

The object of deep-frying is to cook food thoroughly inside while outside it becomes golden and lightly crusted. Most foods that are to be deep-fried are first seasoned, marinated, and dipped into batter. Ideally the oil combines with these other tastes to create new, fresh flavors.

When I wish to make my wok into a deep-fryer I heat it briefly, then pour in 4 to 6 cups of peanut oil and heat the oil to 325°F to 375°F, depending upon what I am cooking. The oil should be heated to a temperature a bit higher than that required for frying the food because, when food is placed in it, the oil temperature will drop. Then it will begin to rise again, so I use a frying thermometer, which I leave in the oil, to help me regulate its temperature.

When the oil reaches the proper temperature, slide the food from the inside edge of the wok into the oil. Remember to keep the temperature of the oil steady by turning the heat up or down as required.

The utensil to use for moving ingredients in deep-frying is the Chinese mesh strainer. Its large surface and stout bamboo handles are ideal for removing foods from oil and straining them as well. In my view, this strainer is far more useful than a slotted spoon.

Oil-Blanching

This relatively simple cooking technique is basically a sealing process. Its aim is to seal in the flavor of vegetables and to retain their bright color. For vegetables, heat the wok, pour 3 cups of peanut oil into it, then heat to exactly 300°F. Vegetables should be added to the oil for no longer than 30 to 45 seconds, then removed with a Chinese strainer. When foods are removed from the oil, the excess oil should be drained off and the oil-blanched foods set aside to be used as required.

Water-Blanching

Water-blanching removes water from vegetables. Pour 3 to 4 cups of water into a wok, add ¼ teaspoon of baking soda, and bring to a boil. The baking soda is optional; it ensures bright color in the vegetables. Place the vegetables in the water and bring the water back to a boil. Immediately drain the vegetables in a strainer, place them in a bowl, and run cold water over them to halt the cooking process. Drain well and set aside.

Steaming

Chinese-style steaming is truly a life-giving process. Natural tastes are preserved when food is steamed. Dry food becomes moist when subjected to steam's wet and penetrating heat. That which is shrunken expands. Steaming bestows a glistening coat of moisture on foods.

It is artful as well, because foods can be arranged in attractive ways within bamboo steamers, and once cooked, they can be served without being transferred to other dishes. Steaming requires virtually no oil, except that which is used to brush the bamboo reeds at the bottoms of the steamers to prevent sticking.

To steam, pour 4 to 5 cups of water into a wok and bring it to a boil. Place the steamers in the wok so that they sit evenly above, but not touching, the water. This can be done by supporting them with a cake rack. You will be able to stack two steamers or more, should you wish. Cover the top one and the contents of all will cook beautifully. Boiling water should be on hand at all times during the steaming process, to replenish any water that evaporates from the wok.

Tempering Dishes for Steaming

Porcelain or Pyrex dishes may be used inside steamers but first should be seasoned and tempered. Fill the wok with 5 to 6 cups of cold water. Place a cake rack in the wok and stack the dishes to be tempered on the rack, making certain they are completely covered by the cold water. Cover with a wok cover and bring the water to a boil. Let the water boil for 10 minutes, turn off the heat, and allow the wok to cool to room temperature. The dishes are then seasoned and can be placed in steamers without fear that they will crack. They may also be used in place of steamers. Foods are put in the seasoned, tempered dishes, which are in turn placed on cake racks within the wok. Cover and steam as described previously. Once tempered, the dishes will remain so for their lifetime. They need not be tempered again.

Dry-Roasting

With this process there is no need for oil, salt, or anything else in the wok.

To dry-roast nuts, heat the wok over high heat for 30 to 45 seconds. Add the nuts and lower the heat to very low. Spread the nuts in a single layer and use a spatula to move them about and turn them over to avoid burning on one side and leaving the other side uncooked. This process takes about 12 to 15 minutes, or until the nuts turn brown. Turn off the heat, remove the nuts from the wok, and allow to cool. Nuts can be dry-roasted 2 to 3 days in advance. After they cool, place them in a sealed jar.

Use the same process to dry-roast sesame seeds, except reduce the roasting time to only 2 to 3 minutes.

Working with the Cleaver

If the wok is an all-purpose cooker, then the cleaver comes close to being the all-purpose cutting utensil. The Chinese kitchen would not be a kitchen without the broad-bladed, wood-handled cleaver, and nobody who cooks Chinese food should be without one. Rather formidable looking, the cleaver occasionally causes trepidation; some people think that the first time they use it they will slice off one or more of their fingers. This is, of course, nonsense. The cleaver, when held correctly so that its weight and balance are well utilized, can do virtually anything a handful of lesser knives can. It slices, shreds, minces, dices, chops, and hacks, all with great ease. It mashes. It scoops. It can function as a dough scraper.

Cleavers come in various sizes and weights, from ¾ pound to as much as 2 pounds. If you are to have a single all-purpose cleaver, I recommend one of stainless steel, weighing about a pound, with a blade about 8 inches long and 3½ inches wide.

There really is no single correct way to hold a cleaver, except that it should be held comfortably and in such a way as to make the weight of the cleaver do the work, firmly and efficiently. There are two basic grips that will be helpful.

The first grip is for chopping and mincing. I grip the handle in a fistlike grasp and swing it straight down. The strokes are long and forceful if I am cutting something quite thick. If I am mincing, the strokes are short, rapid, and controlled. The wrist dictates the force.

The second grip is for slicing, shredding, and dicing. I grip the handle as before but permit the index finger to stretch out along the side of the flat blade to give it guidance. The wrist, which barely moves with this grip, is virtually rigid and becomes almost an extension of the cleaver, as the blade is drawn across the food being cut. When you use this grip, your other hand becomes a guide. Your fingertips should anchor the food to be cut, and your knuckles should guide the cleaver blade, which will brush them ever so slightly as it moves across the food.

Mashing

The handle of the cleaver is used in this technique. Hold the handle firmly, with the index finger and thumb at the base of the blade where it meets the handle. The other fingers are clenched. The blade faces outward. The handle becomes, in effect, a hammer that can be used to make a paste, such as that of fermented black beans and garlic.

Once these simple techniques are mastered, I believe you will agree that there is no mystery to be fathomed when cooking in the Chinese manner. Another path to simplicity is in the preparation of stocks, the very basis of the best in Chinese cooking. Almost every recipe, certainly every soup, in this book utilizes vegetable stock, either as a base, as an ingredient, or as a component of a marinade. I have developed two vegetable stocks. Try them both. Use them both. Or use the one of your choice. Each stock is applicable to any of the recipes.

Vegetable Stocks

I have brewed two stocks, quite alike but with certain differences in ingredients. The first is a more traditional Chinese stock, which includes preserved Chinese red dates and buckthorn seeds, believed by the Chinese to be excellent for your health as well as tasty. It also includes the Scallion Oil I have created and the fried scallions used in the preparation of that oil.

VEGETABLE STOCK I

6 quarts cold water

1½ pounds carrots, peeled and cut into thirds

3½ pounds onions, quartered

1½ pounds scallions, trimmed and cut into thirds

½ pound fresh mushrooms, cut into thirds

12 celery stalks, each cut into thirds

1¼ cups fresh coriander, cut into 3-inch pieces

¼ cup Chinese preserved dates, soaked in hot water 30 minutes
   (see note below)

¼ cup buckthorn seeds, soaked in hot water 30 minutes and washed
   (see note below)

1 teaspoon white peppercorns

¼ pound fresh ginger, cut into chunks, pieces lightly smashed

3 tablespoons Scallion Oil (page 37)

¾ cup fried scallions (see Scallion Oil recipe, page 37)

2 tablespoons salt

1. In a large pot bring the water to a boil. Add all the remaining ingredients to the boiling water, reduce heat, and simmer at a slow boil in a partially covered pot for 5 hours.

2. When the stock is cooked remove from the heat and strain the liquid through a metal strainer. Discard the solids. Store the stock in a plastic container until needed. The stock will keep, refrigerated, for 4 to 5 days, or it can be frozen for 3 to 4 weeks.

Yield: 4 to 4½ quarts

Note: Preserved dates come in 1-pound plastic-wrapped packages labeled either "red dates" or " dates" and can be found in Chinese and Asian markets. After opening the package, place the dates in a glass jar and cover. Store in a cool place. They will keep for 6 months. Buckthorn seeds, so labeled, come in ½-pound to 1-pound packages. Store likewise.

VEGETABLE STOCK II

This second vegetable stock is almost identical to the first. However, it is made without Chinese dates or buckthorn seeds. It does contain my Scallion Oil and the fried scallions; the more familiar pitted, sweet dates sold at most markets; and preserved figs, also widely available.

6 quarts cold water

1½ pounds carrots, peeled and cut into thirds

3 pounds onions, quartered

½ pound fresh mushrooms, halved

1 pound leeks, each cut into 4 pieces

12 celery stalks, cut into thirds

1½ cups fresh coriander, chopped into 3-inch pieces

3 tablespoons Scallion Oil (page 37)

¾ cup fried scallions (see Scallion Oil recipe, page 37)

¼ pound ginger, cut into chunks and lightly smashed

6 preserved figs

7 pitted sweet dates

2 teaspoons white peppercorns

2 tablespoons salt

1. In a large pot, bring the water to a boil. Add all the remaining ingredients to the boiling water, reduce the heat, and simmer at a slow boil in a partially covered pot for 5 hours.

2. When the stock is cooked, remove from the heat and strain the liquid through a metal strainer. Discard the solids. Store stock in a plastic container until needed. The stock will keep, refrigerated, for 4 to 5 days, or it can be frozen for 3 to 4 weeks.

Yield: 4 to 4½ quarts

Of utmost importance in the Chinese kitchen is rice. With virtually every stir-fry preparation in this book I recommend cooked rice. This is the Chinese way of eating.

BASIC COOKED RICE
Bak Fon

The Chinese call cooked rice *bak fon*, or "white rice," for it is the whiteness of cooked rice that is highly prized. In parts of China, brown rice is used, but not nearly as widely as traditional white rice. Here is a foolproof method of cooking this rice, which goes so well with virtually any stir-fry dish.

2 cups rice, extra-long-grain preferred
15 ounces cold water

1. Place the rice in a pot with some cold water and wash it 3 times. As you wash it, rub it between your hands. Drain well after washing. Then add the 15 ounces of cold water and allow the rice to sit 2 hours before cooking. A good ratio of rice to water is 1 cup of rice to 1 cup minus 1 tablespoon of water. (So-called "old rice," which has been lying about in sacks for extended periods, will absorb more water and be easier to cook.)

2. Begin cooking, uncovered, over high heat and bring water to a boil. Stir with chopsticks and cook for about 4 minutes, or until the water evaporates. Even after the water is gone the rice will be quite hard. Cover the pot and cook over low heat for about 8 minutes more, stirring from time to time.

3. After turning off the heat, loosen the rice with chopsticks. This will help retain fluffiness. Cover tightly until ready to serve. Just before serving, stir rice with chopsticks once again. Well-cooked rice will have absorbed the water but will not be lumpy, nor will the grains stick together. They will be firm, fluffy, and separate.

Yield: 4 to 5 cups

Also of basic importance are two ingredients I find indispensable, Ginger Juice and Minced Garlic. Packaged versions of these generally are lacking in intensity. I recommend you make them yourself, in sufficient quantities to have on hand whenever you wish to use them—which, with the recipes in this book, will be often. Neither is difficult to prepare.

GINGER JUICE
Seung Jop

Ginger juice can be bought in jars. I do not recommend using it, however, for often it is mixed with alcohol and/or water. Neither of these benefit the ginger. It is best made fresh.

1 piece of fresh ginger root, 1½ inches long and 1½ inches thick

1. Peel the ginger. Grate it into a pulp using a small, single-panel hand grater. Press the pulp into the well of a garlic press and press the juice into a small bowl.

Yield: About 1½ teaspoons

Note: Occasionally ginger will be dry and will yield less juice. If so, use a larger piece, or augment the juice with the pulp in a recipe. You may make ginger juice up to 2 days in advance. It will not keep longer.

MINCED GARLIC
Seun Yung

Minced garlic is available in jars. However, you will find that such garlic has lost some of its potency. It is best to make it yourself. It is easy to do, and you will have a supply at hand whenever you need it for recipes in this book. It is used constantly.

3 bulbs garlic (6 ounces; ¾ cup tightly packed, minced)
½ cup peanut oil

1. Separate the garlic bulbs into cloves. Smash each clove with the flat side of a cleaver blade. This permits easy removal of the skin. Discard the skins and mince the garlic with the cleaver until you have a mass of minced pieces, about ⅛ inch each. Do not mince more finely than this.

2. Place the minced garlic in a glass jar. Cover with peanut oil. Cover with a lid and refrigerate until use. It will keep 4 to 6 weeks.

Yield: 1 cup

Note: I suggest not using a food processor to mince garlic because you will in all probability end up with garlic puree, which is not desirable.

Throughout this book of Chinese vegetable cookery I use various oils and sauces that I have developed. You will find them, as have I, invaluable to the recipes as ingredients, as bases for soups and for other oils and sauces, or as accompaniments and dips. You will find, I am certain, that they enhance the foods that they touch. Once you've used them, you will find it difficult to cook, or serve, without them.

HOT OIL
Lot Yau

¾ cup hot red pepper flakes
½ cup sesame oil
¾ cup peanut oil

1. Place all the ingredients in a large jar and mix well. Close the jar tightly and place in a cool, dry place for 2 weeks. The oil will then be ready for use. The longer it is stored, the more potent it becomes.

   Yield: 2 cups

   Note: If you prefer not to wait for the oil to mature, here is a quick method of preparing hot oil: Place the pepper flakes in a mixing bowl. Bring the sesame and peanut oils to a boil and pour over flakes. (Caution: Keep your face away from the bowl, for the fumes may cause discomfort to your throat or coughing.) After it cools, the oil is ready for use. Store in the same manner as above.

HOT PEPPER FLAKES

These are called for in several recipes. They are the soaked flakes that will settle at the bottom of your jar of Hot Oil (see above recipe). Use them as indicated, for they are extraordinarily hot.

SCALLION OIL
Chung Yau

Scallion Oil is less an accompaniment than it is an ingredient. It is used widely in this book, to excellent advantage.

2 cups peanut oil
8 to 10 scallions, cut into 3-inch sections, the white portions lightly
    smashed (3 cups)

1. Heat a wok over medium heat. Add the peanut oil, then the scallions. When the scallions turn brown, the oil is done.

2. With a strainer, remove the scallions. Strain the oil through a fine strainer into a mixing bowl and allow to cool to room temperature. Pour the Scallion Oil into a glass jar and store in a cool place until needed. Do not refrigerate.

Yield: 1½ cups

Note: Reserve the cooked scallions for a vegetable stock.

SWEET SCALLION SAUCE
Tim Chung Yau

¼ cup Scallion Oil (see above recipe)
¼ cup double dark soy sauce
¼ cup Vegetable Stock (pages 31–32)
2 tablespoons sugar

1. Heat a wok over medium heat. Pour in the Scallion Oil, soy sauce, stock, and sugar. Stir clockwise (to avoid splattering) until all ingredients are well blended and begin to boil.

2. Turn off the heat. Pour the sauce into a bowl and allow it to come to room temperature. Pour into a glass jar. It will keep in the jar, not refrigerated, for about 4 weeks. Refrigerated, it will keep up to 3 months.

Yield: Slightly more than ¾ cup

SZECHUAN PEPPERCORN OIL
Chin Jiu Yau

I learned the simple basics of creating a fragrant oil from Szechuan peppercorns in Hong Kong. It is truly a fine oil that imparts a distinct flavor to the foods it touches.

1½ tablespoons Szechuan peppercorns
1 cup peanut oil

1. Heat a wok over high heat for 30 seconds. Add the Szechuan peppercorns to the dry wok and stir. Lower the heat to low. Stir for 1½ minutes, or until the peppercorns release their fragrance. Add the peanut oil, raise heat to medium, and allow to come to a boil. Lower the heat and cook for 4 to 5 minutes, or until peppercorns turn black. Turn off the heat and allow the oil to cool. Strain the oil into a glass jar. Reserve for use.

Yield: Just under 1 cup

Note: This oil will keep, in a covered jar in a cool place, for 1 to 2 months.

Note: Do not discard the peppercorns. They may be used when making vegetable stock. Keep stored, refrigerated, until ready for use. They will keep indefinitely.

SZECHUAN PEPPERCORN SALT
Far Jiu Yim

2 teaspoons salt
1 teaspoon 5-spice powder
1 teaspoon whole Szechuan peppercorns, ground

1. Heat a wok over medium heat for 45 seconds to 1 minute. Lower the heat and add all ingredients. Dry-roast, stirring occasionally, until the 5-spice powder turns black. Remove, place in a small dish, and serve. This is ideal with Vegetarian "Oysters" (page 223).

Note: This seasoned salt can be made in advance of use, but it must be kept in a tightly sealed jar. It will keep for 4 to 6 weeks.

綠

油

GREEN OIL
Luk Yau

I call this "Green Oil" simply because of its color, which resembles that of extra-virgin olive oil. The resemblance ends there, however, for mine is based on that fragrant herb, coriander.

1¼ cups peanut oil
1 cup fresh coriander stems, chopped into 2-inch pieces
1 cup tightly packed fresh coriander leaves

1. Make certain the coriander stems and leaves are totally dry. Then heat a wok over high heat for 40 seconds. Add the peanut oil, stir briefly, and add coriander stems. Stir and bring oil to a boil for about 4 minutes. Add the coriander leaves and stir, making certain the leaves are covered with the oil. Cook until the leaves and stems become dull in color, then brownish. Turn off the heat and strain the oil. (The coriander stems and leaves may be reserved for use in your next vegetable stock.)

2. When the oil comes to room temperature, pour into a jar, cover, and store in a cool place until use. It will keep for 6 to 8 weeks.

Yield: About 1 cup

VINEGAR SOY SAUCE
See Cho Yau

This is an easily made dipping sauce that marries well with many dishes, including the Hot Pot (page 150). It can be made ahead, but I prefer to make it as needed to preserve its full strength. In fact, by "ahead" I mean no more than several hours in advance of use, because it loses intensity quickly.

1 tablespoon dark soy sauce
1 tablespoon light soy sauce
1 tablespoon white vinegar
2 tablespoons Vegetable Stock (pages 31–32)
½ teaspoon Hot Oil (page 36)
1 tablespoon trimmed and finely sliced scallions

1. Combine all ingredients in a bowl. Mix well. Allow to marinate for at least 30 minutes. Place in small soy sauce dishes and serve.

   Yield: Slightly more than ¼ cup

GINGER SOY SAUCE
Seung Chung Yau

I prefer to make this accompanying sauce as needed, rather than ahead of time, to retain the pungency of the ginger.

1½ tablespoons shredded fresh ginger
1½ tablespoons dark soy sauce
1½ tablespoons light soy sauce
1 teaspoon sugar
1 teaspoon Scallion Oil (page 37)
3 tablespoons Vegetable Stock (pages 31–32) or 3 tablespoons water
1 scallion, white portion only, sliced into ½-inch lengths
Generous pinch of white pepper

1. Combine all the ingredients in a small bowl and mix well. Allow to stand for 30 minutes before serving.

   Yield: About ¼ cup

CHIU CHOW SWEET SOY
Chiu Chow Tim See Yau

This sauce, which is unique to the kitchens of the Chiu Chow people of southern China, is an integral ingredient in the special Sweet Soy Noodles (page 262) and in other dishes as well. But the sauce, on its own, is fine to use as a dipping sauce.

1½ teaspoons double dark soy sauce
2½ teaspoons sugar
1½ teaspoons light soy sauce
2 teaspoons Shao-Hsing wine or sherry
2 teaspoons sesame oil
1 tablespoon oyster sauce
¼ cup Vegetable Stock (pages 31–32)

1. Mix all the ingredients together until well blended. This is not a sauce to keep. It should be made only as needed.

Yield: ½ cup

SWEET AND SOUR SAUCE
Tim Seun Jung

½ cup red wine vinegar
⅓ cup sugar
1 8-ounce can tomato sauce
⅛ teaspoon salt
2 teaspoons cornstarch mixed with 2 tablespoons cold water
2 tablespoons minced green pepper
2 teaspoons minced fresh coriander

1. In a small saucepan, combine the vinegar, sugar, tomato sauce, salt, and dissolved cornstarch. Bring to a boil over moderately high heat, stirring frequently. Boil for 1 minute. Add the pepper and coriander. Pour into a bowl and serve warm or at room temperature.

Yield: About 1¾ cups

Note: This sauce is a perfect complement to Vegetarian Spring Rolls (page 272).

SOY SESAME SAUCE
See Mah Yau

1½ tablespoons Vegetable Stock (pages 31–32)
1 tablespoon dark soy sauce
1 tablespoon light soy sauce
1 tablespoon white vinegar
1 tablespoon sesame oil
1½ teaspoons crushed hot red pepper
1 tablespoon trimmed and thinly sliced scallions

1. Combine all the ingredients in a small bowl and mix well. Allow to stand for at least 30 minutes to let the flavors blend.

   Yield: ¼ cup

CHILI SOY SAUCE
Lot See Yau

1 tablespoon dark soy sauce
1 tablespoon light soy sauce
1¼ teaspoons minced fresh hot red chilies, or ½ teaspoon crushed hot red pepper
1 tablespoon white vinegar
3 tablespoons Vegetable Stock (pages 31–32)
½ teaspoon sugar
2 teaspoons sesame oil
1½ teaspoons minced garlic
½ teaspoon minced ginger
1 tablespoon trimmed and thinly sliced scallions

1. In a small bowl, combine all the ingredients. Allow to stand for 30 minutes and serve at room temperature.

   Yield: ½ cup

   Note: This sauce is also a fine accompaniment to Vegetarian Spring Rolls (page 272).

水
晶
醬

CRYSTAL SAUCE
Soi Jing Jeung

The words *soi jing* translate as "crystal" or "sparkling," and that is what this sauce is. It is transparent, and it gives no hint, save for the bits of fresh red chilies floating in it, that it is spiced and hot. It is an ideal dip for many of the fried preparations in this book—particularly Spring Rolls (pages 272–77), Bean Curd Balls (page 176), and Vegetarian Eggs (page 206)—as well as for Rice Paper Wrapped Rolls (pages 281–84).

⅓ cup white vinegar
¼ cup water
¼ cup sugar
1 teaspoon salt
1 teaspoon minced fresh red chilies
1½ teaspoons tapioca starch mixed with 2 teaspoons cold water

1. Place the vinegar, water, sugar, salt, and chilies in a small pot. Bring to a boil over medium heat, making certain the sugar and salt dissolve. Pour in the tapioca starch mixture and continue stirring until the sauce thickens and becomes smooth and transparent. Turn off the heat, transfer to a small bowl, and allow to cool.

Yield: About 1 cup

Note: The sauce may be kept refrigerated, in a closed jar, for a week or more.

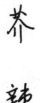

HOT MUSTARD
Gai Lot

There are many prepared hot mustards on the market, but this mix is best made with dry mustard. There are many dry mustards as well, but I prefer that from England, Colman's Mustard Double Superfine Compound. It must be the dry mustard, not the Colman's prepared mustard in jars.

3 tablespoons mustard
3 tablespoons cold water

1. Mix ingredients thoroughly and allow to sit for a while to blend. The mustard may also be mixed with an equal amount of distilled white vinegar, but I prefer the water for its purity of taste.

   There you have the special techniques and flavors basic to the Chinese kitchen. They prepare you well, I believe, for the recipes that follow. As my grandmother would say before each meal, *"ho ho sik,"* or "eat well."

蔬菜 Choi

Vegetables

Choi. Vegetables. In China vegetables are the core of the daily meal. There is, to be sure, the constant presence of rice, but vegetables are truly what the Chinese kitchen depends upon for taste, color, freshness, and reminders of the seasons. In China vegetables go from furrow to table, fruits from the trees into bowls, for eating immediately, with few steps in between. There is no freezing, no processing, no parboiling. Vegetables are picked, cleaned, and cooked. Leaves, discarded stems, and root ends become the bases for stocks. In the preparation vegetables are sliced, diced, julienned, or cut diagonally so that their flavors become more apparent, more accessible.

When vegetables and fruits are to be cooked, they are tossed in a bit of stock, perhaps, or placed in a stock-based broth, or whisked with a spatula through a bit of peanut oil. What could be more healthful? What could be quicker? What could preserve the integrity of the vegetable better? In some European cultures vegetables are boiled for great lengths of time and brought to the table soft. Vegetables so prepared are virtually devoid of nourishment and become mere filler to go along with the main component of the meal, whatever that may be.

Not so in China. It is the vegetable that receives intense attention. Carrots must not be cooked too long or they will lose their crispness, sweetness, and nutrition, their value will be lost, diluted in the broth in which they have been cooked. If you are making soup this is fine, but it isn't if you are stir-frying. Likewise for celery, bok choy, peppers, snow peas, green beans, and all sorts of tender shoots, where freshness and texture are paramount. Freshness unadorned: That is the feeling I have tried to impart to these recipes.

FLOWERS OF JADE
Yuk Far Sah Lut

To the Chinese, broccoli is a symbol of jade, and jade represents youth and rebirth. Broccoli, in some form, is always at the table in the New Year and at birthdays.

1 pound broccoli, separated into flowerets about 1½ inches in diameter
8 cups water
1¼-inch-wide slice fresh ginger
2 garlic cloves
1 teaspoon baking soda, optional (see note below)
3 tablespoons peanut oil
1 teaspoon salt
2 teaspoons minced fresh ginger
1 teaspoon minced garlic

1. In a large pot combine the water, slice of ginger, garlic cloves, and baking soda. Bring to a boil over high heat. Add the broccoli and cook until it turns bright green, about ½ minute. Drain and rinse under cold running water. Drain well and set aside.

2. Heat a wok over high heat for 45 seconds. Add the peanut oil and coat the sides of the wok with a spatula. Add the salt, minced ginger, and minced garlic, and stir-fry until the garlic turns brown, about 30 seconds. Add the broccoli and stir-fry until crisp and tender, 1½ to 2 minutes.

3. Transfer broccoli to a serving dish. Let cool to room temperature before serving. If prepared ahead, this salad should be covered and refrigerated. Allow to come to room temperature, however, before serving.

Serves 4 to 6 as a side dish

Note: The baking soda is added to the water to ensure that the broccoli will remain bright green. It is, of course, optional. The Chinese regard bright color as important to food presentation.

STEAMED BROCCOLI
Jing Sei Lan Far

The Chinese name for this dish translates as "Western broccoli flower," to differentiate it from Chinese broccoli. When Chinese broccoli is prepared, its small, white flowerets are discarded, because when the flowers appear on the plants it is a sign that the broccoli is already too old for use and has perhaps become tough. On Western broccoli the flowerets are green, and are eaten.

¾ pound broccoli flowerets (1 small bunch)
2 tablespoons Ginger Soy Sauce (page 40), or more to taste

1. Wash broccoli thoroughly. Place in a steamer and steam 3 to 4 minutes, until it becomes bright green. Place in a serving dish and toss with the Ginger Soy Sauce. Serve immediately.

Serves 4 to 6

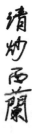

STIR-FRIED BROCCOLI
Ching Chau Sei Lan Far

The Chinese have a humorous name for this dish. Western broccoli is called *sei lan far*, or "foreign broccoli flower." So this dish, to the Chinese, is "plain foreign broccoli flower."

1 tablespoon peanut oil
¼ teaspoon salt
1¼-inch-wide slice fresh ginger
1½ teaspoons minced garlic
1½ cups broccoli flowerets (1 small bunch), each about 1½ by 1½ inches
2 teaspoons white wine

1. Heat a wok over high heat for 45 seconds to 1 minute. Add the peanut oil and coat the wok with a spatula. When a wisp of white smoke appears, add the salt, ginger, and garlic. Cook for 20 seconds, then add the broccoli. Stir-fry together for 1 minute. Add the wine by drizzling it down the side of the wok. Mix well. Cook for 2 more minutes, or until the broccoli turns bright green. Turn off the heat, remove from wok, and serve immediately.

Serves 4 to 6

RED AROUND TWO FLOWERS
Seung Far Bun Hung

This is my variation on a classic dish of Canton. The imagery consists of two "flowers," cauliflower and broccoli, with "red" around them—usually sweet red peppers. I have substituted sun-dried tomatoes for the peppers, making the dish more pungent and quite different indeed.

½ pound cauliflower, cut into flowerets 1½ inches long and 1½ inches wide

½ pound broccoli, cut into flowerets 1½ inches long and 1½ inches wide

1½ tablespoons peanut oil

½ teaspoon salt

1½ teaspoons minced ginger

1½ teaspoons minced garlic

¼ cup julienned sun-dried tomatoes

1 tablespoon white wine

5 tablespoons vegetable stock mixed with 1 teaspoon cornstarch

1. Water-blanch cauliflower for 1 minute. Reserve. Water-blanch broccoli for 1 minute. Reserve.

2. Heat a wok over high heat for 45 seconds. Add the peanut oil and coat the wok with a spatula. When a wisp of white smoke appears, add the salt, ginger, and garlic, and stir. When the garlic turns light brown add the sun-dried tomatoes. Stir for 40 seconds, then add the reserved cauliflower and broccoli. Stir-fry for 1 minute.

3. Add the white wine by drizzling it around the edge of the wok. Mix well with the vegetables for 30 seconds. Make a well in the center of the ingredients, stir the vegetable stock–cornstarch mixture, and pour it into the well. Cover the well with vegetables, then stir everything together until the sauce thickens. Turn off the heat, transfer to a heated serving platter, and serve immediately.

Serves 4 to 6

CAULIFLOWER WITH PEPPERCORN SALT
Jah Yeh Choi Far

This is really a clever play on words, for to the Chinese this dish is "deep-fried floured cabbage flower." The coating resembles that of Japanese tempura and is quite light.

One ½-inch-wide slice fresh ginger, lightly smashed
2 garlic cloves
2 teaspoons salt
¾ pound cauliflower flowerets
6 cups peanut oil
1¼ cups flour
2 large eggs, beaten with a pinch of white pepper

1. In a pot place 2 quarts of water, the ginger, garlic cloves, and salt, and bring to a boil. Allow to boil for 2 minutes. Immerse the cauliflower in the water and water-blanch for 2 minutes, until moderately soft. Turn off the heat, run cold water in the pot, and drain off.

2. Heat the oil in a wok to 350°F. Spread the flour on a large sheet of waxed paper. Keep the beaten egg at hand. Dip the cauliflower into the flour, shake off excess, then dip in the egg to coat well, then back into flour. Shake off excess and lower into the oil with a Chinese strainer, cooking half of the cauliflower pieces at one time. Fry for 4 to 5 minutes, until cauliflower turns golden brown and the coating becomes crisp.

3. Drain on paper towels. Repeat with second batch of cauliflower flowerets. (Keep first batch warm at stoveside. Do not place in oven, for they will become soggy.) Serve immediately with Szechuan Peppercorn Salt (page 38).

Serves 4 to 6

CAULIFLOWER WITH MUSHROOMS
Yeh Choi Far Chau Tung Gu

The cauliflower is not so well known in China, except in cities, such as Canton, Shanghai, and Peking, where there is access to the West. In China it is called *yeh choi far*, or "flower of the cabbage." It is suitable to the Chinese kitchen both for its highly valued whiteness and for its crispness. This dish is an auspicious yin and yang combination for its white and black components.

Sauce ingredients

1 teaspoon light soy sauce
1 teaspoon double dark soy sauce
1½ teaspoons Shao-Hsing wine or sherry
1 teaspoon sesame oil
¾ teaspoon sugar
2½ teaspoons cornstarch
⅓ cup Vegetable Stock (pages 31–32)
Pinch of white pepper

To complete the dish

4 cups cold water
1 teaspoon salt
One slice fresh ginger, 1½ inches thick
¾ pound cauliflower flowerets, 2 inches long and 1 inch wide (see note below)
2 tablespoons Scallion Oil (page 37)
2 teaspoons minced ginger
2 teaspoons minced garlic
¼ teaspoon salt
24 steamed Chinese dried black mushrooms (each about the size of a quarter; see next page)

1. Stir together the sauce ingredients. Reserve.

2. In a pot place the cold water, 1 teaspoon salt, and the slice of ginger, and bring to a boil over high heat. Add the cauliflower and water-blanch for 1½ minutes. Turn off the heat and drain the cauliflower through a strainer.

3. Heat a wok over high heat for 30 seconds and add the Scallion Oil. Coat the wok with a spatula. When a wisp of white smoke appears, add the minced ginger, garlic, and ¼ teaspoon salt. When the garlic turns light brown, add the cauliflower and stir-fry for 1 minute. Add the mushrooms and stir-fry for 2 minutes. Make a well in the center of the mixture, stir the sauce, and pour it in. Mix well. When the sauce begins to bubble and thicken, turn off the heat, transfer to a heated dish, and serve immediately.

Serves 4 to 6

Note: Packaged flowerets are usually available in vegetable markets. However, I prefer to cut them myself because they are fresher and crisper that way.

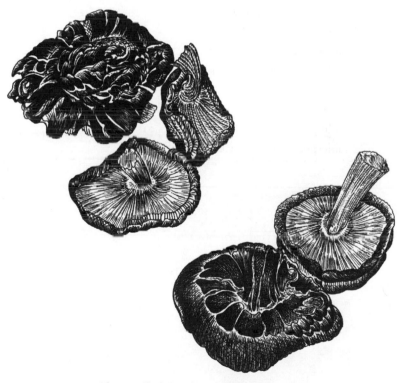

Chinese Black Mushrooms (dried and soaked)

CURRIED CAULIFLOWER
Gah Gee Yeh Choi Far

Curry is not Chinese, but it has come to China by way of Hong Kong and other ports such as Canton and Shanghai, and it is now part of the modern Chinese kitchen.

Curry paste ingredients

1 tablespoon curry powder (see note below)
1 tablespoon Vegetable Stock (pages 31–32)

To complete the dish

4 cups cold water
1¼-inch-wide slice fresh ginger
1¾ teaspoons salt
1 pound caulifower flowerets
3 tablespoons peanut oil
3 tablespoons fresh coriander, finely chopped
1 tablespoon minced ginger
2 teaspoons minced garlic
1 cup onions cut in ¼-inch slices (tightly packed)
2 tablespoons Vegetable Stock (pages 31–32)
2 tablespoons oyster sauce

1. Combine the curry paste ingredients in a bowl. Reserve.

2. In a large pot place the water, ginger, and 1 teaspoon salt. Cover and bring to a boil. Add the cauliflower, stir, and water-blanch for 45 seconds. Turn off the heat. Run cold water into the pot and drain. Reserve. Empty the pot.

3. In the same pot, over high heat, place the peanut oil and the remaining ¾ teaspoon salt. Stir, and when a wisp of white smoke appears, add the coriander, ginger, and garlic. Stir and cook for 10 seconds. Add the curry paste and mix well with other ingredients, about 20 seconds, until the aroma of curry is released. Add the onions and cauliflower and combine well. Add the 2 tablespoons vegetable stock and stir together, making certain the cauliflower and onions are well coated. Add the oyster sauce and blend in. Lower the heat, cover, and allow to cook 7 minutes, or until cauliflower is tender. Stir 3 times during this cooking process, so that the curry is completely absorbed. Turn off heat, transfer to a serving bowl, and serve immediately.

Serves 4 to 6

Note: I prefer the Madras brand of curry, from India, which is available widely. It has pungency, a fine taste, and a balance of spices that is most agreeable.

Ginger Root

TOMATOES STIR-FRIED WITH BROCCOLI
Fon Keh Chau Yuk Far

Tomatoes, those lovely vegetables that moved from the West to the East, were happily adopted by the Chinese. They are called vitamin food and, as my grandmother referred to them, *gum chin gut*, or "golden corn tangerines." Is that not lovely imagery?

Sauce ingredients

1 teaspoon light soy sauce

1 teaspoon double dark soy sauce

2 teaspoons Shao-Hsing wine or sherry

1 teaspoon sesame oil

½ teaspoon salt

1 teaspoon sugar

2 teaspoons cornstarch

Pinch of white pepper

¼ cup Vegetable Stock (pages 31–32)

To complete the dish

2 tomatoes (enough to yield 1½ cups chopped)

2½ tablespoons Scallion Oil (page 37)

1 tablespoon minced fresh ginger

¼ teaspoon salt

1 tablespoon minced garlic

½ cup scallions, white portions only, chopped in 1-inch pieces

1 cup celery, diced in ¼-inch pieces

4 to 5 fresh water chestnuts, peeled and cut into ¼-inch slices (½ cup)

2 cups broccoli flowerets, cut in 2-inch pieces (see note below)

¾ cup canned straw mushrooms, halved lengthwise

2 teaspoons Shao-Hsing wine or sherry

1. Combine the sauce ingredients in a bowl. Reserve.

2. Bring 4 cups of water to a boil. Place the tomatoes in the water. Turn off the heat and allow tomatoes to sit for 10 seconds. Run cold water into the pot and allow to cool. Peel off the skins, quarter the tomatoes, remove the seeds, and cut into 1-inch pieces. Reserve.

3. Heat a wok over high heat for 30 seconds. Add the Scallion Oil and coat the wok with a spatula. When a wisp of white smoke appears, add the ginger and salt and stir. Add the garlic and cook for 10 seconds, then add the scallions and cook for 10 more seconds. Add the celery and water chestnuts and stir-fry for 1 minute, mixing well. Add the broccoli and stir. Add the straw mushrooms and stir. Cook for 1 minute.

4. Add the reserved tomatoes and mix well with other ingredients. Add the wine and stir-fry for 2 minutes. Make a well in the center of the ingredients, stir the sauce, pour it into the well, and mix in. When the sauce thickens and begins to bubble, turn off the heat. Transfer to a preheated serving dish and serve immediately.

Serves 4 to 6

Note: Broccoli flowerets come already cut and bagged. Fresh broccoli is better, and in this book there are many uses for broccoli stems. Tomatoes are peeled and seeded for their appearance, but the dish may be prepared without peeling, if wished.

Water Chestnuts

PISTACHIOS WITH MIXED VEGETABLES
Hoi Sum Guor Chau Jop Choi

The Chinese words for pistachios, *hoi sum guor,* translate as "open heart nut." "Open heart" indicates happiness, meaning that this is a dish of great pleasure.

Sauce ingredients

¾ teaspoon light soy sauce

¾ teaspoon sesame oil

1 tablespoon oyster sauce

½ teaspoon sugar

2 teaspoons cornstarch

Pinch of white pepper

3 tablespoons Vegetable Stock (pages 31–32)

To complete the dish

2½ tablespoons peanut oil

½ teaspoon salt

2 teaspoons minced fresh ginger

¾ large sweet red pepper, cut into ½-inch dice (¾ cup)

1 medium stalk celery, cut into ½-inch dice (½ cup)

3 ounces string beans, ends removed, chopped into ½-inch pieces (¾ cup)

¼ cup bamboo shoots, cut into ½-inch dice

1 to 2 scallions, white portions only, chopped into ½-inch pieces (¼ cup)

2 fresh water chestnuts, peeled and cut into ¼-inch dice

2 teaspoons minced garlic

½ cup shelled pistachio nuts (with inner skin left on)

1. Combine the sauce ingredients in a bowl. Reserve.

2. Heat a wok over high heat for 45 seconds. Add 1½ tablespoons peanut oil and coat the wok with a spatula. When a wisp of white smoke appears, add salt and ginger. When ginger turns light brown, add all the vegetables except the pistachios and the garlic. Stir-fry for 1½ to 2 minutes, or until the string beans turn bright green. Remove the ingredients from the wok. Reserve.

3. Clean the wok and spatula with paper towels. Reheat the wok over high heat. Add the remaining peanut oil and coat the wok. When a wisp of white smoke

appears, stir in garlic. When garlic turns light brown, add the pistachios. Stir briefly, then add the reserved vegetables. Cook together for about 1½ minutes. Stir the sauce, make a well in the center of the vegetable mixture, and pour in the sauce. Mix thoroughly. When the sauce begins to bubble and thicken, remove from the heat. Transfer to a heated serving dish and serve immediately.

Serves 4 to 6

SNOW PEA SHOOTS
Ching Chau Dau Mui

Snow pea shoots are a true delicacy in China, and in Chinese and Asian markets, the tender shoots and their tips have been available for years. But it is only lately that Western cooks have discovered these sweet, utterly delicious vegetables after being unaware of them for so long.

8 cups cold water
1 teaspoon salt
1¼-inch-wide slice fresh ginger
½ teaspoon baking soda, optional (see note below)
1 pound snow pea shoots, drained
2 tablespoons peanut oil
One ½-inch-wide slice fresh ginger
2 whole garlic cloves
¾ teaspoon salt

1. In a pot place the water, 1 teaspoon salt, ¼-inch slice of ginger, and baking soda, and bring to a boil over high heat. Add the snow pea shoots and water-blanch for 30 seconds. The shoots should be bright green. Turn off the heat, run cold water into the pot, and drain. Repeat, then drain until all water runs off.

2. Heat a wok over high heat for 30 seconds, add the peanut oil, and coat the wok with a spatula. Add the ½-inch slice of ginger and stir for 20 seconds. Add the garlic cloves, stir, and when the garlic turns light brown, add the ¾ teaspoon salt. Stir. Add the shoots and mix well. Cook for 3 minutes. Turn off heat, transfer to a heated serving dish, discard garlic and ginger, and serve.

Serves 4 to 6

Note: The baking soda is added to the water to ensure that the snow pea shoots will remain bright green. It is, of course, optional. The Chinese regard bright color as important to food presentation.

SNOW PEAS WITH GINGER
Ji Seung Chau Sut Dau

Young ginger, that which is not mature, is recognizable by its tender texture, its pinkish color, and its almost translucent appearance. It is mild and quite crisp. It is available three times each year here; in China there are usually two crops per year. It is available more often because of hothouses and West Coast growing. Look for it—the search is worth the effort.

2½ tablespoons peanut oil

½ teaspoon salt, or to taste

3 tablespoons young ginger, sliced into pieces ½ by 1½ inches

¾ pound snow peas, both ends and strings removed, cut in half on the diagonal

1 tablespoon Shao-Hsing wine or sherry

1. Heat a wok over high heat for 30 seconds. Add the peanut oil and salt, and coat the wok with a spatula. When a wisp of white smoke appears, add the ginger slices. Stir-fry for 10 seconds, then add the snow peas. Stir-fry for 20 seconds. Add the wine by drizzling it down the side of the wok. Mix well. Stir until snow peas turn bright green and the mixture is very hot. Turn off the heat, transfer to a heated serving dish, and serve immediately.

Serves 4 to 6

SNOW PEAS STIR-FRIED WITH GARLIC
Soon Chau Soot Dau

Snow peas are highly thought of in China, both for their pods and for their shoots. Their name translates as "snow peas," but they are also known as *hoh lan dau*, or "Holland peas," in honor of their lineage.

2½ tablespoons Szechuan Peppercorn Oil (page 38)

½ teaspoon salt

2 cloves garlic, lightly smashed

¾ pound snow peas, strings removed on both sides, and cut into julienne

1. Heat a wok over high heat for 30 seconds. Add the oil and salt and coat the wok with a spatula. When a wisp of white smoke appears, add the garlic and stir. When garlic turns light brown, add the snow peas and stir-fry together. When the snow peas turn bright green, turn off the heat, transfer to a heated serving dish, and serve immediately.

Serves 4 to 6

Two Pearls in Sweet Soy
Tim Yau Chau Seung Jiu

In China green peas are "jade pearls" and white corn kernels are "white pearls." Binding them together in this recipe is a sauce based on the Chiu Chow–inspired sauce that I have developed. If you cannot find white corn then yellow will do, because in China it too is a pearl, a "golden pearl."

2 tablespoons Scallion Oil (page 37)
¼ teaspoon salt
1½ teaspoons minced fresh ginger
1 cup fresh or frozen green peas (see note below)
1¼ cup fresh or frozen white corn kernels (see note below)
⅓ cup Cinnamon-Roasted Soybeans (page 311)
2 tablespoons Chiu Chow Sweet Soy (page 41)

1. Heat a wok over high heat for 30 seconds. Add the Scallion Oil and coat the wok with a spatula. When a wisp of white smoke appears, add the salt and ginger. Stir briefly. Add the peas and corn and stir-fry for 1½ minutes. Add the soybeans and stir-fry for 1 minute more. Add the sweet soy and mix in well, until the liquid is absorbed. Turn off the heat, transfer to a heated dish, and serve immediately.

Serves 4 to 6

Note: If fresh peas and corn are used, they should be water-blanched in gently boiling water for about ½ minute, then drained thoroughly and cooled to room temperature. If frozen peas and corn are used, allow to come to room temperature before use.

SOYBEAN SPROUTS WITH FENNEL
Dai Dau Choi Chau Wui Hung

This dish is familiar to the Chinese when the soybean sprouts are cooked with Chinese celery, as is traditional. Fennel seed is widely used in China as a flavoring, but the stalk itself is relatively rare. In Hong Kong, where it is more familiar, it is known as "fragrant return." I have made this adaptation of the traditional dish, and it is a most happy blend.

6 cups cold water
1¼-inch-wide slice fresh ginger
1½ teaspoons salt
1 pound soybean sprouts, washed and drained
2 tablespoons peanut oil
One ½-inch-wide slice fresh ginger
½ cup fresh julienned fennel
1 cup green portion of scallions, cut into 2-inch pieces

1. In a pot place the cold water, ¼-inch slice ginger, and ¾ teaspoon salt. Bring to a boil. Add the soybean sprouts and water-blanch for 20 seconds. Turn off the heat, run cold water into the pot, and drain well. This should be done 1 hour before further preparation to ensure that the sprouts dry completely. Occasionally loosen the sprouts with chopsticks to help drying.

2. Heat a wok over high heat for 30 seconds, add the peanut oil, and coat the wok with a spatula. When a wisp of white smoke appears, add the ½-inch slice of ginger and remaining ¾ teaspoon salt. Stir briefly, then add the fennel and stir-fry for 30 seconds. Add the bean sprouts, mix well, and cook for 1½ minutes. Add the scallions and mix well. When the scallions turn bright green, turn off the heat, transfer to a heated serving dish, and serve immediately.

Serves 4 to 6

Note: This dish may also be served at room temperature or cold, as a salad.

BEAN SPROUTS WITH YELLOW CHIVES
Gau Wong Chau Nga Choi

Yellow chives have been part of the Chinese kitchen for countless years. They are simply garlic chives that have been deprived of sunlight and thus remain yellow instead of becoming green. They made their appearance in the West about fifteen years ago when the so-called Vietnamese-Chinese "boat people" immigrated to the West. Growing and selling yellow chives became a way of making a living, and a "new" ingredient came into the modern Western kitchen.

8 cups cold water

1 pound bean sprouts, washed and picked clean

3 tablespoons peanut oil

¼ teaspoon salt, or to taste

½ tablespoon shredded fresh ginger

¼ pound yellow chives, washed and cut into ½-inch sections (if
    unavailable, use regular chives)

2 tablespoons whole fresh coriander leaves

1. Bring the cold water to a boil. Add sprouts and water-blanch for 5 seconds. Turn off the heat, run cold water into the pot, and drain. This should be done 1 hour before further preparation to ensure that the sprouts dry completely. Occasionally loosen the sprouts with chopsticks to help drying.

2. Heat a wok over high heat for 30 seconds. Add the peanut oil and salt, stir, and coat the wok with a spatula. When a wisp of white smoke appears, add the ginger and stir. Add yellow chives and mix well. Add the bean sprouts and stir-fry together for 1½ minutes, until very hot. Turn off the heat, transfer to a serving dish, sprinkle coriander leaves on top, and serve immediately.

Serves 4 to 6

GREEN OIL BEAN SPROUTS
Chau Ngah Choi

The green oil from fresh coriander will not color these so-called "silver needles," but the flavor given off is unusual indeed, quite different from a simple stir-fry with peanut or vegetable oil.

1 pound bean sprouts
2 tablespoons Green Oil (page 39)
½ teaspoon salt
1 tablespoon julienned fresh ginger

1. Wash the bean sprouts. Remove remnants of skin that adhere to the sprouts but leave the buds on the stalks. Allow to drain and dry completely. Loosen to help with drying.

2. Heat a wok over high heat for 30 seconds. Add the green oil and salt and coat the wok with a spatula. When a wisp of white smoke appears, add the ginger and stir briefly. Add the bean sprouts and stir-fry together for 2 to 3 minutes, or until sprouts wilt and turn from white to an off-white color. Turn off heat, transfer to a heated serving dish, and serve immediately.

Serves 4 to 6

Mung Bean Sprouts

清
炒
拾
菜

CHIVES STIR-FRIED WITH BEAN SPROUTS
Ching Chau Sub Choi

This dish is enjoyed in China not only for its taste but for its humor. The Chinese translates as "stir-fried ten vegetables." The word for chives is *gau choi*, which also means "nine vegetables"; thus chives plus one more vegetable, bean sprouts, equals ten.

4 cups cold water

¾ pound bean sprouts

1½ tablespoons peanut oil

½ teaspoon salt

2 teaspoons minced ginger

1¼ cups chives, cut into 1-inch pieces (discard about ⅛ inch of the hard end)

1. In a large pot, bring the water to a boil. Place the bean sprouts in the water and cook, stirring, for no longer than 20 seconds. Turn the heat off, run cold water into the pot, and drain. Run more cold water into the pot and drain excess water. Set aside. This should be done 1 hour before further preparation to ensure that the sprouts dry completely. Occasionally loosen the sprouts with chopsticks to help drying.

2. Heat a wok over high heat for 1 minute. Add the peanut oil and coat the wok with a spatula. When a wisp of white smoke appears, add salt and ginger. When the ginger turns light brown, add the chives. Stir well for about 30 seconds, or until the chives turn bright green. Add the bean sprouts, stir well, and cook for 1 minute. Turn off heat. Transfer to a serving dish and serve immediately.

Serves 4 to 6

SWEET SCALLION BEAN SPROUTS
Tim Chung Nga Choi

This is a simple and quite refreshing summer dish. It is, at the same time, a small cooking lesson. I prefer not to cook vegetables with soy sauce; though it is widely practiced, it is not the true Chinese way of cooking. Soy should be mixed with other ingredients to make a sauce, which is then combined with still other ingredients. In this particular dish the soy mix is tossed with the vegetables, not cooked with them, but the principle remains the same.

Sauce ingredients

2 tablespoons Sweet Scallion Sauce (page 37)
½ tablespoon Green Oil (page 39)
¼ teaspoon salt
3 tablespoons finely sliced scallion greens

To complete the dish

8 cups cold water
One ½-inch-wide slice fresh ginger
1 pound bean sprouts

1. Combine the sauce ingredients in a bowl. Reserve.

2. Place the cold water in a large pot. Add the ginger. Cover and bring to a boil over high heat. Add the bean sprouts. Use a chopstick or wooden spoon to ensure that the sprouts are completely submerged. Cook for 10 seconds. Turn off the heat and drain the water completely.

3. Place the bean sprouts in a large bowl. Stir sauce and pour into sprouts. Mix well so that sprouts are thoroughly coated. Transfer to a serving dish and serve at room temperature.

Serves 4 to 6

炒
西
洋
菜

STIR-FRIED WATERCRESS
Chau Sei Yung Choi

Watercress stir-fried alone is delicious, because of its pungency. It is also used in elaborate banquets and dishes as a decorative food, often as a border around or a divider between other foods, even as a bed on which other foods rest. I prefer it unadorned, as it is.

8 cups water
1¼-inch-wide slice fresh ginger
½ teaspoon baking soda (optional)
2 teaspoons salt
3 bunches fresh watercress
2 tablespoons peanut oil
1 teaspoon sesame oil
¼ teaspoon salt, or to taste

1. In a pot place the water, ginger, baking soda, and 2 teaspoons salt, and bring to a boil over high heat. Immerse the watercress and water-blanch for ½ minute. The watercress should become bright green. Turn off the heat, run cold water into the pot, and allow to drain for 10 to 15 minutes, tossing occasionally.

2. Heat a wok over high heat for 30 seconds. Add the peanut and sesame oils and coat the wok with a spatula. When a wisp of white smoke appears, add ¼ teaspoon salt and stir. Add the watercress. You may need a chopstick to loosen the watercress. Stir-fry for 2 to 3 minutes, until hot. Turn off the heat, transfer to a heated serving dish, and serve immediately.

Serves 4 to 6

CHICORY WITH SCALLION OIL
Suk Goi Chung Yau

Chicory, or curly endive, has until recently not been well known in China. But in Hong Kong all foods can be found. It is a fine leaf to cook in combination with other vegetables and seasonings because of its pleasant taste. Its bitterness is almost completely removed when it is blanched.

8 cups cold water

One ½-inch-wide slice fresh ginger, lightly smashed

1 teaspoon salt

¼ teaspoon baking soda, optional (see note below)

1½ pounds chicory, tender stalks only, halved (save core and old outer
 stalks for another use)

2 tablespoons Scallion Oil (page 37)

¼ teaspoon salt, or to taste

1. Place the water in a large pot with the ginger, 1 teaspoon salt, and baking soda. Cover and bring to a boil over high heat. Add the chicory and blanch for 10 seconds, until bright green. Turn off the heat, run cold water into the pot, and drain well.

2. Heat a wok over high heat. Add the Scallion Oil and ¼ teaspoon salt. Coat the wok with a spatula. When a wisp of white smoke appears, add the chicory and toss well in the oil. (A chopstick may be needed to loosen the chicory.) Stir-fry for about 1½ minutes, until very hot. Taste a piece of chicory; an additional bit of salt may be necessary. Turn off the heat. Transfer to a heated dish and serve immediately.

Serves 4 to 6

Note: The baking soda is added to the water to ensure that the chicory will remain bright green. It is, of course, optional. The Chinese regard bright color as important to food presentation.

SPINACH WITH GARLIC
Chau Bor Choi

In Chinese, spinach is called *bor choi*, or "wavy vegetable," which describes it most accurately. The fine taste of spinach is best enjoyed in a simple manner, accented with the strength of garlic. Often, cooked spinach is used as a bed for other foods on decorative platters because of its bright green color. You may wish to do the same.

8 cups cold water
1¼ teaspoons salt
1¼-inch-wide slice fresh ginger
¼ teaspoon baking soda, optional (see note below)
1 pound spinach
2 tablespoons peanut oil
1 tablespoon minced garlic

1. In a pot place the water, 1 teaspoon salt, ginger, and baking soda. Bring to a boil. Add the spinach, completely submerge it, and water-blanch for 30 seconds. Turn off the heat and run cold water into the pot. Drain the spinach completely. Reserve.

2. Heat a wok over high heat for 30 seconds. Add the peanut oil and remaining ¼ teaspoon salt, or more to taste, and coat the wok with a spatula. When a wisp of white smoke appears, add the garlic and stir for about 30 seconds, or until the garlic turns light brown. Add the spinach and stir-fry together for 2 to 3 minutes, until very hot. Make certain to keep spinach leaves as separate as possible so they will become coated with the minced garlic and the oil. Turn off the heat, transfer to a heated serving dish, and serve immediately.

Serves 4 to 6

Note: The baking soda is added to the water to ensure that the spinach will remain bright green. It is, of course, optional. The Chinese regard bright color as important to food presentation.

STIR-FRIED LETTUCE
Ho Yau Sahng Choi

Here is a quick and easy stir-fry that uses that most mundane of vegetables, iceberg lettuce. But with a good sauce it becomes a special dish indeed. Use only light green leaves, not the darker green outer leaves or the white inner leaves. A 2-pound head will usually yield a pound of light green leaves.

1 pound iceberg lettuce (see comment above)

Sauce ingredients

1 teaspoon sesame oil
1½ teaspoons dark soy sauce
1½ tablespoons oyster sauce
¾ teaspoon sugar
1½ tablespoons cornstarch
Pinch of white pepper
½ cup Vegetable Stock (pages 31–32)

To complete the dish

8 cups cold water
½ teaspoon baking soda, optional (see note below)
2 tablespoons peanut oil
1 teaspoon minced ginger

1. Wash the lettuce leaves several times. Break each into 3 pieces. Drain and reserve.

2. Combine the sauce ingredients and reserve.

3. Place the water in a large pot with the baking soda and bring to a boil. Drop the lettuce into the water, immersing the leaves. Cook for $1/2$ minute, until the leaves soften and become bright green. Place the pot under cold running water to cool. Drain. Loosen the leaves with chopsticks and drain thoroughly through a strainer. Reserve.

4. Heat a wok over high heat for 45 seconds and add the peanut oil. Coat the sides of the wok with a spatula. When a wisp of white smoke appears, add the ginger. When the ginger turns light brown, add the lettuce leaves and stir together. Cook for 1 to $1\frac{1}{2}$ minutes. Make a well in the center of the lettuce leaves, stir the sauce, and pour it into the well. Stir and cook until the sauce thickens and turns brown. Remove to a preheated serving dish and serve immediately.

Serves 4 to 6

Note: The baking soda is added to the water to ensure that the lettuce will remain bright green. It is, of course, optional. The Chinese regard bright color as important to food presentation.

ROMAINE LETTUCE WITH BLACK BEANS
Dau See Chau Sang Choi

In China there is a species of lettuce that is almost identical to romaine. To the Chinese all lettuce is *sang choi*. This particular lettuce looks like romaine but has a texture somewhat like iceberg lettuce. It is called *bor lei sang choi*, or "glass lettuce." This recipe for glass lettuce is just fine with romaine.

1¼ pounds romaine lettuce
8 cups cold water
1 teaspoon salt
¼ teaspoon baking soda, optional (see note below)

Sauce ingredients

2 teaspoons Shao-Hsing wine or sherry
1½ tablespoons oyster sauce
1 teaspoon sesame oil
2 teaspoons soy sauce
1 teaspoon sugar
Pinch of white pepper
2 teaspoons cornstarch
2 tablespoons Vegetable Stock (pages 31–32)

To complete the dish

2½ tablespoons peanut oil
¼ teaspoon salt
3 cloves garlic, lightly smashed
1 tablespoon fermented black beans, washed twice and drained

1. Wash the lettuce well and drain. Cut into 2-inch pieces, separating the stalk sections from the leaves and discard old wilted leaves. After preparation, the 1¼ pounds should yield 1 pound.

2. Place the water in a pot, add the salt and baking soda, cover, and bring to a boil. Add the lettuce stalks first, stir for 5 seconds, then add the leaves. Submerge completely in water and cook for 5 seconds. Turn off the heat. Run cold water into the pot. Drain thoroughly. Toss the lettuce to ensure dryness. Reserve.

3. Combine the sauce ingredients in a bowl. Reserve.

4. Heat a wok over high heat for 30 seconds. Add the peanut oil and salt, and coat the wok with a spatula. When a wisp of white smoke appears, add the garlic and black beans. Stir and mix well, about 20 seconds, until garlic turns light brown. Add the reserved lettuce and mix thoroughly, making certain the leaves and stalks are coated and very hot, about 1½ minutes. Make a well in the center of the mixture, stir the sauce, pour it in, and mix well. When the sauce thickens and bubbles, turn off the heat, transfer to a heated serving dish, and serve immediately (see note below).

Serves 4 to 6

Note: Baking soda is added to enhance the green of the lettuce and to make it tender. It is optional, if your preference is not to use it.

Note: After lettuce has been transferred to the serving dish, liquid will be released because the lettuce contains much water. This will thin the sauce but not alter it. The dish is best served, with the sauce, over cooked rice.

STIR-FRIED CARROTS AND CELERY
Sai Con Chau Gum Sun

Carrots, the "golden shoots" of China, marry well with celery. In China there are two celeries: the kind that all of us are familiar with, and Chinese celery, which is small and very thin with a pronounced celery aroma. Chinese celery is available in Chinese and Asian markets, and if you find it I recommend you use it for this recipe. If not, then the celery you are used to will be just fine.

1½ tablespoons peanut oil

½ teaspoon salt

2 to 3 large scallions, white and green parts separated and sliced diagonally into ½-inch pieces (⅓ cup white and ½ cup green)

3 large carrots, peeled, halved lengthwise, and sliced across into half-moons (1½ cups)

4 large stalks celery, diagonally sliced into ⅓-inch pieces (1½ cups)(see note below)

1. Heat a wok over high heat for 30 seconds. Add the peanut oil and salt and coat the wok with a spatula. When a wisp of white smoke appears, add the white portions of the scallions and stir-fry for 15 seconds. Add the carrots and celery and stir-fry all together for 3 minutes. Add the green portions of the scallions and toss together. When the green portions become bright green, turn off the heat, transfer to a heated serving dish, and serve immediately.

Serves 4 to 6

Note: When cooked, Chinese celery tends to shrink. So if you use Chinese celery, add ¼ cup more to the recipe and cut into 1-inch, rather than ⅓-inch, pieces.

雙
椒
炒
椰
菜

STIR-FRIED CABBAGE AND PEPPERS
Seung Jiu Chu Yeh Choi

Cabbage is plentiful throughout China and most reasonably priced. Thus it is widely used. It is also, at its best, quite sweet, and stir-frying releases that sweetness. Its name is almost a misnomer—the words for cabbage, *yeh choi*, sound like the words for "grandfather vegetable."

1 teaspoon Scallion Oil (page 37)

½ teaspoon sesame oil

½ tablespoon finely shredded ginger

½ teaspoon salt

¾ pound cabbage, inner white tender portions only, cut into ¼-inch-by-3-
   inch pieces (4 cups packed tightly)

1 tablespoon Shao-Hsing wine or sherry

½ cup julienned sweet red peppers

½ cup julienned green peppers

3 tablespoons Vegetable Stock (pages 31–32)

1. Heat a wok over high heat for 30 seconds. Add the scallion and sesame oils and coat the wok with a spatula. When a wisp of white smoke appears, add the ginger and salt and stir briefly. Add the cabbage and stir-fry for 30 seconds. Add the wine by drizzling it down the side of the wok. Mix well. Add the peppers and stir-fry for 1 minute. Add 2 tablespoons vegetable stock and stir into vegetables.

2. Cook for 7 minutes, stirring frequently. If the stock is absorbed, add the remaining tablespoon of stock. Cook until the cabbage is tender. Turn off the heat, transfer to a heated serving dish, and serve immediately.

Serves 4 to 6

STIR-FRIED RED CABBAGE
Chau Hung Yeh Choi

Red cabbage is seldom seen in much of China, where white cabbage abounds. It is more common as one nears Hong Kong, for in these fields vegetables are grown for that city's Western population—including the red cabbage favored by those early Western immigrants to Hong Kong, the so-called White Russians.

2½ tablespoons peanut oil

1¼-inch-wide slice fresh ginger

¾ teaspoon salt, or to taste

1 pound red cabbage, outer leaves removed, inner tender portions cut into
 ¼-inch-by-3-inch strips (5¼ cups tightly packed)

2 to 3 tablespoons Vegetable Stock (pages 31–32), if needed

4 to 5 scallions, green parts cut into 2-inch pieces (1 cup)

1. Heat a wok over high heat for 30 seconds. Add the peanut oil and coat the wok with a spatula. When a wisp of white smoke appears, add the ginger and salt. When ginger turns light brown, add the cabbage. Stir-fry for about 7 minutes, until the cabbage is softened. If too dry, add 2 to 3 tablespoons vegetable stock to moisten. Add the scallions and stir-fry for 1 minute, or until scallions turn bright green. Turn off the heat, transfer to a heated serving dish, and serve immediately.

Serves 4 to 6

STIR-FRIED BOK CHOY
Ching Chau Bok Choy

Is there anyone who does not know of the ubiquitous bok choy? This sweet Chinese stalk vegetable has even made its way into the French kitchen these days, and to good advantage.

Sauce ingredients

⅓ cup Vegetable Stock (pages 31–32)

1 tablespoon cornstarch

1 teaspoon dark soy sauce

1 tablespoon oyster sauce

To complete the dish

2 tablespoons Scallion Oil (page 37)

1¼-inch-wide slice fresh ginger

½ teaspoon salt

1½ pounds bok choy, separated into white stalks and green leaves and cut
　　into 1-inch pieces (this should yield about 4 cups of stalks and 6
　　cups of leaves, tightly packed)

1. Combine the sauce ingredients in a bowl. Reserve.

2. Heat a wok over high heat for 30 seconds. Add the Scallion Oil. When a wisp
of white smoke appears, add the ginger and salt. When ginger turns light brown,
add the white stalks of bok choy and stir-fry for about 1 minute. Add the leaves
and stir-fry to mix well. If too dry, sprinkle a bit of cold water on leaves. The
leaves should be bright green. Make a well in the center of the mixture, stir the
sauce, and pour it in. Stir-fry until the sauce thickens and begins to bubble.
Turn off the heat, remove to a heated serving dish, and serve immediately.

Serves 4 to 6

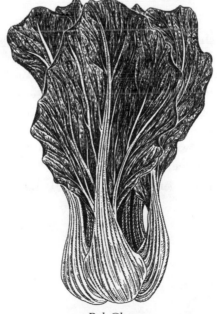

Bok Choy

Bok Choy Stir-Fried with Bamboo Shoots and Mushrooms
Bok Choy Chau Seung Tung

Seung Tung, the name for this classic stir-fry, translates as "double winter." It signifies that winter bamboo shoots and Chinese dried black mushrooms—the name for which is *tung gu*, or "winter mushrooms"—together make a "double winter stir-fry."

Sauce ingredients

⅓ cup Vegetable Stock (pages 31–32)

1½ tablespoons oyster sauce

1 teaspoon sesame oil

1 teaspoon dark soy sauce

1 teaspoon light soy sauce

1 teaspoon sugar

Pinch of white pepper

2½ teaspoons cornstarch

To complete the dish

3 tablespoons Scallion Oil (page 37)

One ½-inch-wide slice fresh ginger, lightly smashed

¼ teaspoon salt

12 medium Chinese dried black mushrooms, soaked for 1½ hours in hot
water, water squeezed off, stems discarded, and caps quartered

1 pound bok choy, stalks and leaves separated, cut diagonally into ½-inch
pieces

⅔ cup canned winter bamboo shoots, thinly sliced crosswise

1 tablespoon Shao-Hsing wine or sherry

4 tablespoons Vegetable Stock (pages 31–32)

1. Combine the sauce ingredients in a bowl. Reserve.

2. Heat a wok over high heat for 30 seconds. Add the Scallion Oil and coat the wok with a spatula. When a wisp of white smoke appears, add the ginger and salt. Stir briefly, add the mushrooms, and cook for 1 minute. Add the bok choy stalks and stir. Cook for 30 seconds. Add the bamboo shoots, stir briefly, and add the wine. Mix well. Add the bok choy leaves and stir. Add 2 tablespoons vegetable stock and mix well.

3. Cover the wok. Allow to cook for 2 minutes. Check the mixture to see if any liquid remains in the wok. (If not, add the remaining vegetable stock.) Cover the wok again and cook for 1 minute more until the stalks are tender. Make a well in the center of the mixture. Stir the sauce and pour it in. Mix well. When the sauce begins to bubble and turn brown, turn off the heat. Transfer to a heated dish and serve immediately with cooked rice.

Serves 4 to 6

SHANGHAI BOK CHOY
Shanghai Bok Choy Ho Jop

This is a special vegetable, native to Shanghai and the region around it. It is, however, widely available in the United States, and we are fortunate for this.

Sauce ingredients

½ teaspoon dark soy sauce

2 teaspoons oyster sauce

¼ teaspoon salt

½ teaspoon sugar

½ teaspoon Shao-Hsing wine or sherry

⅛ teaspoon white pepper

2 teaspoons cornstarch

½ cup Vegetable Stock (pages 31–32)

To complete the dish

6 heads Shanghai bok choy, about 2½ pounds

6 cups water

½ teaspoon baking soda, optional (see note below)

1 teaspoon salt

2 tablespoons peanut oil

Shanghai Bok Choy

1. Combine the sauce ingredients in a bowl. Reserve.

2. Remove any discolored leaves from the outer part of the bok choy and cut each head lengthwise into quarters. Remove most of the leaves. Wash the bok choy well under running water to remove sand and grit. Drain. Heat the water in a wok and add the baking soda and salt. When the water boils, add the bok choy and bring back to a boil. Then immediately turn off the heat. Run cold water into the wok and drain. Run cold water in again and drain.

3. Dry the wok thoroughly. Place over high heat for 45 seconds. Add the peanut oil and coat the sides of the wok with a spatula. When a wisp of white smoke appears, add the bok choy. Stir-fry for 4 minutes, or until hot. Make a well in the center of the bok choy, stir the sauce, and pour it in. Stir until the sauce thickens. Turn off the heat, transfer the bok choy to a heated serving platter, and serve.

Serves 4 to 6

Note: The baking soda is added to the water to ensure that the bok choy will remain bright green. It is, of course, optional. The Chinese regard bright color as important to food presentation.

STIR-FRIED CHOI SUM
Ching Chau Yau Choi

Choi Sum is one of the most delicious of Chinese vegetables. It is bright green, resembling Chinese broccoli, but has small yellow flower buds. It is available in Asian markets. When cooked it is very sweet.

2 bunches *choi sum*
1¼-inch-wide slice fresh ginger
8 cups cold water
½ teaspoon baking soda, optional (see note below)
2½ tablespoons peanut oil
¼ teaspoon salt
2 teaspoons minced ginger

Choi Sum

1. Wash the *choi sum*. Break off the tender top portions, about 4 to 5 inches. Discard the large leaves and flowers. Set aside.

2. In a large pot place the ginger slice, water, and baking soda, and bring to a boil. Add the *choi sum* and water-blanch until it becomes bright green, about 1 minute. Turn off the heat, remove the pot from the stove, and pour through a strainer. Run under cold water for 1 minute, then set aside. The *choi sum* must drain thoroughly, so allow it to sit for 1 to 1½ hours.

3. Heat a wok over high heat. Add the peanut oil and coat the wok with a spatula. Add the salt and minced ginger. Stir, and when the ginger turns brown, add the *choi sum*. Stir-fry for 2 to 3 minutes, until hot. Transfer to a serving dish and serve immediately.

Serves 4 to 6

Note: The baking soda is added to the water to ensure that the *choi sum* will remain bright green. It is, of course, optional. The Chinese regard bright color as important to food presentation.

STIR-FRIED TIENTSIN BOK CHOY
Siu Chau Tientsin Bok Choy

In China this vegetable, a cabbage, is variously called Peking bok choy and Shantung bok choy. It is also known as celery cabbage or Napa cabbage. It picks up the tastes of whatever it is cooked with. This is how it is prepared in Peking.

Sauce ingredients

2 teaspoons dark soy sauce

1 teaspoon sugar

½ teaspoon salt

2 teaspoons cornstarch

½ teaspoon sesame oil

½ teaspoon white vinegar

2 teaspoons Shao-Hsing wine or sherry

3 tablespoons Vegetable Stock (pages 31–32)

To complete the dish

1 pound Tientsin bok choy, also called Napa cabbage

2 tablespoons peanut oil

2 teaspoons minced ginger

8 Chinese dried black mushrooms, soaked in hot water for 30 minutes, stems discarded, and caps julienned

½ cup julienned bamboo shoots

¼ cup seeded and julienned sweet red peppers

1. Combine the sauce ingredients in a bowl. Reserve.

2. Separate the bok choy into individual leaves. Wash thoroughly and drain off excess water. Using a knife, cut the ribs from the leaves. Cut the ribs into julienne; thinly slice the leaves. Reserve the ribs and leaves separately.

3. Heat a wok over high heat for 1 minute. Add the peanut oil. Coat the wok with a spatula. Add the ginger and stir-fry for 20 seconds. Add the ribs of bok choy and mushrooms and stir well. Add the bamboo shoots and stir well. Add the bok choy leaves, mix well, and cook for 1 minute. Add the red peppers, mix thoroughly, and cook for 2 minutes more.

4. Make a well in the center of the mixture. Stir the sauce, pour it into the well, and mix thoroughly until the sauce thickens. Remove from wok and serve immediately.

Serves 4 to 6

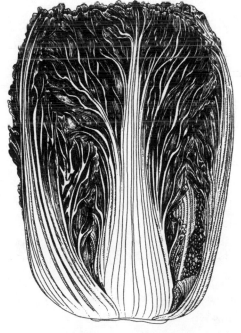

Tientsin Bok Choy

FOUR-SEASON BEANS
Sei Guai Dau

The Chinese call string beans "four-season beans" because they are available throughout the year. This is how string beans are prepared in Szechuan.

Sauce ingredients

1 tablespoon Oyster Sauce (page 15)

1 teaspoon dark soy sauce

¾ teaspoon sugar

⅛ teaspoon salt

1 teaspoon sesame oil

½ teaspoon white vinegar

1½ teaspoons Shao-Hsing wine or sherry

½ to ¾ teaspoon soaked hot pepper flakes from bottom of Hot Oil (page 36)

1½ teaspoons cornstarch

3 tablespoons Vegetable Stock (pages 31–32)

Pinch of white pepper

To complete the dish

12 ounces fresh green string beans, both ends removed, and dried very thoroughly (since they are to be oil-blanched)

3 cups plus 1½ tablespoons peanut oil

2 teaspoons minced ginger

2 teaspoons minced garlic

1. Combine the sauce ingredients in a bowl. Reserve.

2. Heat a wok over high heat for 40 seconds. Add 3 cups peanut oil. When a wisp of white smoke appears, lower the beans into the oil with a Chinese strainer and oil-blanch for 2 minutes, or until beans soften. Remove with a strainer and drain over a bowl.

3. Pour off the oil from the wok. Add the remaining 1½ tablespoons oil to the wok. Over high heat add the ginger and stir; add the garlic and stir. When the garlic browns add the beans, mix well, and cook for 1 minute. Make a well in the center. Stir the sauce and then pour it into the well. Mix all the ingredients thoroughly. When the sauce thickens and bubbles, turn off the heat. Remove the beans from the wok and serve.

Serves 4 to 6

圓
鍋
荳

TWICE-FRIED CHINESE LONG BEANS
Wui Wor Dau

Long beans, known as *dau gok*, or "bean horns," because of their shape and length, grow in China to 1 to 3 feet in length. In the West, in this country, the longest you will find them is about 2 feet. They are of the bean family, taste quite similar, and string beans may be used in their place in this recipe (see note below).

Sauce ingredients

1 teaspoon dark soy sauce
1 teaspoon light soy sauce
1 teaspoon sugar
1 tablespoon oyster sauce
¾ teaspoon sesame oil
½ tablespoon Shao-Hsing wine or sherry
1½ teaspoons cornstarch
1 teaspoon white vinegar
⅛ teaspoon ground Szechuan peppercorns
3 tablespoons Vegetable Stock (pages 31–32)

To complete the dish

3½ cups peanut oil
1 pound long beans, both ends removed, dried thoroughly and cut into
    2½-inch lengths
2 teaspoons minced ginger
2 teaspoons minced garlic

1. Combine the sauce ingredients in a bowl. Reserve.
2. Heat a wok over high heat for 40 seconds. Add the peanut oil and heat to 350°F. Place the long beans in a Chinese strainer and lower into the oil. Oil-blanch for 1½ minutes, until softened. Remove and drain over a bowl.

3. Pour all but 1½ tablespoons of the oil from the wok. Over high heat add the ginger and garlic and stir. When the garlic becomes brown, add the long beans and stir-fry for 2 minutes. Make a well in the center of the mixture, stir the sauce, and pour it in. Mix well, making certain the beans are coated. When the sauce thickens and begins to bubble, turn off the heat, transfer to a heated serving dish, and serve immediately.

Serves 4 to 6

Note: When buying long beans, look for a deep green color and for thinness. When long beans are pale and fat, they are old and will be soft. As mentioned, this recipe may be made with string beans. If used, however, the string beans should be left whole, with both ends removed, and blanched for 3 minutes rather than 2.

Chinese Long Beans

STIR-FRIED STRING BEANS
Ching Chau See Guai Dau

As a child I grew up knowing of the Chinese long beans, the pods of which can be as long as 2 feet. The string bean is its cousin, and the two taste very much alike. Thus, for this recipe either string beans or long beans (which are available both in Asian specialty shops and in regular food markets) may be used.

2 tablespoons peanut oil
1 tablespoon julienned ginger
2 teaspoons sliced garlic
¾ teaspoon salt, or to taste
1 pound string beans, both ends removed, cut into 1½-inch pieces
1 to 2 tablespoons Vegetable Stock, if needed (pages 31–32)

1. Heat a wok over high heat for 30 seconds. Add the peanut oil and coat the wok with a spatula. When a wisp of white smoke appears, add the ginger, garlic, and salt. When the garlic turns light brown and releases its fragrance, add the string beans. Stir-fry and cook for 5 to 6 minutes, or until the string beans turn bright green. If they become dry, add the vegetable stock to moisten. Turn off the heat, transfer to a heated serving dish, and serve immediately.

Serves 4 to 6

SESAME STRING BEANS
Jee Mah Sei Guai Dau

Sesame seeds are utilized widely in the Chinese kitchen, especially in the vegetarian kitchen, because of the taste, aroma, and texture they impart. They do indeed combine nicely with the crispness of fresh string beans.

2 tablespoons Szechuan Peppercorn Oil (page 38)
¼ teaspoon salt, or to taste
2 tablespoons minced shallots
¾ pound string beans, both ends removed, cut into 1½-inch lengths
1 tablespoon white sesame seeds, dry-roasted (page 28)

1. Heat a wok over high heat for 30 seconds. Add the peanut oil and salt, mix, and coat the wok with a spatula. When a wisp of white smoke appears, add the shallots. Stir and cook for 2 minutes, until shallots release their aroma. Add the string beans and stir-fry for 3 to 4 minutes. Turn off the heat, transfer to a heated serving dish, sprinkle with the sesame seeds, and serve immediately.

Serves 4 to 6

STIR-FRIED CORN
Chau Gum Jue

In China, corn, that gift from the West, is known as *gum jue*, or "golden pearls." It is usually eaten in the summer, fresh, usually off the ear, sometimes on. Occasionally an ear of corn is steamed on a rack above a wok full of cooking rice. It is then eaten on the cob at room temperature, as a snack. When corn is to be part of a meal, the kernels are stripped from the ears and stir-fried to be eaten hot.

3½ teaspoons peanut oil
1½ teaspoons minced garlic
¼ teaspoon salt, or to taste
2½ cups fresh corn stripped from the cob (or use frozen; see note below)
1½ tablespoons cold water
1 scallion, green portion only finely sliced (3 tablespoons)

1. Heat a wok over high heat for 30 seconds. Add the peanut oil and coat the wok with a spatula. When a wisp of white smoke appears, add garlic and salt. Stir. When garlic turns light brown, add the corn, stir, and cook for 1 minute. Add the cold water and stir in. Cover wok and bring to a boil; this will take about 2 to 3 minutes. Remove the cover and stir the corn. Lower the heat, cover again, and cook for 3 minutes more, or until corn is tender. Turn off the heat, transfer to a heated dish, sprinkle with scallions, and serve immediately.

Serves 4 to 6

Note: If you use frozen corn, the dish is cooked differently. No water need be added, nor does the corn have to be covered and cooked after stir-frying. Just stir-fry until very hot, remove from the heat, and serve as indicated.

西蘭珍珠筍

BABY CORN WITH BROCCOLI STEMS

Sei Lam Sum Sum Jue Shun

These miniature ears of corn are sweet and increasingly available these days in specialty food shops. They also come canned. This dish, like the combination of asparagus and fresh corn in the next recipe, relies on texture and color, as well as taste, for its appeal. The recipe is also a perfect use of broccoli stems that are left over after you have used the flowerets in another dish.

3 cups water
1 teaspoon salt
¾ cup fresh baby corn, 8 to 10 ears (or use canned; see note below)
1½ tablespoons peanut oil
One ½-inch-wide slice fresh ginger, lightly smashed
2 cups broccoli stems, peeled and cut diagonally into ¼-inch slices
1½ medium-sized carrots, cut diagonally into ¼-inch slices (¾ cup)
2 teaspoons Shao-Hsing wine or sherry

1. If canned corn is used, skip to the next step. Bring the water to a boil with ½ teaspoon salt. Add the corn and boil for 2 minutes, or until tender. Turn off the heat and run cold water into the pot to cool the corn. Drain. Allow to cool, then cut each ear into 3 sections on the diagonal. Reserve.

2. Heat a wok over high heat for 30 seconds. Add the peanut oil and coat the wok with a spatula. When a wisp of white smoke appears, add the ginger and remaining ½ teaspoon salt. When the ginger turns light brown, add broccoli stems and carrots. Stir-fry for 1 minute. Add the corn. Stir-fry briefly, then add the wine and mix well. Cook for about 2 minutes, until the broccoli and carrots are tender but still crisp. Turn off the heat. Transfer to a heated serving dish and serve immediately.

Serves 4 to 6

Note: Any canned ears that remain may be kept in fresh water in a plastic container in the refrigerator. They will keep 3 to 4 weeks, but the water must be changed daily.

CORN WITH ASPARAGUS
Lo Sun Wui Gum Jue

In this preparation the crispness and green of the asparagus complement the yellow corn. This dish is a good example of the accommodation to be found in the Chinese kitchen. Both corn and asparagus are new to China. I had not tasted asparagus in China, and it was not until I moved to Hong Kong that I made its acquaintance.

2 tablespoons peanut oil
One ½-inch-thick slice fresh ginger
½ teaspoon salt
2 cups asparagus, cut diagonally into ¾-inch slices
10 ounces sweet corn kernels, fresh or frozen and thawed
1 to 2 tablespoons Vegetable Stock, if needed (pages 31–32)

1. Heat a wok over high heat for 30 seconds. Add the peanut oil and coat the wok with a spatula. When a wisp of white smoke appears, add the ginger and salt. When ginger turns light brown, add the asparagus. Stir-fry for 3 minutes, or until the asparagus turn bright green. Add the corn, mix, and stir-fry for 3 minutes more. If too dry, add 1 to 2 tablespoons vegetable stock. Turn off the heat, discard the ginger, transfer to a heated serving dish, and serve immediately.

Serves 4 to 6

STEAMED ASPARAGUS
Jing Lo Shun

The Chinese words for asparagus translate as "shoots of the mist," a lovely phrase, the source of which I do not know. But these spears, steamed and served with my Sweet Scallion Sauce, are not misty at all. They are quite direct.

1 pound asparagus, tender portions only (it may be necessary
    to buy 1¼ pounds to yield 1 pound trimmed)
2 tablespoons Sweet Scallion Sauce (page 37)

1. Remove the tiny scales from the asparagus stalks. These are easily removed with a thumbnail or a paring knife. Then cut off the hard, stringy bottoms. Wash.
2. Place in a steamer and steam for 3 to 5 minutes, until the stalks become light green. Remove from the steamer and cut each, on a board, in 2-inch lengths on the diagonal. Toss these in a bowl with the Sweet Scallion Sauce. Serve immediately.

Serves 4 to 6

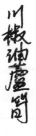

ASPARAGUS STIR-FRIED WITH SZECHUAN PEPPERCORN OIL
Chin Jiu Yau Lo Sun

This is a perfect example of how Szechuan Peppercorn Oil can enhance an essentially simple dish. The asparagus, already tasty, become doubly so with this fragrant and assertive oil.

2 tablespoons Szechuan Peppercorn Oil (page 38)
¼ teaspoon salt
½ pound asparagus, tender portions only, cut diagonally into ¾-inch slices
    (3 cups)
2 tablespoons minced carrots

1. Heat a wok over high heat for 30 seconds. Add the Peppercorn Oil and salt and coat the wok with a spatula. When a wisp of white smoke appears, add the asparagus. Stir-fry for 3 to 4 minutes, or until the pieces become tender and bright green. Add the carrots and stir-fry with asparagus for 1 minute, until well mixed. Turn off the heat, transfer to a heated serving dish, and serve immediately.

Serves 4 to 6

ASPARAGUS WITH FRESH MUSHROOMS
Lo Sun Chau Sin Gu

Fresh, fresh, fresh. This dish is best made with the vegetables just out of the ground. That is the very essence of the Chinese stir-fry.

2½ tablespoons Szechuan Peppercorn Oil (page 38)

¼ teaspoon salt, or to taste

3 tablespoons minced shallots

½ pound asparagus, tender portions only, cut diagonally into ¾-inch pieces

20 fresh mushroom caps, halved

1 tablespoon Shao-Hsing wine or sherry

1. Heat a wok over high heat for 30 seconds. Add Peppercorn Oil and salt and coat the wok with a spatula. When a wisp of white smoke appears, add the shallots. Stir-fry for 2 minutes, until the shallots soften and release their fragrance. Add the asparagus and stir-fry for 2 minutes. Add the mushrooms and stir-fry for 1 minute. Add the wine to the mixture by drizzling it down the side of the wok, and mix thoroughly. Cook for 2 minutes, until very hot. Turn off the heat, transfer to a heated serving dish, and serve immediately.

Serves 4 to 6

鮮
菇
炒
玉
花

MUSHROOMS WITH BROCCOLI
Sin Gu Chau Yuk Far

This is one of those deceptively simple stir-fries, with ingredients that are accessible always. The Chinese love it, and I believe you will too.

Sauce ingredients

⅓ cup Vegetable Stock (pages 31–32)

1 teaspoon light soy sauce

1 teaspoon double dark soy sauce

1½ teaspoons Shao-Hsing wine or sherry

½ teaspoon sugar

2½ teaspoons cornstarch

Pinch of white pepper

⅛ teaspoon salt

To complete the dish

3 quarts water

One slice fresh ginger, ½-inch thick

2 teaspoons salt

¾ pound fresh mushrooms, each about the size of a quarter, stems
     removed

¾ pound broccoli flowerets

2 tablespoons Scallion Oil (page 37)

2 teaspoons minced ginger

2 teaspoons minced garlic

¼ teaspoon salt

1. Combine the sauce ingredients in a bowl. Reserve.

2. In a large pot place the water, the slice of ginger, and 2 teaspoons of salt, and bring to a boil. Add the mushroom caps by lowering them into the water with a wire mesh strainer, and water-blanch for 1 minute. Remove from the pot and strain over a bowl. Allow the water in the pot to come back to a boil, add the broccoli, and water-blanch for 30 seconds until it turns bright green. Remove from the pot and strain.

3. Heat a wok over high heat for 30 seconds, add the Scallion Oil, and coat the wok with a spatula. When a wisp of white smoke appears, add minced ginger, garlic, and salt, and stir. When the garlic turns light brown, add the mushroom caps and the broccoli and stir-fry together for 2 minutes. Make a well in the center, stir the sauce, and pour it in. Stir all the ingredients well. When sauce begins to bubble and thicken, turn off the heat, remove from wok, transfer to a heated serving dish, and serve immediately.

Serves 4 to 6

CHINESE MUSHROOMS STIR-FRIED WITH CABBAGE
Dong Gu Chau Yeh Choi

The intense flavor of the mushrooms complements the texture and the fresh taste of the cabbage. This is a good example of the Chinese combination of opposites to create harmony.

2 tablespoons peanut oil
One ½-inch-wide slice fresh ginger, lightly smashed
½ teaspoon salt
1 pound cabbage, julienned (5½ cups tightly packed)
½ cup julienned and steamed Chinese dried black mushrooms (page 95)
2 to 3 tablespoons Vegetable Stock (pages 31–32)
5 to 6 scallions, green portions only, cut into 1½-inch sections (1 cup)

1. Heat a wok over high heat for 30 seconds. Add the peanut oil, ginger, and salt. Coat the wok with a spatula. When a wisp of white smoke appears, add the cabbage. Stir-fry for 1 minute. Add 2 tablespoons of vegetable stock. Mix well. Add the mushrooms, stir together, and cook for 5 minutes, or until cabbage softens. If the mixture is too dry add 1 more tablespoon of vegetable stock and mix well. Add the scallions and stir together. When the scallions turn bright green, turn off the heat, transfer to a heated serving dish, and serve immediately.

Serves 4 to 6

ASPARAGUS WITH STRAW MUSHROOMS
Lo Sun Chau Cho Gu

Here is a fine and tasty stir-fry with a basic ingredient, asparagus, that is only now becoming widely known in China. The importance of contrasting textures in a stir-fry is well illustrated in this dish—the crispness of the asparagus, the softness of the straw mushrooms, and the somewhat elastic bite of the gingko nuts.

Sauce ingredients

2 teaspoons soy sauce

2 teaspoons Shao-Hsing wine or sherry

1½ tablespoons oyster sauce

1 teaspoon white vinegar

1 teaspoon sesame oil

1 teaspoon sugar

⅛ teaspoon salt

1 tablespoon cornstarch

Pinch of white pepper

½ cup Vegetable Stock (pages 31–32)

To complete the dish

2 tablespoons peanut oil

2 teaspoons minced ginger

2 teaspoons minced garlic

⅛ teaspoon salt

12 asparagus spears, cut diagonally into ¼-inch pieces (1½ cups)

One 8-ounce can straw mushrooms, each mushroom halved lengthwise

½ cup lotus root, peeled and halved lengthwise into half-moons

10 baby corn, cut in half lengthwise

⅔ cup julienned sweet red peppers

½ cup fresh gingko nuts (page 100, or use canned if fresh are unavailable)

1 ounce bean threads, soaked in water for 30 minutes, drained, and cut into 4-inch lengths

2 tablespoons Vegetable Stock (pages 31–32)

1. Combine the sauce ingredients in a bowl. Reserve.

2. Heat a wok over high heat for 30 seconds. Add the peanut oil and coat the wok with a spatula. When a wisp of white smoke appears, add the ginger, garlic, and salt, and stir. When the garlic turns light brown, add the asparagus, then stir and cook for 30 seconds. Add straw mushrooms and stir together. Add the lotus root, baby corn, peppers, and gingko nuts, and stir-fry together for 3 minutes. Add the bean threads and mix well. Add the vegetable stock and cook all together for 3 minutes. Make a well in the center of the mixture, stir the sauce, and pour it in. When the sauce bubbles and begins to thicken, turn off the heat, transfer to a heated dish, and serve immediately.

Serves 4 to 6

蒸
冬
菇

STEAMED BLACK MUSHROOMS
Jing Dong Gu

These mushrooms are delightful eaten just as they come out of the steamer, as part of a larger meal. They may be eaten hot or cool and, as you will discover, are marvelous additions to other dishes.

24 Chinese dried black mushrooms, each the about the size of a silver
    dollar
½ teaspoon salt
1½ teaspoons sugar
4 teaspoons dark soy sauce
2 tablespoons Shao-Hsing wine or sherry
½ cup Vegetable Stock (pages 31–32)
2 scallions, trimmed and cut into 2-inch pieces
One slice fresh ginger, 1-inch thick, smashed

1. Soak the mushrooms in hot water for 1 hour. Wash thoroughly and squeeze out the excess water. Remove the stems and place the mushrooms in a heatproof dish. (It should be noted that after soaking, the mushrooms increase in size.)

2. Add the salt, sugar, soy sauce, wine, and stock, and toss with the mushrooms. Sprinkle the scallions atop the mushrooms and add the ginger. In a steamer, steam the mushrooms for 30 minutes.

3. Turn off the heat and remove from the steamer. Discard the scallions and ginger and gently toss mushrooms in the remaining liquid. Serve immediately, hot, or allow to cool before serving.

Serves 4 to 6

Note: These mushrooms will keep, refrigerated and covered with plastic wrap, for 4 to 5 days.

STUFFED MUSHROOMS I
Yeung Sin Gu

Stuffing mushrooms with mushrooms is a delightful concept, though not a new one. Yet this recipe differs from the traditional way of cooking stuffed mushrooms. In China, stuffed mushrooms are always fried. Baking these, with the addition of Szechuan Peppercorn Oil, imbues them completely with flavor, different indeed.

24 fresh mushroom caps (each about 1½ inches in diameter)
3 tablespoons Szechuan Peppercorn Oil (page 38)
2 large onions, cut into ¼-inch pieces (2 cups)
½ teaspoon salt
12 to 15 mushrooms, diced into ¼-inch pieces (1½ cups)
Pinch of ground Szechuan peppercorns
2½ tablespoons minced fresh coriander
2 tablespoons peanut oil

1. Heat a wok over high heat for 30 seconds. Add the Szechuan Peppercorn Oil and coat the wok with a spatula. When a wisp of white smoke appears, add the onions and salt. Stir, lower the heat to medium, and cook for 15 minutes, stirring frequently. The onions will be reduced by half. Raise the heat back to high, add the diced mushrooms, and stir, mixing well. Cook for 1½ minutes, then lower the heat and cook for 15 to 20 minutes. Stir frequently to prevent sticking. The onion-mushroom mixture will reduce to 1 cup. Add a pinch of Szechuan peppercorns and stir in. Add the coriander and mix well. Turn off the heat, transfer to a shallow dish, and reserve.

2. Coat the mushroom caps with peanut oil. Place on a nonstick baking sheet. Stuff each cap with 2 teaspoons of the stuffing. Pat firmly with a butter knife.

3. Preheat oven to 400°F for 20 minutes. Into the oven place the baking sheets with the stuffed mushrooms and bake for 30 minutes, until browned. Remove from the oven, transfer to a heated platter, and serve immediately.

Serves 4 to 6

STUFFED MUSHROOMS II
Yeung Tung Gu

Here is another stuffed mushroom preparation, utilizing Chinese dried black mushrooms instead of fresh ones. This dish is pure Chinese tradition.

3 tablespoons peanut oil

3 tablespoons minced fresh coriander

1½ cups onions cut into ¼-inch dice

1 cake fresh bean curd, mashed (to make ¾ cup)

2 fresh water chestnuts, peeled and cut into ⅛-inch dice

½ tablespoon minced carrots

¾ teaspoon salt

¾ teaspoon sugar

1 teaspoon Green Oil (page 39)

½ teaspoon soy sauce

½ teaspoon white vinegar

Pinch of white pepper

18 Chinese dried black mushrooms, each about 1½ inches in diameter,
        soaked in hot water for 2 hours, squeezed dry, stems removed

2 teaspoons cornstarch

1. Heat a wok over high heat for 30 seconds. Add 2 tablespoons of the peanut oil and coat the wok with a spatula. When a wisp of white smoke appears, add the coriander, then stir and cook for 15 seconds. Add onions, stir, lower heat to medium, and cook for 10 minutes. The onions should reduce to ¾ cup. Turn off the heat and transfer to a bowl. Combine with all other ingredients except the peanut oil, mushrooms, and cornstarch. Mix well. Reserve.

2. Place the mushrooms in a large dish, caps up. Lightly sprinkle cornstarch inside the caps. Place about 1 tablespoon of filling in each cap and pat down firmly. Any leftover filling may be used to fill additional caps.

3. In a nonstick frying pan add the remaining tablespoon of peanut oil. Place 9 of the stuffed caps, stuffed side down, in the pan and fry over medium heat for 3 to 4 minutes. Turn over and fry for another 2 to 3 minutes. Transfer to a heated serving dish. Fry the remaining 9 caps in the same manner. A bit more oil may be needed.

4. Serve immediately. I recommend these with Hot Mustard (page 44) that has been lightly touched with a hot pepper sauce, such as Tabasco.

Serves 4 to 6

Note: These stuffed mushrooms may also be steamed. The preparation is identical, except that the steaming process replaces frying. Steamed, the mushrooms taste quite different, and they are well worth trying. If steaming, I suggest that the caps be sprinkled with 3 tablespoons of minced carrots, for color as well as for texture. Steam the mushrooms for 20 to 25 minutes, until they soften.

黑
白
冬
菇

BLACK AND WHITE MUSHROOMS
Hok Bok Tung Gu

In China mushrooms are eaten widely, alone or in combination with other foods. Putting fresh together with dried—the mild and the pronounced, the black and the white—is an illustration of the yin and the yang of the Chinese kitchen.

Sauce ingredients

1 teaspoon light soy sauce

1 teaspoon dark soy sauce

1 teaspoon sugar

1 teaspoon sesame oil

1 tablespoon cornstarch

¼ cup mushroom liquid

Pinch of white pepper

To complete the dish

20 Chinese dried black mushrooms, each about the size of a half-dollar, soaked in hot water for 30 minutes, stems removed

2 scallions, trimmed and cut into 3 pieces each

One slice fresh ginger, 1-inch thick

1 teaspoon sugar

2 tablespoons dark soy sauce

1 tablespoons Shao-Hsing wine or sherry

1 teaspoon sesame oil

½ cup Vegetable Stock (pages 31–32)

4 tablespoons Scallion Oil (page 37)

20 fresh mushrooms, about silver dollar size, brushed clean and stems removed

2 teaspoons minced garlic

2 teaspoons minced ginger

Sprigs of fresh coriander

1. Place the black mushrooms, scallions, ginger, sugar, dark soy sauce, wine, sesame oil, vegetable stock, and 2 tablespoons of Scallion Oil in a heatproof dish. Mix thoroughly so the mushrooms are well coated. Steam over high heat for 20 minutes. Remove from the heat and allow to cool. Drain off and reserve the steaming liquid for the sauce. Reserve the mushrooms. Discard the ginger and scallions.

2. Combine the sauce ingredients in a bowl. Reserve.

3. Add the fresh mushrooms to a pot of 6 cups of water and put over high heat. Water-blanch until the water boils. Turn off the heat. Run cold water into the pot, then drain. Remove the mushrooms and reserve.

4. Heat a wok over high heat for 45 seconds. Add the remaining 2 tablespoons Scallion Oil and coat the wok with a spatula. Add the garlic and ginger. When the garlic browns, add the blanched fresh mushrooms. Stir for 2 minutes. Add the black mushrooms and stir-fry for 1½ to 2 minutes, until very hot.

5. Make a well in the center of the mixture, stir the sauce, pour it into the well, and mix thoroughly. When the sauce thickens, turns brown, and bubbles, turn off the heat. Remove the mushrooms from the wok and serve, garnished with coriander.

Serves 4 to 6

GINGKO NUTS
Bok Guah

These nuts, so dear to the Chinese and strange to Westerners, are not even referred to as nuts in China, where they are known as "white fruit." They are never eaten alone as nuts, either raw or cooked, but are always combined with other ingredients. However, because they are important to several recipes in this book, the method of preparing them properly is essential.

3 ounces gingko nuts, unshelled and uncooked (see note below)
4 cups water

1. The shell of the gingko nut is quite hard. With the seam of the nut facing up, tap gently with a hammer on the seam to crack the shell. The nut inside must be intact. Once all the nuts are shelled, place 4 cups of water in a pot, bring to a boil, and add the nuts. Return to a boil. Lower the heat and cover the pot, leaving a slight opening. Allow to cook for 30 minutes. Turn off the heat and run cold water into the pot to cool. Remove the skin from the gingko nuts. Drain and reserve.

Note: Gingko nuts also come cooked, in cans. They are softer and lack the bite and more defined taste of freshly prepared nuts.

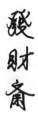

BUDDHA'S DELIGHT
Fat Choi Jai

Every New Year celebration should have this vegetable dish, which is an aspect of homage to Buddha. Its name, indeed, is a wish for prosperity in the New Year.

½ cup thinly sliced lotus root (4 to 5 ounces)

½ cup thinly sliced carrots

½ cup thinly sliced bamboo shoots

2 water chestnuts, peeled and thinly sliced

6 Chinese dried black mushrooms, soaked in hot water for 30 minutes until softened, stems removed

15 pieces tiger lily buds, soaked, bottom ends cut off

2 tablespoons celery, julienned into 1½-inch strips

⅓ cup snow peas, trimmed and thinly sliced

2 slices dried bean curd, soaked for 20 minutes and sliced into ¼-inch strips

¼ cup gingko nuts, shelled, peeled, and boiled (see page 100 for directions)

Sauce ingredients

¼ teaspoon salt

¾ teaspoon sugar

½ teaspoon sesame oil

¾ teaspoon dark soy sauce

½ tablespoon cornstarch

Pinch of white pepper

¼ cup Vegetable Stock (pages 31–32)

To complete the dish

2 tablespoons peanut oil

2 teaspoons minced ginger

¼ teaspoon salt

¼ cup water

½ package (1 ounce) bean thread noodles, soaked for 30 minutes and drained

1. Arrange the vegetables, bean curd, and gingko nuts in mounds on a platter. Combine the sauce ingredients in a bowl. Reserve.

2. Heat wok over high heat for 45 seconds, then add peanut oil, ginger, and salt. Coat the wok with a spatula. Begin adding vegetables. First stir-fry lotus root, then add carrots, then remaining vegetables, bean curd, and gingko nuts. Stir-fry continuously until snow peas turn bright green.

3. As you stir-fry, add ¼ cup water, a little at a time, to create steam for the cooking. Add the soaked, drained bean thread noodles and stir-fry them into the mix.

4. Make a well in the center of the ingredients. Stir the sauce and pour it into the well. Stir-fry for 2 more minutes. Turn off the heat, remove the ingredients from the wok, place in a serving dish, and serve immediately.

Serves 4 to 6

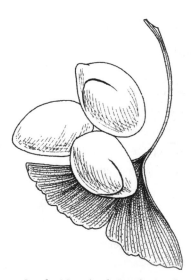

Gingko Nuts (with Gingko Leaf)

HAIR SEAWEED WITH MIXED VEGETABLES

Lor Horn Jai

Though it can be eaten anytime, of course, hair seaweed is usually eaten during the New Year celebration, at birthdays, and on special occasions. Its name, *fat choi*, sounds like the words for "prosperity" and is part of the name for Buddha's Delight (page 101). This is because that dish usually contains hair seaweed, though bean threads can be substituted. Similarly in this dish, the hair seaweed, if unobtainable, can be replaced with bean threads.

Sauce ingredients

2 teaspoons soy sauce

1 tablespoon Shao-Hsing wine or sherry

1½ tablespoons oyster sauce

1 teaspoon white vinegar

1 teaspoon sesame oil

1 teaspoon sugar

Pinch of white pepper

1 tablespoon cornstarch

⅛ teaspoon salt

½ cup Vegetable Stock (pages 31–32)

To complete the dish

2 tablespoons peanut oil

2½ teaspoons minced fresh ginger

⅛ teaspoon salt

2 teaspoons minced garlic

16 to 18 fresh quarter-sized white mushrooms, stemmed (1½ cups)

⅔ cup fresh carrots, peeled, washed, cut in half lengthwise, and thinly sliced into half-moons

½ cup celery, cut crosswise into ¼-inch slices

4 to 5 ounces lotus root, peeled, washed, cut in half lengthwise, and thinly sliced into half-moons (½ cup)

½ cup fresh gingko nuts, shelled, peeled, and boiled (page 100)

½ ounce hair seaweed, soaked in hot water for 45 minutes, drained, and cut into 2-inch lengths

3 tablespoons Vegetable Stock (pages 31–32)

1. Combine the sauce ingredients in a bowl. Reserve.

2. Heat a wok over high heat for 30 seconds. Add the peanut oil and coat the wok with a spatula. When a wisp of white smoke appears, add the ginger, salt, and garlic, and stir. When the garlic turns light brown, add the mushroom caps and stir. Add the carrots and stir. Add the celery and stir. Add the lotus roots and gingko nuts and stir. Add the hair seaweed and mix all the ingredients together well. Add the vegetable stock, stir, and cook for 3 minutes. Make a well in the center of the ingredients, stir the sauce, and pour it into the well. Stir together for 3 minutes. When the sauce begins to bubble and thicken, turn off the heat, transfer to a heated dish, and serve immediately.

Serves 4 to 6

Note: Hair seaweed comes in packages of various sizes. It is because of its black strands that the Chinese call it "hair." Unused seaweed will keep indefinitely in a closed jar.

Lotus Root

Two-Zucchini Stir-Fry
Chau Yee Dai Lei Gua

The Chinese name for zucchini, *yee dai lei gua*, translates as "squash of Italy." There is, however, nothing at all Italian about this stir-fry mix of green and yellow zucchini, which is a colorful and traditional summer dish of Canton.

½ pound green zucchini
½ pound yellow zucchini
2½ tablespoons peanut oil
1½ tablespoons julienned ginger
1½ teaspoons minced garlic
½ teaspoon salt
3 tablespoons Vegetable Stock (pages 31–32)
¼ cup trimmed and finely sliced scallions

1. Cut each zucchini lengthwise. Then slice across at ⅛-inch intervals to create half-moon slices.

2. Heat a wok over high heat for 30 seconds. Add the peanut oil and coat the wok with a spatula. When a wisp of white smoke appears, add ginger, garlic, and salt. Stir briefly. Add the zucchini slices and stir-fry for 1 minute. Add 2 tablespoons of vegetable stock and mix well. Cook for 3 minutes. If the mixture is too dry, add the remaining vegetable stock. Stir-fry until the zucchini is tender, about 1 minute more. Turn off the heat. Place on a heated platter, sprinkle scallions on top, and serve immediately.

Serves 4 to 6

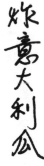

Batter-Fried Zucchini
Jah Ee Dai Lei Guah

This recipe, at first glance, might be thought of as the traditional Italian recipe for fried zucchini. It is not, however. The batter is thin and clings more to the zucchini than does the simple egg wash used in the Italian kitchen, and the zucchini about doubles in size after preparation.

Batter ingredients

1 cup tapioca starch (if unavailable, use cornstarch)

1 cup flour

5 teaspoons baking powder

1½ cups cool water (plus 2 tablespoons, if needed)

3 tablespoons peanut oil

To complete the dish

6 cups peanut oil, for deep-frying

3 tablespoons flour

1 pound zucchini, cut into pieces ½ inch thick by 3 inches long

Szechuan Peppercorn Salt (page 38), for serving

1. In a bowl place the tapioca starch, 1 cup flour, and baking powder, and mix together. Slowly pour in 1½ cups water, mixing with a wooden spoon as you do so. Continue mixing until smoothly blended. Add 3 tablespoons peanut oil, stirring continuously to blend well. The batter should be thin, not thick. If too thick, add the extra tablespoons of water one at a time (as needed) until smooth and thin. Reserve.

2. Heat a wok over high heat for 40 seconds. Add 6 cups of peanut oil and heat to 350°F to 375°F. As the oil heats, coat the zucchini pieces with 3 tablespoons flour, shake off the excess, and dip into the batter. If smoke is seen coming from the oil, do not add the zucchini, because it is too hot. Turn off the heat, allow the oil to cool a bit to the proper temperature, then cook the zucchini pieces 6 at a time, adjusting the heat as necessary. Fry until the zucchini are light brown, about 2 minutes. Remove from the oil and strain. Continue until all the pieces are cooked. (**Note:** The cooking process up to this point may be done an hour in advance.)

3. To complete cooking: Put half of the zucchini pieces back into the oil and deep-fry a second time until browned and crisp. Remove and drain on paper towels. Repeat with the second half. Serve immediately with Szechuan Peppercorn Salt lightly sprinkled on top.

Serves 4 to 6

STEWED HAIRY MELON
Jiu Jeet Guah See

This is a favored food of Buddhist monks and nuns, a melon that when properly cooked and seasoned becomes very sweet. This dish is a virtual stew and has a good bit of sauce. The Buddhist religious like to eat such dishes with cooked rice and congee, a rice porridge.

Sauce ingredients

1 teaspoon light soy sauce

1 teaspoon double dark soy sauce

2 teaspoons Shao-Hsing wine or sherry

1 teaspoon sugar

¼ teaspoon salt

1 teaspoon sesame oil

1 teaspoon cornstarch

Pinch of white pepper

¼ cup Vegetable Stock (pages 31–32)

To complete the dish

3 tablespoons Scallion Oil (page 37)

1 tablespoon minced ginger

2 teaspoons minced garlic

½ teaspoon salt

One 2-pound hairy melon, peeled, sliced into ⅓-inch rounds, then cut into ⅓-inch strips (3 cups; see note below)

4 to 5 Chinese dried black mushrooms, soaked in hot water for 30 minutes, squeezed dry, steams removed, and julienned (½ cup)

¾ cup Vegetable Stock (pages 31–32)

5 slices dried bean curd, soaked in hot water for 30 minutes and cut into ¼-inch strips

5 to 6 scallions, green portions only, cut into 1-inch pieces (1 cup)

One 2-ounce package bean threads, soaked in hot water for 30 minutes, drained, and cut into 4-inch lengths

1. Combine the sauce ingredients in a bowl. Reserve.

2. Heat a wok over high heat for 30 seconds, add the Scallion Oil, and coat the wok with a spatula. Add the ginger, garlic, and salt, and stir. When garlic turns light brown, add sliced melon and mushrooms and stir-fry for 2 minutes. Add the stock, cover the wok, and cook for 10 to 12 minutes. Stir frequently. When melon softens, add the bean curd, stir, cover, and cook for 2 minutes more. Add the scallions and mix well. Make a well in the center of the mixture, stir the sauce, and pour it into the well. Mix well. Add the bean threads and mix. When the sauce begins to bubble and thicken, turn off the heat, transfer to a heated serving dish, and serve immediately.

Note: Hairy melon is available in Chinese and Asian markets, but if you cannot find it, this recipe can be made perfectly with zucchini.

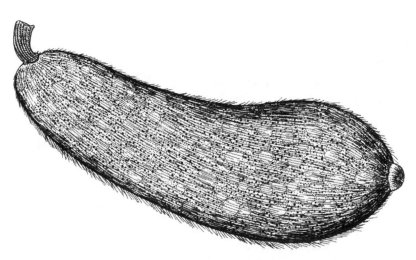

Hairy Melon (Fuzzy Melon)

HAIRY-MELON PANCAKES
Jeet Guah Bang

This is another use for the versatile and sweet hairy melon, which combines so well with other vegetables. These pancakes are fine as part of a several-course lunch, or as a snack.

1 pound hairy melon, peeled, cut into ¼-inch rounds, then cut into
        ¼-inch strips
½ cup trimmed and sliced scallions
2 fresh water chestnuts, peeled and cut into matchsticks
1 teaspoon grated fresh ginger
2 teaspoons Shao-Hsing wine or sherry
2 teaspoons sesame oil
1 teaspoon soy sauce
½ teaspoon salt
1½ teaspoons sugar
½ cup flour
1 teaspoon baking powder
6 tablespoons Vegetable Stock (pages 31–32)
4 tablespoons peanut oil

1. In a large mixing bowl combine all ingredients except the peanut oil. Mix thoroughly and divide into 2 equal portions.

2. Heat a wok over high heat for 30 seconds. Add 1 tablespoon of peanut oil and coat the wok with a spatula. When a wisp of white smoke appears, place 1 portion of the melon mixture in the wok and spread in a thin layer about 8 inches in diameter. Lower the heat and cook for 1 minute, tipping the wok from side to side to ensure evenness of cooking. Cook for 2 minutes, then add ½ tablespoon of peanut oil by drizzling it down the side of the wok. Cook for another 2 minutes, until underside is golden brown.

3. Slide the pancake onto a large dish. Place another dish of the same size over it and invert the pancake. Slide the pancake back into the wok and cook this side as you did the first. Remove from wok and keep warm at stoveside. Do not place in the oven, for it will become soggy and watery.

4. Repeat procedure with the second pancake. You may need an additional ½ tablespoon of peanut oil to complete cooking. When the pancakes are cooked to a golden brown, transfer to a heated serving dish and serve immediately.

Serves 4 to 6

STIR-FRIED SILK SQUASH
Chau See Guah

The silk squash is an odd-looking vegetable, like a cucumber but with ridges along its length. These must be pared before use. It is worth the effort to pare and cut up the silk squash because it is the sweetest of vegetables. I recall as a young girl eagerly awaiting late spring and early summer, when it was available.

1¾ pounds silk squash, ridges pared, with some of the green left on (see note below)
2 tablespoons Scallion Oil (page 37)
1¼-inch-wide slice fresh ginger
¾ teaspoon salt, or to taste
2 tablespoons Vegetable Stock, if needed (pages 31–32)

1. Starting at one end, cut the silk squash diagonally into ¾-inch slices. Turn the squash a quarter-turn between each cut. You will end up with pieces shaped like tiny axe blades, the traditional shape favored by the Chinese.

2. Heat a wok over high heat for 30 seconds. Add the Scallion Oil and coat the wok with a spatula. When a wisp of white smoke appears, add ginger and salt. Stir, and when ginger turns light brown add silk squash. Stir-fry for about 5 minutes, or until it is very tender. If too dry, add the vegetable stock. Turn off the heat, remove to a heated serving dish, and serve immediately.

Serves 4 to 6

Note: Silk squash is available the year round in Chinese markets. Select small, young squashes, for they are the sweetest.

SQUASH PANCAKES
Jdai Lei Guah Bok Bang

This dish, from the southern Chinese coast, is usually made with water squash. The closest vegetable to it in the West is the zucchini, which has a similar texture.

2 tablespoons raw peanuts

1½ cups zucchini, peeled, sliced into ½-inch rounds, then julienned into
    ¼-inch sticks

2 tablespoons scallions, ends discarded, cut into ¼-inch rounds

1 egg, beaten

½ teaspoon sugar

1 tablespoon soy sauce

½ tablespoon Shao-Hsing wine or sherry

Pinch of white pepper

4½ tablespoons flour

3½ tablespoons peanut oil, plus 1½ tablespoons if needed

1. Dry-roast peanuts (page 28). Remove from the wok and allow to cool. Place on a sheet of waxed paper and with a rolling pin crush the peanuts coarsely.

2. Place the peanuts and all the remaining ingredients, except peanut oil, in a large mixing bowl. Mix well to create a smooth batter.

3. Heat a wok over high heat for 1 minute. Add 3½ tablespoons peanut oil and coat the wok with a spatula. Pour in the batter and spread into a layer. Take both wok handles and move the wok about in a circular manner so that the pancake moves around and does not stick. Cook for about 2 minutes.

4. Slide the pancake onto a large dish. Cover with another dish the same size. Turn the pancake over and then slide it back into the wok. Lower the heat to medium and cook. Pat down with a spatula. If the wok becomes too dry, add an additional 1½ tablespoons peanut oil. Cook until the zucchini softens. Turn off the heat. Slide the pancake onto a heated platter and serve immediately.

Serves 4 to 6

Braised Chinese Turnips with Vegetables
Mun Lor Bok

The Chinese turnip is quite different from the turnip most of us are familiar with. It is like a long, thick, white radish, and its taste is quite like that of a radish. It can be sweet or a bit hot, or both simultaneously. It is widely available and quite versatile—fine in soups, salads, and stews, or when braised as in this recipe.

Sauce ingredients

1½ teaspoons sesame oil

1½ tablespoons oyster sauce

2 teaspoons Shao-Hsing wine or sherry

1 teaspoon soy sauce

1 teaspoon sugar

1 tablespoon cornstarch

4 tablespoons Vegetable Stock (pages 31–32)

To complete the dish

3½ tablespoons peanut oil

One ½-inch-wide slice fresh ginger, lightly smashed

6 to 8 medium shallots, peeled and chopped into ¼-inch dice (½ cup)

1 pound Chinese turnips, peeled, sliced into ¼-inch rounds, then cut into
    ¼-inch julienne

1 medium-sized carrot, peeled and cut into 2-inch matchsticks

¾ cup thinly sliced sweet green peppers

6 tablespoons Vegetable Stock (pages 31–32)

⅛ teaspoon salt

⅛ teaspoon freshly ground Szechuan peppercorns

1. Combine the sauce ingredients in a bowl. Reserve.

2. Heat a wok over high heat for 30 seconds. Add the peanut oil and coat the wok with a spatula. When a wisp of white smoke appears, add the ginger and cook for 30 seconds. Add the shallots, stir, and cook for 2 minutes. Add the turnips, carrots, and peppers, stir together, and cook for 1 minute. Add the vegetable stock, salt, and Szechuan peppercorns. Stir and mix well. Cover the wok, lower the heat to medium, and cook for 7 to 10 minutes, or until the turnips become tender. During this cooking time, stir the mixture 3 times.

3. Remove the cover. Raise the heat back to high. Make a well in the center of the mixture, stir the sauce, and pour it in. Mix thoroughly. When the sauce begins to thicken and bubble, turn off the heat. Transfer to a heated serving dish and serve immediately.

Serves 4 to 6

Chinese Turnip (Daikon)

TURNIP CAKE
Lor Bok Goh

This cake is one of the symbols of the Lunar New Year. The *goh*, or cake, represents one's fortune, job, or business, and as the cake rises during baking, one's good fortune is said to be rising as well.

1 pound 5 ounces (about 4 cups) Chinese turnips, peeled and grated coarsely (see note below)

3 cups plus 2 tablespoons cold water

1¼-inch-wide slice fresh ginger, mashed

2 tablespoons white wine

1 clove garlic

Pinch of white pepper

1 cup onions, cut into ¼-inch dice

1 tablespoon peanut oil

⅓ cup raw peanuts, dry roasted (page 28)

1 pound rice powder (see note below)

2 cups plus 2 tablespoons cold water

¼ teaspoon white pepper

1 tablespoon salt

½ cup Scallion Oil (page 37)

Garnishes

1 to 2 tablespoons sesame seeds, dry-roasted (page 28)

4 to 6 scallions, trimmed and finely sliced

1 tablespoon fresh coriander, finely minced (optional)

1. In a large pot place the turnips, water, ginger, wine, garlic, and white pepper. Cover the pot and bring to a boil over high heat. Lower the heat and simmer, with the lid partially open, for 20 minutes. Remove the turnip mixture from the stove, allow it to cool, and discard the ginger and garlic.

2. As the turnip mixture simmers and cools, cook the diced onions in a wok in 1 tablespoon of peanut oil over medium heat until softened and translucent, about 2 to 3 minutes. Remove and reserve. Wash and dry the wok and spatula thoroughly and dry-roast the peanuts (page 28). Remove from the wok, crush, and reserve.

3. In a large mixing bowl, mix the rice powder with 2 cups water. (Use the extra 2 tablespoons of water, if necessary, to make the mixture smooth.) Add the reserved onions and peanuts, the white pepper, salt, and Scallion Oil. Mix well, then add the cooked turnips and mix again until well blended.

4. Place the turnip mixture in a greased 9-inch round cake pan, place the pan in a steamer, and steam for 1 to 1½ hours. During steaming, keep boiling water at hand to replenish that which might evaporate. To learn whether the cake is cooked, insert a chopstick into the center. If the chopstick is clean when pulled out, the cake is done. If a residue remains, continue to steam until the cake tests as done.

5. Remove cake from steamer and allow to cool slightly. Just before serving, sprinkle with sesame seeds, then scallions, and finally coriander. Serve immediately, in slices, as you would a cake.

Serves 4 to 6

Note: Be certain to use rice powder and not glutinous rice powder, which comes in a similar wrapping. If Chinese turnips are unavailable, small white radishes may be substituted. I do not recommend them as highly as the turnips for flavor, however.

Turnip cake may be refrigerated (but not frozen), either whole or in slices. To reheat, allow the cake to come to room temperature, then steam for 2 to 3 minutes, or until heated through. Also, the cake may be reheated by pan-frying. (See Pan-Fried Turnip Cake, page 116.)

PAN-FRIED TURNIP CAKE
Jin Lor Bok Goh

If you wish to pan-fry turnip cake, prepare the cake a day before you plan to serve it, and refrigerate it overnight. If you pan-fry, do not use the sesame seed or scallion garnishes before frying, since both will "pop" in the oil. You may, however, top the cake slices, once fried, with any of the three garnishes.

1 Turnip Cake (page 114)
Peanut oil, as needed

Garnishes

1 to 2 tablespoons sesame seeds, dry-roasted (page 28)
4 to 6 scallions, trimmed and finely sliced
1 tablespoon fresh coriander, finely minced (optional)

1. Cut the cake into slices, ¼ inch thick by 2½ inches long by 2 inches wide. In a cast-iron skillet fry the slices in enough peanut oil to cover the bottom of the skillet for about 2½ minutes on each side, until light brown. Drain, garnish as desired, and serve immediately.

Serves 4 to 6

ONION PANCAKES
Chung Yau Bang

These onion pancakes come from Shanghai, where they are made with scallions and lard. This "foreign onion bread," as the Chinese call it, is faithful to tradition, but my adaptation is considerably lighter.

3 cups flour
5 tablespoons peanut oil
¼ teaspoon salt
8 ounces hot water
3½ cups onions, cut into ¼-inch dice
3½ tablespoons peanut oil
¾ teaspoon salt
½ cup peanut oil (for frying)

1. Mound the flour onto a work surface. Make a well, add the 5 tablespoons peanut oil and salt, and mix well with your fingers. Again make a well and pour hot water in with one hand, using fingers of the other to mix. When the water has been added, knead into a dough. Using a scraper, pick up the dough and continue to knead for 5 to 7 minutes, until it is smooth and elastic. If it is too moist, sprinkle with additional flour. Cover the dough with a damp cloth and allow to rest for at least 30 minutes.

2. As the dough rests, prepare the onions. Heat a wok over high heat for 30 seconds. Add 3½ tablespoons of peanut oil and salt and coat the wok with a spatula. When a wisp of white smoke appears, add the onions and cook about 10 minutes, until they become translucent. After cooking, there should be about 1¾ cups.

3. Divide the dough into 4 equal pieces. To prevent sticking as you roll out the dough, flour the work surface and the rolling pin frequently. Shape each piece into a 10-inch-long roll, 1 inch in diameter. Cut each roll into five 2-inch-long pieces. With a rolling pin, roll each piece to measure 9 by 3 inches, with rounded edges.

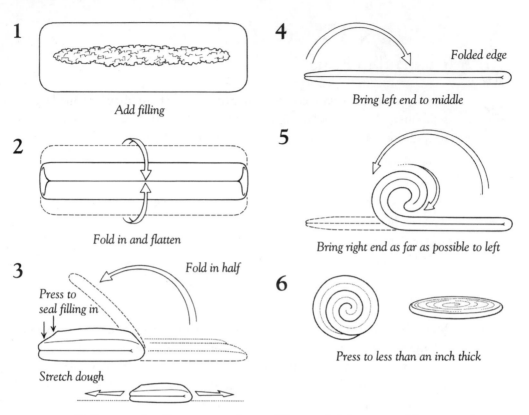

1 Add filling

2 Fold in and flatten

3 Press to seal filling in
Stretch dough

4 Folded edge
Bring left end to middle

5 Bring right end as far as possible to left

Fold in half

6 Press to less than an inch thick

4. Following the illustrations above, (1) spread 1 heaping tablespoon of onion filling along center of each piece of dough. (2) Fold both sides so they meet over the filling, then flatten gently. (3) Fold in half lengthwise and press again to seal the filling in. Pick up the dough by the ends and gently stretch it, hitting it lightly on the work surface at the same time. Placing the folded edge outward, (4) bring the left end to the middle, creating a circle. (5) Bring the right end around as far as possible to the left, creating a shape like a jelly roll. Slip the end between the folds of dough and press gently. (6) Press again, so roll becomes a solid pancake less than an inch thick. Repeat until all pieces of dough are used. As you work, the remaining dough should always be covered with a damp cloth.

5. Fry the pancakes in the peanut oil in a heavy skillet, preferably cast iron, until golden brown on both sides. Use 3 tablespoons to begin, then replenish as needed. Remove, drain, and serve immediately.

Serves 4 to 6

Note: Both the dough and the filling may be made a day ahead of time and refrigerated. Or you may proceed through the entire recipe but only lightly brown the pancakes. Refrigerate them until needed. Then bring to room temperature and fry as indicated, to a golden brown.

STIR-FRIED ONIONS AND PEPPERS WITH BLACK BEANS
See Jiu Chau Yung Chung

The bond between the onions and the peppers in this recipe is provided by the black beans, truly an ingredient that enhances many, many dishes in the Chinese repertoire. It is astonishing that these salted beans go so well with virtually any vegetable anyone might care to cook them with.

1½ tablespoons peanut oil

⅛ teaspoon salt

2 teaspoons minced garlic

1 tablespoon fermented black beans, washed twice and drained

1¾ cups onions, cut into ¾-inch cubes

1½ large green peppers, washed, dried, seeded, and cut into 1-inch cubes
       (1½ cups)

1 tablespoon oyster sauce

1. Heat a wok over high heat for 30 seconds. Add the peanut oil and salt and stir. Coat the wok with a spatula. When a wisp of white smoke appears, add the garlic. When garlic turns light brown, add the black beans. When the beans release their aroma, add the onions and stir together. Cook for 1 minute, add the peppers, and stir-fry together for 2 minutes. Add oyster sauce, mix well, and cook for 1 minute more. Turn off the heat, transfer to a heated serving dish, and serve immediately.

Serves 4 to 6

SPICED THREE-COLOR PEPPERS
Cha Sam Sing

The Chinese for this dish translates as "stir-fried three stars." The stars refer to this dish's three colors, which for the Chinese represent good luck, particularly at the New Year—red for continued good luck, green for youth and long life, and yellow, the color of gold, for prosperity.

1½ tablespoons peanut oil
½ teaspoon salt
1 tablespoon minced garlic
1¼ large sweet red peppers, cut into ½-inch squares (1¼ cups)
¾ large sweet green pepper, cut into ½-inch squares (¾ cup)
1 large sweet yellow pepper, cut into ½-inch squares (1 cup)
1 small jalapeño pepper, minced

1. Heat a wok over high heat for 30 seconds. Add the peanut oil and salt and coat the wok with a spatula. When a wisp of white smoke appears, add the garlic and stir briefly. Add all the peppers and stir-fry for 2 minutes, or until very hot. Remove from the heat, transfer to a heated serving dish, and serve immediately.

Serves 4 to 6

STEAMED CHINESE EGGPLANT
Jing Ai Guah

Chinese eggplants are sweeter than Western eggplants and have tender skins, which are eaten. In China they are generally white; elsewhere they are light purple.

1 pound small Chinese eggplants (3 to 4), stems removed
2 tablespoons peanut oil
½ cup plus 3 tablespoons shallots, cut into ⅛-inch dice
1 tablespoon sesame seed paste
¼ cup Vegetable Stock (pages 31–32)
1 tablespoon Shao-Hsing wine or sherry
1½ teaspoons sugar
¾ teaspoon salt
1 teaspoon white vinegar
½ teaspoon Hot Pepper Flakes (page 36)
1 tablespoon Green Oil (page 39)

Chinese Eggplant

1. Place the whole eggplants in a steamer. Steam for 4 to 5 minutes, until tender. Test by inserting a chopstick into the flesh; it should go in easily. Remove from the heat and place on a serving dish. With a chopstick "cut" along the length of each, open, then with chopsticks draw lengthwise along the eggplants again to create strips. Reserve.

2. As the eggplants steam, prepare the sauce. Heat a wok over high heat for 30 seconds. Add the peanut oil and coat the wok with a spatula. When a wisp of white smoke appears, add ½ cup shallots. Stir, lower the heat to medium, and cook for 3 minutes, until soft. Add the sesame seed paste and vegetable stock and mix well. Add all the other ingredients except the reserved shallots, and mix together thoroughly. When the sauce bubbles, turn off the heat. Pour the sauce atop the eggplant strips, sprinkle with remaining 3 tablespoons of minced shallots, and serve immediately.

Serves 4 to 6

EGGPLANT WITH GARLIC SAUCE
Yue Hung Keh Tzi

Eggplants came from India, via Southeast Asia, to China many centuries ago. It is still highly prized, and I remember my family eagerly awaiting the first eggplant of the year.

Sauce ingredients

1 tablespoon dark soy sauce

1 teaspoon light soy sauce

½ teaspoon soaked pepper flakes from bottom of Hot Oil (page 36)

2 teaspoons sugar

1 teaspoon white vinegar

¼ teaspoon salt

1½ teaspoons cornstarch mixed with 3 tablespoons Vegetable Stock
    (pages 31–32)

1 teaspoon Shao-Hsing wine or sherry

To complete the dish

3 cups peanut oil

1 pound eggplant, peeled and sliced lengthwise into ½-inch strips

2 teaspoons minced garlic

1. Combine the sauce ingredients in a bowl. Reserve.

2. Heat a wok over high heat for 45 seconds. Add the peanut oil and coat the wok with a spatula. When a wisp of white smoke appears, place the eggplant strips in a strainer and lower into the oil. Cook for 1 minute, or until the eggplant softens. Remove, drain, and reserve.

3. Empty all but 1½ tablespoons of the oil from wok. Over high heat add the minced garlic. Stir until it browns, then place the eggplant in the wok. Stir together and cook for 1½ minutes. Make a well in the center of the mixture. Stir the sauce and pour it in. Stir until the sauce thickens and bubbles. Remove from the heat and serve immediately.

Serves 4 to 6

蒸
搞
瓜
红
椒

STEAMED EGGPLANT WITH RED PEPPERS

Ai Guah Yeung Hong Jiu

For this dish I use the large Western eggplant, because of the greater amount of interior pith. The cooked eggplant, with its sesame seed paste taste and its overtones of garlic, contrasts well with the crispness of the uncooked peppers. This is a fine and unusual first course.

1 pound eggplant
4 small sweet red peppers
1 tablespoon sesame seed paste
2 teaspoons minced garlic
1 tablespoon Green Oil (page 39)
1 teaspoon sugar
½ teaspoon salt
1½ teaspoons mushroom soy sauce
1 teaspoon white vinegar
½ teaspoon hot pepper flakes (from bottom of Hot Oil, page 36)
Pinch of white pepper
1 large scallion, green portion only, finely sliced (¼ cup)

1. Peel, wash, and dry the eggplant. Cut into 2-inch cubes. Place in a steamproof dish and steam for about 7 minutes, or until very tender. Turn off the heat. Strain off all liquid. Place the eggplant in a bowl.

2. As the eggplant steams, wash and dry the peppers and cut in half lengthwise. Remove the seeds. Reserve.

3. Into the bowl with the eggplant add the sesame paste. Cover with the still-warm eggplant so that the heat of the eggplant softens the paste. Then add all other ingredients except scallions, and mix together thoroughly. As you mix, the eggplant will come apart and soften.

4. Stuff each pepper half with the eggplant mixture. Sprinkle with the sliced scallions and serve at room temperature.

Serves 4 to 6

Note: This dish may also be eaten cold after refrigeration. When cold the taste is somewhat different and the garlic predominates. So enjoy this dish either way.

PINEAPPLE WITH MIXED VEGETABLES
Bor Law Chau Jop Choi

Not only do fine, sweet pineapples come into China from Taiwan, they also come from Southeast Asia and are grown in China's south, around Canton. The sweetness of these "phoenix pears," as they are called, contrasts well with the tastes and textures of the vegetables.

3 tablespoons peanut oil

1¼-inch-wide slice fresh ginger

½ teaspoon salt

20 fresh mushroom caps, each the size of a quarter, cut in half

2 to 3 shiitake (or porcini) mushrooms, cut into 1-inch pieces (⅔ cup)

1 medium-sized carrot, peeled, washed, cut in half lengthwise, then cut
    into half-moons ¼ inch thick (¾ cup)

1 small stalk celery, sliced on the diagonal into ½-inch pieces (½ cup)

½ large sweet green pepper, cut into ½-inch pieces (½ cup)

4 to 5 fresh water chestnuts, cut into ¼-inch slices (½ cup)

1 tablespoon Shao-Hsing wine or sherry

¼ whole fresh pineapple, cut into pieces 1 inch by ⅓ inch (1 cup)

2 teaspoons cornstarch mixed with 2 teaspoons cold water

1 teaspoon sesame oil

1. Heat a wok over high heat for 30 seconds. Add the peanut oil and coat the wok with a spatula. Add the ginger and salt and stir. When the ginger turns light brown, add the two kinds of mushrooms. Stir for 1 minute. Add the carrots and celery and stir-fry for 30 seconds. Add the peppers and water chestnuts and stir-fry for 1 minute. Combine all the vegetables well.

2. Add the wine to the mixture and mix well. Add the pineapple and stir together for 1½ minutes. Make a well in the center of the mixture, stir the cornstarch-water mix, and pour it in. Mix well and cook until the liquid bubbles and begins to thicken. Add the sesame oil and mix thoroughly. Turn off heat, transfer to a heated serving dish, and serve immediately.

Serves 4 to 6

白

飯 Fon

Rice

As with other foods in China, rice, *fon*, is both symbol and nourishment. To the Chinese rice represents well-being in its broadest sense. If one is healthy, is provided for, if one has work, it is said that one's "rice bowl is full." The reverse is also true. If one is in the midst of hard times one has "a broken rice bowl."

While rice has always been the basic food of choice in southern China, where it is harvested twice each year, rice historically was only an occasional treat in the wheat culture of northern China. In Canton, where I grew up, no day passed without each man, woman, and child having rice at least twice, for it was believed that unless a person ate rice twice daily, he or she would have no energy.

Traditionally we ate rice in several ways. In the mornings we had it as congee, a souplike breakfast porridge, either plain or with vegetables added. Or we might have a bowl of cooked rice to accompany a stir-fried vegetable. At noon we ate a meal called not lunch but *n'fon*, or "afternoon rice," and in the evening we ate *mon fon*, or "evening rice." The words signifying that a meal is to be eaten are *sik fon*, which translates as "eat rice." These days, congee is often eaten as a lighter evening meal as well.

At a family celebration it was customary, it still is, to wish each older person at the table *sik fon*, and nobody was supposed to eat until all the *sik fons* had been wished. I can remember an occasion sitting at a table with my grandmother, Ah Paw, my mother and father, my older brother, two aunts and two uncles, and five older cousins and having to wish each of them *sik fon*. It was an occasion of thirteen wishes, and I felt sorry for two younger cousins at the same table, who had go through all the wishes and then wish me *sik fon* as well.

The rice we ate and to which I remain loyal is the long-grain variety grown in southern China. It was said to have been cultivated first in the region that today is Laos. Today the long-grain and extra-long-grain varieties are grown in Thailand as well, and in Texas. In fact, Texas-grown extra-long-grain rice is of exceptionally high quality. The rice I ate, and eat, is white, cooked plainly with water, and prepared properly so that each grain is fluffy and separate from other grains, and so that the rice, though not moist, has absorbed all of the water in which it has been cooked. The recipe for foolproof cooked rice can be found in this book on page 33.

The Chinese prize white, glistening rice for its taste and for its connotation of purity. In most of China brown rice, whose outer husk has been milled off but whose inner husk remains, is regarded as inferior rice. It is known—and accepted—that some of rice's protein is lost in the milling to whiteness, but what has been lost is replenished with the foods eaten with the rice.

Various rices are available both in Asian markets and in supermarkets:

Extra-long-grain and long-grain. There is a distinction between these two varieties in Asian markets, but no distinction is made in Western markets. The basic long-grain is generally about four times as long as it is wide. Extra-long-grain is slightly longer and thinner than long-grain. When properly cooked the grains are separate and fluffy and have a pleasing bite. There is also a red long-grain rice grown in China, but it is used mainly for decorative dishes.

Jasmine. This is an extremely fragrant extra long-grain rice that is imported from Thailand. When it cooks and when it is eaten, it emits the sweet aroma of jasmine. It is a delicious rice. Indian basmati rice may be substituted for it, but most basmatis do not have the fragrance of the jasmine long-grain.

Short-grain. Short, round, and plump, these grains are soft when cooked and stick together in clumps. This rice is favored in Japan and Taiwan and among some Chinese. It is usually available in Asian markets. Short-grain rice grown in California is an excellent substitute for the short-grain grown in Asia. I use short-grain rice mixed with glutinous rice to make congee.

Glutinous. This is often referred to as "sticky rice" or "sweet rice." It is short-grained and when cooked becomes a cohesive mass. Because it can be molded it is often used in stuffed dishes. Although it is not generally eaten with other foods, as is long-grain rice, it is occasionally stir-fried. In Southeast Asia there is a long-grain black glutinous rice, usually labeled "black sweet rice," that becomes sticky when cooked. Thailand also has a white long-grain glutinous rice called "special long-grain." Both of these are used most often in sweet desserts. The more familiar glutinous rice is used most often wrapped with other foods in lotus leaves or bamboo leaves, then steamed.

In this section I have illustrated the many uses and varieties of rice. Most people eat cooked rice, plain or as fried rice, and I have recognized the latter with several modern adaptations of classic fried rice. There are also congees and wrapped glutinous rice bundles. Enjoy. *Sik fon.*

FRIED RICE WITH SUN-DRIED TOMATOES
Tai Gawn Keh Chau Fon

To me this is an exciting dish. Customarily, fried rice is made with familiar ingredients, the most familiar being roast pork. I have substituted sun-dried tomatoes for pork. It looks like bits of pork are mixed into the rice, but there's a surprise in the mouth!

1 Basic Cooked Rice recipe (page 33)

Sauce ingredients

1½ tablespoons oyster sauce

1 tablespoon Vegetable Stock (pages 31–32)

2 teaspoons soy sauce

1 teaspoon white wine

¾ teaspoon sugar

Pinch of white pepper

½ teaspoon sesame oil

To complete the dish

2 teaspoons Scallion Oil (page 37)

3 large eggs, beaten with a pinch of white pepper and salt

1½ teaspoons minced ginger

1¼ cups peeled broccoli stems, cut into ¼-inch dice

¼ cup sun-dried tomatoes, soaked in warm water for 1 minute and cut into ½-inch by ¼-inch pieces (see note below)

2 to 3 scallions, trimmed and finely sliced (½ cup)

3 tablespoons minced fresh coriander

1. Prepare the basic rice recipe. Allow to cool. Reserve. As the rice cooks, combine the sauce ingredients in a bowl. Reserve.

2. Also as the rice cooks, heat a wok over high heat for 30 seconds, add 1 teaspoon of Scallion Oil, and coat the wok with a spatula. When a wisp of white smoke appears, add the eggs and scramble. Turn off the heat, transfer to a bowl, and cut the eggs into small pieces. Reserve.

3. Heat the wok over high heat for 30 seconds, add the other teaspoon of Scallion Oil, and coat the wok with a spatula. When a wisp of white smoke appears, add the minced ginger, then stir and cook for 10 seconds. Add the broccoli stems, then stir and cook for 20 seconds. Add the reserved rice and mix well, cooking for 5 minutes, or until the rice mixture is very hot.

4. Stir the sauce and pour it over the rice. Mix thoroughly. Add the eggs and stir; add the sun-dried tomatoes and mix very well, making certain the tomatoes and other ingredients are blended. Add scallions and coriander and toss with the rice. Turn off the heat, transfer to a heated serving dish, and serve immediately.

Serves 4 to 6

Note: Sun-dried tomatoes are quite pungent. Their taste permeates this dish. If you desire an even stronger taste, you may use ⅓ cup rather than the ¼ cup called for.

If the sun-dried tomatoes are of recent vintage they will be soft, and a simple washing will soften them further, sufficient to cook. If hard, they have been on the shelf for a long time. These need to be soaked in warm water first for 1 to 2 minutes until they soften. *Do not* use those soaked in oil for this recipe.

FRIED RICE WITH TOMATOES
Wai Tah Min Chau Fon

As they do with many dishes, the Chinese inject some basic humor into this dish. The tomato is known by several names in China, not the least of which is *wai tah min*, or "vitamin food." I recall that my cousin, who loved to go to the markets and took me many times, loved tomatoes and called them "foods with vitamins." And so they are.

1 Basic Cooked Rice recipe (page 33)
3 tomatoes (to yield 2 cups; see instructions)

Sauce ingredients

2 teaspoons soy sauce
2 teaspoons Shao-Hsing wine or sherry
1½ teaspoons sugar
1 teaspoon salt
⅛ teaspoon white pepper
4 to 5 scallions, trimmed and finely sliced (1 cup)

To complete the dish

3½ tablespoons Scallion Oil (page 37)
1 tablespoon minced ginger
2 teaspoons minced garlic
10 to 12 shallots, peeled and cut into ¼-inch dice (¾ cup)
4 to 5 fresh water chestnuts, peeled and cut into ⅓-inch dice (⅔ cup)
¾ cup peeled broccoli stems, cut into ⅓-inch dice

1. Prepare the basic rice recipe. Allow to come to room temperature. Reserve. Meanwhile, bring 4 cups water to a boil in a pot, then add the tomatoes. Turn off the heat and allow the tomatoes to sit for 10 seconds. Run cold water into the pot. Cool the tomatoes, then peel off the skins. Quarter the tomatoes, remove the seeds, and cut into ½-inch cubes. Reserve.

2. Combine the sauce ingredients in a bowl. Reserve.

3. Heat a wok over high heat for 30 seconds, add the Scallion Oil, and coat the wok with a spatula. When a wisp of white smoke appears, add the minced ginger and stir. Add the minced garlic, stir and cook for 10 seconds, then add the shallots. Cook for 2 minutes, then add water chestnuts and broccoli and stir-fry for 2 more minutes. Add the reserved tomatoes and mix well. When the mixture begins to bubble, stir the sauce and pour it in.

4. When the sauce begins to bubble and thicken, add the reserved cooked rice. Stir well, mixing and tossing, to ensure that all the ingredients are well blended. Cook for about 5 minutes, until the rice is very hot and well mixed. Add the scallions and toss to mix. Turn off the heat, transfer to a heated serving dish, and serve immediately.

Serves 4 to 6

PINEAPPLE FRIED RICE
Bor Law Chau Fou

The pineapple came to mainland China from Taiwan, which to this day is famed for the sweetness of its pineapples. Taiwan is equally famous for the fine quality of its short-grain rice, a heritage from its long association with Japan. Think of this dish as a gift from Taiwan.

1½ cups short-grain rice

1½ cups cold water

½ cup steamed mushrooms (4 or 5; pages 127–28)

Sauce ingredients

1½ tablespoons steamed mushroom liquid (reserved from steamed mushrooms, above)

1½ teaspoons soy sauce

1 teaspoon Shao-Hsing wine or sherry

½ teaspoon sesame oil

¾ teaspoon sugar

¾ teaspoon salt

Pinch of white pepper

To complete the dish

3 tablespoons peanut oil

¾ teaspoon salt

1½ teaspoons minced ginger

1½ teaspoons minced garlic

½ cup green peas, fresh or frozen (see note below)

3 fresh water chestnuts, peeled and cut into ¼-inch dice

¾ cup fresh pineapple chunks (1 inch by ¼ inch)

2 to 3 scallions, trimmed and finely sliced (½ cup)

3 tablespoons minced fresh coriander

1. Place the rice in a bowl, run cold water in, and wash 3 times, rubbing between your hands. Drain well. Place in a round 9-inch cake pan and add 1½ cups cold water. Allow to sit for 2 hours. Then steam for 25 minutes (see note). Loosen the rice with chopsticks and allow to cool to room temperature. Reserve.

2. As the rice is being prepared, steam the mushrooms and reserve. Combine the sauce ingredients in a bowl, using the liquid from the steamed mushrooms. Reserve.

3. Heat a wok over high heat for 30 seconds. Add the peanut oil and coat the wok with a spatula. When a wisp of white smoke appears, add the salt and stir, then add the ginger and garlic and stir. Cook for 10 seconds, add the peas and mix, then add the mushrooms and stir for 20 seconds. Add the rice and mix well, breaking up lumps as you mix. Cook for 5 minutes, or until the rice is very hot. Add the water chestnuts and mix in. Stir the sauce, pour it into the rice, and stir thoroughly. Add the pineapple and stir together for 2 minutes. Add the scallions and coriander and mix well into rice. Turn off the heat, transfer to a heated dish, and serve immediately.

Serves 4 to 6

Note: The reason for steaming short-grain rice instead of cooking it in the basic manner is that it has a high degree of gluten in it. In a pot, unless it is carefully and constantly watched, it can easily burn on the bottom.

Note: If the peas are fresh, they should be water-blanched for 2 minutes; if frozen, allow to defrost and come to room temperature before use.

FRIED RICE WITH GREEN PEAS
Ching Dau Chau Fou

The aim of fried rice, which is made most often with leftover rice, is to give the rice not only added taste but textural interest. Green peas do that.

1 Basic Cooked Rice recipe (page 33)

Sauce ingredients

1 tablespoon Vegetable Stock (pages 31–32)

1½ tablespoons oyster sauce

2 teaspoons soy sauce

1 teaspoon white wine

¾ teaspoon sugar

½ teaspoon sesame oil

To complete the dish

1 tablespoon plus 2 teaspoons peanut oil

3 large eggs, beaten with a pinch of white pepper and salt

1½ teaspoons minced ginger

1¼ cups green peas, fresh or frozen

2 to 3 scallions, trimmed and finely sliced (½ cup)

3 tablespoons minced fresh coriander

1. Prepare the basic rice recipe. Allow to cool. Reserve. As the rice cooks, combine the sauce ingredients in a bowl. Reserve.

2. Also while the rice cooks, heat a wok over high heat for 30 seconds, add 2 teaspoons of peanut oil, and coat the wok with a spatula. When a wisp of white smoke appears, add the beaten eggs and scramble them. Turn off the heat, transfer to a bowl, cut the eggs into small pieces, and reserve.

3. Heat the wok over high heat for 30 seconds, add the remaining tablespoon of peanut oil, and coat the wok with a spatula. When a wisp of white smoke appears, add the ginger. Stir and cook for 10 seconds. Add the peas, stir together, and cook for 20 seconds. Add the cooked rice and mix well, cooking for 5 minutes, or until the rice mixture is very hot.

4. Stir the sauce and pour it over the rice. Mix thoroughly. Add the scrambled eggs and mix well with the rice. Add the scallions and coriander and mix well. Turn off the heat, transfer to a heated serving dish, and serve immediately.

Serves 4 to 6

CONGEE
Jook

This soup, or porridge, is a Chinese universal. It is almost always the morning meal, with other ingredients added, and it is the all-purpose restorative. Congee reduces the body's heat and is usually the only food taken when one has a fever. Just a bit of salt should be added to it. Short-grain rice is preferred over long-grain for this dish. It blends better with glutinous rice.

½ cup rice
¼ cup glutinous rice
8½ cups cold water
salt to taste

1. In a large pot place both kinds of rice. Wash the rice 3 times under water, rubbing between your hands. Drain.

2. Return the rice to the pot, add the 8½ cups water, cover, and bring to a boil. Leave the lid open a crack. Reduce the heat to medium-low and cook for 1 to 1½ hours, stirring occasionally to prevent the rice from sticking to the bottom of the pot. Cook until the rice thickens almost to the consistency of porridge. Add salt to taste, and stir. Turn off the heat and serve.

Serves 4 to 6

LETTUCE CONGEE
Sang Choi Jook

Virtually any food can be added to one's breakfast congee in China. What you might add to it depends upon your preferences. Here is one of mine.

1 Congee recipe (page 135)

1 large head romaine lettuce, cut into ½-inch strips (6 cups)

1½ to 2 teaspoons salt

2 teaspoons soy sauce

Pinch of white pepper

One slice fresh ginger, ½-inch thick

2 to 3 tablespoons Scallion Oil (page 37)

1. Prepare the congee.

2. When the congee is done, add the lettuce strips, salt, soy sauce, white pepper, and ginger. Mix thoroughly, then bring the congee back to a boil, stirring constantly. Turn off the heat, then add the Scallion Oil and stir it well into the mixture. Serve hot.

Serves 4 to 6

CONGEE WITH TIENTSIN BOK CHOY
Tin Jun Bok Choy Jook

Tientsin bok choy, which is also known as Tianjin bok choy as well as Napa cabbage and celery cabbage, is an extraordinarily sweet leafy vegetable. It is a perfect complement to cooked congee.

1 Congee recipe (page 135)

1 large head Tientsin bok choy, separated into white stalks (3 cups) and leaves (5 cups)

1½ to 2 teaspoons salt

2 teaspoons soy sauce

Pinch of white pepper

One slice fresh ginger, ½-inch thick

2 to 3 tablespoons Scallion Oil (page 37)

1. Prepare the basic congee. As the congee is cooking, wash the Tientsin bok choy stalks and leaves. Cut the leaves into ¼-inch by 4-inch slices, and the stalks into ¼-inch pieces. Reserve.

2. About 7 minutes before the congee is completely cooked, add the Tientsin bok choy stalks, salt, soy sauce, white pepper, and ginger. Mix together thoroughly and bring the congee to a boil, stirring constantly. Reduce the heat, add the bok choy leaves, and cook for 2 to 3 minutes longer. Turn off the heat, then add the Scallion Oil and stir it well into the mixture. Serve hot.

Serves 4 to 6

Note: A fine complement to this congee is Sweet Scallion Sauce (page 37), which can be added, to taste, to individual bowls of congee.

ALMOND RICE WITH CAPERS
Hung Yun Chau Fon

Almonds are used widely in China; most often the nuts are ground and become the bases for sweet soups. They are also used whole in soups, for the Chinese believe the almond is a food of good health. It is, I find, just as delicious in rice.

2 cups short-grain rice

15 ounces cold water

½ cup slivered almonds, dry-roasted (page 28; see note below)

8 mushrooms, steamed (pages 27–28) and cut into ½-inch pieces (¾ cup)

Sauce ingredients

2 teaspoons soy sauce

2 tablespoons oyster sauce

2 teaspoons Shao-Hsing wine or sherry

1 teaspoon sesame oil

¾ teaspoon sugar

Pinch of white pepper

To complete the dish

3 tablespoons peanut oil

2 teaspoons minced ginger

2 teaspoons minced garlic

2 onions, cut into ¼-inch pieces (1½ cups)

3½ tablespoons capers

4 to 5 scallions, trimmed and finely sliced (1 cup)

3 to 4 fresh water chestnuts, peeled and cut into ¼-inch pieces (½ cup)

1. Wash the rice in cold water 3 times by rubbing it between your hands. Drain well. Place the rice in a 9-inch round cake pan, add the 15 ounces cold water, and allow to soak for 2 hours. Steam for 25 minutes. Allow to cool. Loosen with chopsticks. Reserve.

2. As rice soaks and steams, prepare the almonds and mushrooms. Reserve. Combine the sauce ingredients in a bowl. Reserve.

3. Heat a wok over high heat for 30 seconds, add 2 tablespoons of peanut oil, and coat the wok with a spatula. When a wisp of white smoke appears, add the ginger and garlic and stir. Add the onions, stir, lower the heat to medium, and cook for 7 minutes. Raise the heat back to high and add the rice. Mix well with the onions. If the rice begins to stick to the wok, add the remaining 1 tablespoon of peanut oil and mix. Add the capers, mushrooms, and water chestnuts; stir, and cook for 2 minutes. Stir the sauce, add to the rice, and mix thoroughly. Add the scallions and mix together. Add the almonds and mix well into the rice. Turn off the heat, transfer to a heated dish, and serve immediately.

Serves 4 to 6

Note: If slivered almonds are unavailable, use whole skinless almonds and crush them after dry-roasting.

JASMINE FRIED RICE

Heung Fon

This "fragrant rice" is made from that absolutely wonderful Thai jasmine rice. Other than for the use of this special rice, this dish is a variation of the traditional fried rice.

1½ cups jasmine rice

3 tablespoons peanut oil

3 large eggs, beaten with a pinch of white pepper and salt

Sauce ingredients

2 teaspoons soy sauce

1½ teaspoons Shao-Hsing wine or sherry

1 tablespoon oyster sauce

1 teaspoon sesame oil

½ teaspoon sugar

Pinch of white pepper

Marinade for shrimp

½ teaspoon Ginger Juice (page 34) mixed with ½ teaspoon Shao-Hsing
　　wine or sherry

1 teaspoon soy sauce

¾ teaspoon sugar

½ tablespoon oyster sauce

Pinch of white pepper

1 teaspoon sesame oil

To complete the dish

6 ounces shrimp, shelled, deveined, and halved

2 teaspoons minced ginger

2 teaspoons minced garlic

½ teaspoon salt

1 to 2 broccoli stems, peeled and cut into ⅓-inch pieces (1 cup)

4 to 5 scallions, trimmed and finely sliced (1 cup)

1. Prepare the rice according to the Basic Cooked Rice recipe (page 33), using 2 cups minus 1 tablespoon water. Reserve.

2. Combine the sauce ingredients in a bowl. Reserve.

3. Heat a wok over high heat for 30 seconds, add ½ tablespoon peanut oil, and coat the wok with a spatula. When a wisp of white smoke appears, add the beaten eggs. Scramble the eggs, turn off the heat, remove to a bowl, and cut into small pieces. Reserve.

4. Combine the shrimp marinade ingredients and add the shrimp. Allow to stand for 10 minutes. Wipe the wok and spatula with paper towels. Heat the wok over high heat for 20 seconds, add ½ tablespoon peanut oil, and coat the wok with a spatula. When a wisp of white smoke appears, add 1 teaspoon of the minced ginger and 1 teaspoon of the minced garlic, and stir. Add the shrimp and marinade, spread in a thin layer, and cook for 1 minute. Turn over and stir. When the shrimp turn pink, turn off the heat, remove from the wok, and reserve. Wipe off the wok and spatula with paper towels.

5. Turn the heat back to high, add remaining 2 tablespoons peanut oil, and coat the wok with a spatula. Add the remaining ginger and garlic, and the salt, and stir together. When the garlic turns light brown, add the broccoli stems. Stir and cook for 1 minute. Add the rice and mix well, cooking for 3 minutes. Add the reserved shrimp and mix thoroughly. Stir the sauce, pour it into the rice, and mix well. Add the scrambled eggs and combine well. Add the scallions and mix well. Turn off the heat, transfer to a heated dish, and serve immediately.

Serves 4 to 6

CURRIED JASMINE RICE
Gah Lei Heung Fon

In China, *heung* means "perfume" or "fragrance." This dish utilizes the extra-long-grain rice, usually grown in Thailand, that has the lovely scent of jasmine. The rice suits the curry so well.

2 cups jasmine rice

3 tablespoons curry powder

2½ cups Vegetable Stock (pages 31–32)

3 tablespoons peanut oil

1½ tablespoons minced ginger

1 tablespoon minced garlic

¼ teaspoon salt

2½ onions, cut into ¼-inch dice (2 cups)

2 tomatoes, cut into ½-inch pieces (1 cup)

3½ tablespoons oyster sauce

3½ tablespoons minced fresh coriander

2 tablespoons Scallion Oil (page 37)

¾ large sweet red pepper, minced (½ cup), for garnish

¾ large sweet green pepper, minced (½ cup), for garnish

½ cup minced fresh coriander, for garnish

1. Prepare the rice. Wash 3 times, rubbing between hands. Drain rice thoroughly and place in pot, adding 2 cups vegetable stock. Allow to sit for 1 hour.

2. In a small bowl place the curry powder and 3 tablespoons vegetable stock and mix into a paste. Heat a small saucepan over high heat for 30 seconds and add 1½ tablespoons peanut oil. When a wisp of white smoke appears, add the ginger and garlic and stir. When the garlic turns light brown, add the curry paste, stir, and cook for 1 minute. Add 5 more tablespoons of vegetable stock and mix well. Cook for 2 minutes, then lower heat to medium and cook for 15 minutes, stirring occasionally to avoid sticking. Turn off the heat. Reserve.

3. Heat a wok over high heat for 30 seconds. Add the remaining 1½ tablespoons peanut oil and coat the wok with a spatula. Add the salt. When a wisp of white smoke appears, add the onions, stir, and cook for 30 seconds. Lower the heat and cook for 5 minutes. Raise the heat back to high, add the tomatoes, stir, and cook for 2 minutes. Add the curry paste mixture and stir. Cook for 1 minute.

4. Pour the contents of the wok into the rice and mix well. Add the oyster sauce, the 3½ tablespoons minced coriander, and the Scallion Oil and mix thoroughly. Bring the pot to a boil over high heat, stirring often to prevent sticking, and cook for 3 minutes. Reduce heat to low, cover, and cook the rice until it is tender and firm, 8 to 10 minutes. Stir 3 times while it is cooking.

5. Stir in the pepper and coriander garnishes, transfer to a heated bowl, and serve immediately.

Serves 4 to 6

STUFFED LOTUS LEAVES
Liu Bau Nor Mai Fou

Wrapping rice in lotus leaves is a Cantonese and Southeast Asian practice. I recall that my father used this technique to do many variations of this preparation. Here is one of them.

5 cups cold water

⅓ cup peeled raw chestnuts

¼ cup skinned raw peanuts

1 cup glutinous rice, washed 3 times and drained

2 large lotus leaves (see note below)

¼ cup straw mushrooms, cut into ¼-inch dice

¼ cup fresh mushrooms, cut into ¼-inch dice

¼ cup bamboo shoots, cut into ¼-inch dice

2 fresh water chestnuts, peeled and cut into ¼-inch pieces

2 scallions, trimmed and cut into ⅛-inch pieces

½ teaspoon salt

1 teaspoon sugar

1 teaspoon light soy sauce

¾ teaspoon dark soy sauce

1 teaspoon sesame oil

1 tablespoon Scallion Oil (page 37)

Pinch of white pepper

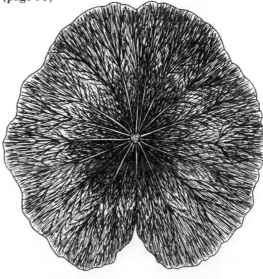

Lotus Leaf

1. Place 2 cups of the cold water in a pot. Add the chestnuts, bring to a boil, lower the heat, partially cover, and cook for 1 hour, until the chestnuts are tender. Allow to cool, then cut into ½-inch pieces. Reserve. Repeat the process with the peanuts but do not cut them up. Reserve.

2. Place the drained glutinous rice in a round 9-inch cake pan, add 1 cup cold water to the rice, put the cake pan in the wok, and steam for 30 minutes, covered. Reserve. While the rice is cooking, soak the lotus leaves in hot water for 30 minutes. Wash and reserve.

3. When the rice is cooked, place it in a large bowl and add all the prepared and remaining ingredients, except the lotus leaves. Mix thoroughly with your hands. Place 1 lotus leaf atop the other, positioning them so no holes can be seen. Mound the rice mixture on the leaves. Make a package by folding the leaves to cover the rice on all four sides. Place the package, folded side down, on a steamer and steam, covered, for 35 minutes, until hot, to allow all flavors to blend.

4. Transfer the package from the steamer to a dish. Cut a round hole in the top of the package and serve.

Serves 4 to 6

Note: Bamboo leaves may be substituted for lotus leaves. However, because of their smaller size, it is necessary to make 3 small packages instead of 1 large package. Use 6 bamboo leaves of the largest size possible.

BAMBOO-LEAF RICE
Juk Yip Fon

This rice is usually made for the annual Dragon Boat Festival in spring. In the traditional dish, raw glutinous rice is used with lye water and salted duck eggs. I have made this adaptation, which is true to the spirit of the dish but suited to the Western kitchen. For this dish only bamboo leaves should be used, to keep the spirit.

2 cups glutinous rice

2 cups water

12 large bamboo leaves

⅔ cup steamed mushrooms (pages 27–28)

¼ cup pine nuts, dry-roasted (page 28)

¼ cup peanuts, dry-roasted (page 28)

3 to 4 fresh water chestnuts, peeled and cut into ¼-inch dice (½ cup)

6 to 7 scallions, trimmed and finely sliced (1¼ cups)

2 tablespoons oyster sauce

1 teaspoon sugar

1 teaspoon light soy sauce

1 teaspoon double dark soy sauce

2 tablespoons Scallion Oil (page 37)

1 teaspoon sesame oil

¼ teaspoon salt

Pinch of white pepper

1. In a bowl, combine the rice and enough water to cover. Wash the rice 3 times by rubbing between the hands. Drain well. Transfer the rice to an 9-inch round cake pan. Add the 2 cups water and set aside to soak for 2 hours.

2. Place the cake pan with rice in a steamer, cover, and steam until the rice is soft and sticky, about 25 minutes. Remove the steamer from the wok, fluff the rice with a chopstick, and set aside to cool for 5 minutes.

3. While the rice steams, place the bamboo leaves in a large bowl or in the sink and add hot water to cover. Allow to soak for 30 minutes, or until ready for use.

4. In a large bowl place the rice and all other ingredients, except the bamboo leaves, and mix thoroughly. Divide into 6 equal portions.

5. Place 2 bamboo leaves on a flat surface, overlapping. Place a portion of the rice mixture in the center of the leaves. Fold the sides up, then the two ends in, to create a square bundle. Tie with a string, if necessary. Repeat until you have 6 bundles. Place the bundles in a steamer and steam for 35 minutes, until they are hot and flavors are blended. Remove from steamer and serve individually.

Serves 4 to 6

BASIC SIZZLING RICE PREPARATION FOR WOR BAH DISHES

½ cup extra-long-grain (or long-grain) rice
½ cup water

1. Place the rice in a bowl with cold water and wash 3 times, rubbing between the hands. Drain. Place the drained rice in a 10-inch nonstick skillet. Add ½ cup cold water. Spread the rice in a thin even layer. Allow to sit for 1½ hours. Most of the water will be absorbed.

2. Place the pan over medium heat, cover, and cook for 5 minutes. Lower the heat to low and cook 2 minutes more. The rice should be white and translucent. Remove the cover. Continue cooking over low heat for 2 to 3 minutes more. Gently move the pan from side to side to loosen rice. If it is loose and it moves, it is done. Turn off the heat and allow to cool in the pan.

3. Place a large plate over the pan and invert the pan so the rice round falls onto the plate. It should be dry and hard, though cooked. This rice round is ready for use in *wor bah* dishes. It can be made up to a week in advance.

Makes 1 cake

Note: This is my way of preparing this rice. Traditionally it is made in this manner: After rice is cooked in a pot and removed, a layer remains on the bottom of the pot. Customarily this is heated, in the pot, until it becomes hard and crisp. Unfortunately, often it burns. My way is foolproof.

锅
吧
汤

SIZZLING RICE SOUP

Wor Bah Tong

Sizzling rice soup is a preparation quite popular in central and northern China, particularly in the north where rice itself is a treat. It is a dramatic dish; it sizzles and steams when hot soup meets hot rice.

½ recipe Basic Sizzling Rice (page 147)

3 tablespoons peanut oil

1 tablespoon minced ginger

1 tablespoon minced garlic

4 onions, cut into ¼-inch dice (2 cups)

8 fresh tomatoes, cut into ½-inch dice (4 cups)

3 cups Vegetable Stock (pages 31–32)

½ cup (4 ounces) tomato sauce

1 teaspoon salt

1½ teaspoons sugar

⅛ teaspoon white pepper

2 teaspoons double dark soy sauce

3 cups peanut oil, for deep-frying

2 to 3 scallions, green portions only, finely sliced (½ cup)

1. Heat a large pot over high heat for 30 seconds. Add the 3 tablespoons peanut oil. When a wisp of white smoke appears, add the ginger, stir, and cook for 30 seconds. Add the garlic and stir. When the garlic turns light brown, add the onions and stir. Lower heat to medium and cook for 5 minutes, stirring occasionally. Turn heat back to high and add the tomatoes. Stir and cook for 2 minutes, then add the stock, tomato sauce, salt, sugar, white pepper, and soy sauce. Stir all the ingredients together well and bring back to a boil. Then lower the heat and cover, leaving a small opening at the lid. Cook for 20 minutes.

2. Halfway through the cooking of the soup, heat a wok over high heat for 45 seconds. Add the 3 cups peanut oil. When a wisp of white smoke appears, lower the sizzling rice round into the oil with a Chinese strainer. Deep-fry for 3 minutes, or until it expands to about double its size. Turn off the heat. Place the strainer over a bowl to drain.

3. Place the hot rice in a soup tureen and pour the soup over it. There will be a sizzling sound, as well as steam. Stir in the scallions and serve.

Serves 4 to 6

湯

麵 Tong

Soup

In China's history soup has always been venerated as a representation of the simple life. Confucius continually encouraged soup consumption for those looking for simplicity in their lives, or as an antidote for the often excessive feasting and the rich foods associated with the imperial court and with the official class, the Mandarins. A Sung dynasty poet, Su Shih, even wrote a poem in which he celebrated a soup made with vegetables for its natural character. I do not disagree with Su Shih.

In my girlhood home in Sun Tak we did not consider a meal to be complete unless a component of it was soup, whether it was a souplike congee at breakfast, or a plain broth. At other meals, either we ate bowls of soup enriched with all manner of vegetables, or we took occasional tastes of broth throughout our meal from a communal bowl of hot soup set in the middle of our table. We were encouraged to drink this soup as a beverage to accompany the meal.

In summer we believed that eating hot soup would cool our bodies despite the heat of the day. In winter we ate rich soups like sizzling rice soups or hot pots, these to ward off winter chills. And if we became ill, soup was often the answer. Winter melon, boiled down to a clear broth with water chestnuts, would, we believed, lower a fever. And the same soup, with sugarcane sugar added, was a perfect treatment for measles. In general, soup was believed to be a cleansing agent for the system.

Buckthorn seeds and red dates in soup were said to be good for the eyes and lungs, respectively. Whether this is precisely true or not, I believe in the efficacy of these two ingredients, and they are present in one of the stocks I have made for use with the recipes in this book.

There is an art to making soup, the Chinese believe, one that is urged upon new brides. A saying goes that if good soup is not being made at home, then a husband might seek out *ah yee lang tong,* or "beautiful soup from number two." The meaning is plain. If number one is not making good soup, then a husband might seek better soup from number two.

The range of soups in China is limitless. You will find a wide variety in this section, from traditional and perhaps familiar soups such as hot pot, hot and sour, winter melon, and corn chowder, to others I have created using my stock and a broad range of available vegetables. Make these and you will not find your spouse looking for better soup from number two.

VEGETABLE HOT POT
Chai Dah Pin Lo

Contrary to what most people believe, the hot pot is not limited to Mongolia, in northernmost China. Both Shanghai and Canton have versions of the hot pot, with and without meats and fish. What I have created is a vegetable version that would be most at home in Canton.

6 ounces bean thread noodles, soaked for ½ an hour and cut into 5-inch threads

8 cakes bean curd, cubed

1 pound spinach, cut into pieces

3 bunches watercress, cut into pieces

1 pound romaine lettuce, cut into 2-inch pieces

1 head fennel, cut into 2-inch by 1-inch pieces

2 cups broccoli stems, peeled and diagonally sliced into ⅓-inch pieces

1 pound cabbage, cut into 2-inch by 3-inch slices

1 recipe Ginger Soy Sauce, for dipping (page 40)

Broth ingredients

8 cups Vegetable Stock (pages 31–32)

1 piece fresh ginger, 2 by 2 inches

4 cloves garlic

½ cup chopped fresh coriander

1 tablespoon sesame oil

1 tablespoon Scallion Oil (page 37)

1. Each of the vegetables, as well as the bean curd and the noodles, should be placed in its own bowl or plate and arranged around a hot pot (available in Asian markets) or an electric frying pan.

2. Heat 4 cups of the stock in the hot pot or electric frying pan. Add the ginger and garlic. When it comes to a boil add the coriander, sesame oil, and Scallion Oil. Stir, cook for 3 minutes for best aroma.

3. Eat as you wish, by placing the vegetable of your choice, or noodle, into the boiling broth and cooking it. I recommend using small, strainerlike spoons made of wire, which are available in Asian markets. If unavailable you may use ordinary slotted spoons. Dip the cooked foods in the ginger soy sauce, and eat.

4. Keep replenishing the stock. When the vegetables and noodles have been consumed, pour the remaining broth into small bowls and drink it as the final taste of the hot pot.

Serves 4 to 6

HOT AND SOUR SOUP
Seun Lot Tong

This is a traditional favorite of the Chinese kitchen. It is served in the western part of the country, in Hunan and Szechuan, and in the north, in Peking, and is always made in the same manner, usually with pork added. I have removed the pork and used my vegetable stock instead of the chicken stock it is traditionally made with, for a soup that is as intense and tasty as the original.

4 cups Vegetable Stock (pages 31–32)

1 cup cold water

One slice fresh ginger, ½-inch thick

1 teaspoon salt, or to taste

1 clove garlic

4 to 5 Chinese dried black mushrooms, soaked in hot water for 30 minutes until soft, stems removed, caps shredded (½ cup)

⅓ cup tiger lily buds, soaked in hot water for 30 minutes until soft, hard ends cut off, and halved

3 tablespoons shredded Szechuan mustard pickle

6 thin slices dried bean curd, soaked in hot water for 30 minutes, until soft

3 tablespoons red wine vinegar

3 tablespoons Scallion Oil (page 37)

5 tablespoons cornstarch mixed with 5 tablespoons cold water

1 teaspoon Hot Oil (page 36)

½ teaspoon hot pepper flakes from bottom of Hot Oil (page 36)

2 cakes fresh bean curd, sliced into strips

1 teaspoon dark soy sauce

1 small scallion, trimmed and finely sliced (3 tablespoons)

1. Place the stock, water, ginger, salt, and garlic in a pot. Bring to a boil and add the shredded mushrooms. Cook 5 minutes. Add the tiger lily buds, mustard pickle, and softened dry bean curd and cook another 2 minutes. Add the vinegar and Scallion Oil and stir. Add the cornstarch mixture, stirring constantly, and bring to a boil. Add the Hot Oil and hot pepper flakes and mix well. Add the fresh bean curd and soy sauce, mix, and bring back to a boil. Turn off the heat and serve immediately in individual bowls, sprinkled with sliced scallions.

Serves 4 to 6

Corn Chowder with Egg Whites

Suk Mai Dan Bak Tong

This is my variation on a classic Cantonese soup. Who has not had, in his or her local restaurant, corn soup with crabmeat, or with chicken, or whatever? This simple soup concentrates on the sweetness of the corn and its lovely yellow color.

1 pound corn kernels, fresh or frozen (fresh preferred)
4 cups Vegetable Stock (pages 31–32)
½ teaspoon grated fresh ginger
⅛ teaspoon white pepper
¼ teaspoon salt
3 large egg whites, beaten lightly
2 small scallions, trimmed and finely sliced (¼ cup)

1. Place ¾ pound corn kernels and ¾ cup stock in a blender and puree. Do not liquefy totally; leave some pieces in the puree.

2. Place remaining vegetable stock in a pot with the ginger, white pepper, and salt and bring to a boil over high heat. Add remaining ¼ pound corn kernels and return to a boil. Cover the pot, lower the heat, and simmer for 5 minutes. Raise the heat back to high, add the pureed corn, mix well, and bring back to a boil. Cook for 2 minutes, stirring frequently to avoid sticking. Fold in the egg whites. Turn off the heat, transfer to a heated tureen, sprinkle with scallions, and serve immediately.

Serves 4 to 6

Tiger Lily Buds (dried and soaked)

WINTER MELON SOUP
Seung Tung Tong

The winter melon is a versatile vegetable. Because it has virtually no taste of its own, it absorbs the tastes of what it is cooked with, either in a stir-fry or in a soup. What it does have is a pleasing texture, like a watermelon, and when it is grated, as it often is, it gives a dish a pureed consistency. But it is winter melon's ability to absorb tastes that makes it quite special.

1½ pounds winter melon

2 tablespoons peanut oil

⅛ teaspoon salt, or to taste

14 to 16 shallots, peeled and cut into ¼-inch dice (1 cup)

6 Chinese dried black mushrooms, each 1½ inches in diameter, steamed
    (pages 27–28) and diced

1 tablespoon Shao-Hsing wine or sherry

4½ cups Vegetable Stock (pages 31–32)

1½-inch-wide slice fresh ginger

½ teaspoon sugar

Pinch of white pepper

1 teaspoon sesame oil

3 tablespoons finely chopped fresh coriander

1. Seed, peel, and coarsely grate the winter melon into a bowl so as not to lose the juice. Reserve.

2. Heat a large pot over high heat for 20 seconds. Add the peanut oil and salt and stir. When a wisp of white smoke appears, add the shallots. Stir and cook 3 minutes. Add the mushrooms and stir. Add the winter melon and its liquid and mix well. Add the wine and blend. Add the vegetable stock, ginger, and sugar and continue to blend.

3. Cover the pot and bring to a boil. Lower the heat and cook for 45 minutes, stirring occasionally. Just before turning off the heat, add white pepper and sesame oil and stir into the soup. Turn off the heat, transfer to a heated tureen, sprinkle with chopped coriander, and serve immediately.

Serves 4 to 6

Note: In China this soup would be called, in a humorous play on words, "soup of double winter." The name for winter melon is *tung guah*, and mushrooms are *tung gu*. Together they are "double *tung*," or "double winter." The dish, of course, has nothing at all to do with winter—the ingredients are available the year round—but its name makes us laugh.

Note: When buying winter melon, you buy it in long wedges sliced from the large melon. You should ask for a 1½-pound piece. You will probably receive a bit more, perhaps as much as 1¾ pounds. You can use all of it in the recipe. There is no need to be precise in the amount you use, or to discard any melon over 1½ pounds.

WATERCRESS SOUP WITH BEAN CURD
Sai Yeung Choi Daufu Tong

Watercress will, the Chinese believe, cool one's system and thus provide wanted interior balance. It might well be true; I know my grandmother believed it to be so. It is a fine vegetable with which to balance because it is available virtually the year round.

4 cups Vegetable Stock (pages 31–32)
1¼-inch-wide slice fresh ginger, lightly smashed
2 large bunches watercress, washed thoroughly, each broken in half
2 cakes fresh bean curd, cut into ½-inch cubes
¼ teaspoon salt, or to taste
2 tablespoons Scallion Oil (page 37)
1 teaspoon sesame oil

1. In a large pot, place the vegetable stock and ginger and bring to a boil over high heat. Add the watercress and stir, making certain the cress is immersed in the liquid. Add the bean curd and bring back to a boil. Add the salt, if necessary. Add the Scallion Oil and sesame oil and stir thoroughly. Turn off the heat, remove to a heated tureen, and serve immediately.

Serves 4 to 6

Note: To give watercress a bright green color, add ¼ teaspoon baking soda at the same time as the stock and ginger. Using this technique, you will be able to make the soup hours in advance and the watercress will remain bright green.

BOK CHOY SOUP
Bok Choy Tong

A soup of bok choy is a tradition of home cookery in China, particularly in the summer months in Canton. At that time of the year the bok choy stalks and leaves are the sweetest and tenderest.

3 tablespoons Green Oil (page 39)

2 teaspoons minced ginger

1 teaspoon minced garlic

½ teaspoon salt, or to taste

4 soybean cakes (⅔ package), thinly sliced

1½ pounds bok choy, leaves and stalks separated, each cut diagonally into
    ¼-inch pieces

2 tablespoons Shao-Hsing wine or sherry

5½ cups Vegetable Stock (pages 31–32)

2 teaspoons soy sauce

3½ tablespoons fresh coriander, finely chopped

1. Heat a pot over high heat for 40 seconds. Add the Green Oil, ginger, garlic, and salt and stir. When the garlic turns light brown, add the soybean cake slices and stir. Cook for 1 minute. Add the bok choy stalks and stir briefly. Add the wine to the mixture. Add the stock and stir well. Cover and allow to come to a boil. Lower the heat and let the soup cook 15 minutes, until the stalks are tender. Raise the heat, add the bok choy leaves, bring back to a boil, and allow to cook 4 to 5 minutes, until leaves are tender. Turn off the heat. Stir in soy sauce and coriander. Transfer to a heated tureen and serve immediately.

Serves 4 to 6

青
豆
湯

GREEN PEA SOUP
Ching Dau Tong

Sweet green peas are prized in China, particularly in Hong Kong, where they have been used more and more in recent years. Often they are added to modernized versions of fried rice, cooked with shrimp, and added to soups for their color as well as for their taste. This soup recognizes the pea for itself alone.

1 Basic Sizzling Rice recipe (page 147; see note below)

2½ tablespoons peanut oil

¼ teaspoon salt, or to taste

1½-inch-wide slice fresh ginger, lightly smashed

2 onions, cut into ¼-inch dice (1½ cups)

2½ cups green peas, fresh or frozen (if frozen, allow to come to room
    temperature)

1½ to 2 yellow peppers, cut into ¼-inch dice (1½ cups)

1 tablespoon Shao-Hsing wine or sherry

6 cups Vegetable Stock (pages 31–32)

3 cups peanut oil (to deep-fry)

1. Make the sizzling rice recipe. Reserve.

2. Heat a large pot over high heat for 40 seconds. Add the peanut oil, salt, and ginger. Stir. When the ginger turns light brown, add the onions, stir, and cook until the onions are translucent, about 2 minutes. Add the peas and cook for 1 minute more. Add the peppers, stir briefly, and add the wine. Stir the vegetable stock into the mixture. Cover and bring to a boil. Lower the heat and simmer for 5 minutes. Turn off the heat. Taste the soup for seasoning.

3. Heat a wok over high heat for 45 seconds; add the 3 cups peanut oil. When a wisp of white smoke appears, lower the rice round into the oil with a Chinese strainer. Deep-fry for 3 minutes, or until it expands to about double its size. Turn off heat. Place in strainer to drain and cool.

4. Place the soup into 6 individual soup bowls. Serve with the crisp rice as an accompaniment, either broken into the soup or alongside as a sort of cracker.

Serves 4 to 6

Note: The sizzling *wor bah* rice may be made in advance. It will keep in a tightly closed container for up to 2 months. It need not be refrigerated.

CHINESE TURNIP AND GREEN PEA SOUP
Hong Luk Bok Tong

I call this soup *hong luk bok*, which means "red, green, and white" soup. The peas are green, the turnips white, and the carrots, while orange in color, are often called "red turnips" in China. My husband insists that this soup is a tacit recognition of the Italian flag.

3 tablespoons Scallion Oil (page 37)

2 tablespoons minced fresh ginger

1 teaspoon salt, or to taste

1 pound Chinese turnips, peeled, both ends trimmed, cut into ⅓-inch dice

2 carrots, peeled and cut into ⅓-inch dice (1 cup)

1½ cups green peas, fresh or frozen (if frozen, allow to come to room temperature)

2 tablespoons Shao-Hsing wine or sherry

5½ cups Vegetable Stock (pages 31–32)

⅛ teaspoon white pepper

1. Heat a large pot over high heat for 40 seconds. Add Scallion Oil, ginger, and salt and stir. Add the turnips and stir briefly. Add the carrots and stir briefly. Add the peas and stir briefly. Add the wine and mix. Add vegetable stock and mix well. Cover the pot and bring to a boil over high heat. Lower the heat and cook for 7 minutes, until the turnips and carrots are tender. Turn off the heat and stir in the white pepper. Transfer to a heated tureen and serve immediately.

Serves 4 to 6

SILK SQUASH AND FRESH MUSHROOM SOUP
See Guah Sin Gu Tong

This squash is combined with a variety of other vegetables in China, particularly in soups, because of its sweetness. I chose fresh mushrooms for their contrast and texture.

1½ pounds silk squash

2 cups fresh mushrooms, each the size of a quarter

3 tablespoons peanut oil

1¼-inch-wide slice fresh ginger

¼ teaspoon salt

3 cups Vegetable Stock (pages 31–32)

2 cups cold water

1 tablespoon Shao-Hsing wine or sherry

1 teaspoon sesame oil

1. Clean and wash the squash. Pare down the ridges but do not remove all of the green. Roll-cut squash: Starting at one end, cut diagonally into ¾-inch slices. Turn the squash a quarter-turn between each cut. The slices will resemble tiny axe blades. Set aside. Cut the mushrooms in half. Set aside.

2. Heat the wok over high heat for 30 seconds. Add peanut oil and coat the wok with a spatula. When a wisp of white smoke appears, add the ginger and salt and stir. When the ginger turns light brown, add the squash and mushrooms. Stir-fry for 2 minutes.

3. Place the squash and mushrooms in a pot. Add the vegetable stock and water. Cover the pot and bring to a boil. Lower heat to medium and allow to cook 5 to 7 minutes, or until squash is tender. Turn the heat back to high, add the wine, and stir well. Add the sesame oil and mix well. Turn off the heat, transfer to a heated tureen, and serve immediately.

Serves 4 to 6

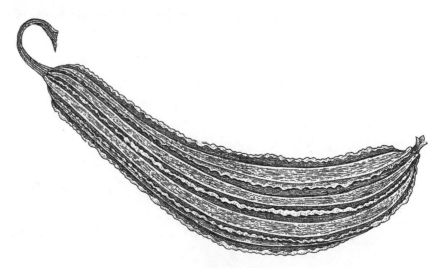

Silk Squash

STEAMED HAIRY MELON SOUP
Jeet Guah Jung

These zucchini-like melons, when ripe, have a kind of fuzz on their skins, thus their name. They are versatile, and the Chinese steam, bake, boil, fry, and stuff them. They are relatively small, less than a foot in length and about 3 inches in diameter. As they get older, they yellow and become round and softer, so young hairy melon are best for this visually spectacular dish. Each melon is its own tureen.

3 hairy melons, each 12 inches long by 3 inches in diameter

3 fresh water chestnuts, peeled and minced

3 Chinese dried black mushrooms, each 1½ inches in diameter, soaked in
    hot water for 30 minutes, stems removed, caps cut into ⅛-inch dice

½ carrot, peeled and cut into ⅛-inch dice (3 tablespoons)

3 cups Vegetable Stock (pages 31–32)

1 scallion, green portion only, finely sliced (1 tablespoon)

1. Wash the melons. Cut in half, crosswise, then with a grapefruit knife scoop out the seeds and center core of all 6 halves. Wrap the base of each in a cloth and wedge it into a small heatproof dish so that it stands firmly.

2. Divide all the ingredients, except the scallions, evenly among melon halves. Place the halves, still in their heatproof dishes, in a steamer or a clam pot and steam for 1½ hours, or until the melons soften but do not lose their shape. Remove from the steamer, sprinkle with scallions, and serve individually. Eat with a small spoon, shaving melon flesh from the sides as you eat the soup.

Serves 4 to 6

CUCUMBER WITH BEAN CURD SOUP
Chang Gua Daufu Tong

This is a simple soup and a popular one, particularly in the summer. The Chinese believe that cucumbers tend to bring the body's temperature down, and the more so in soup. It is believed a hot soup, with the proper ingredients, will cool the body in summer. At least that is what my grandmother told me.

1½ cups Vegetable Stock (pages 31–32)

1½ cups cold water

1¼-inch-wide slice fresh ginger, lightly smashed

Salt to taste

2 cakes fresh bean curd, cut into julienne

1 large cucumber, peeled, cut in half lengthwise, seeds removed, then cut
    crosswise into ¼-inch slices to create half-moons (1¼ cups)

¼ cup celery leaves

1. Place the vegetable stock and water in a pot with the ginger and salt. Bring to a boil. Add the bean curd and allow to return to a boil. Add the cucumbers and allow to return to a boil. Cook for about 1 minute, until the cucumbers become tender. Add the celery leaves and stir into the soup. Taste for salt. Turn off the heat, transfer to a heated tureen, and serve.

Serves 4 to 6

莞
荽
湯

Coriander Soup with Bean Curd
Yeun Sai Tong

Fresh coriander is used extensively throughout China and Asia, usually as an enhancing ingredient or as a garnish. It is the center of attention in this soup, which utilizes its texture as well as its scent.

3½ tablespoons Green Oil (page 39)

½ teaspoon salt, or to taste

1½-inch-wide slice fresh ginger, lightly smashed

4½ tablespoons fresh coriander roots and stems, minced

3 onions, cut into ¼-inch dice (2 cups)

2 to 3 stalks celery, cut into ¼-inch dice (1½ cups)

4½ cups Vegetable Stock (pages 31–32)

1 cup cold water

3 cakes fresh bean curd, cut into ¼-inch dice

½ cup fresh coriander leaves, finely chopped

1. Heat a large pot over high heat for 30 seconds. Add the Green Oil, salt, and ginger and stir. When a wisp of white smoke appears, add the coriander stems and roots. Cook for 20 seconds. Add the onions, stir, and cook for about 3 minutes, until onions become translucent. Add the celery, stir, and cook for 1 minute. Add the vegetable stock and water and mix well.

2. Cover the pot and bring to a boil. Lower the heat to medium and cook 7 to 10 minutes, until the celery is tender. Raise the heat back to high and add the bean curd. Bring back to a boil and boil for 2 minutes. Turn off the heat, add the coriander leaves, and mix well. Transfer to a heated tureen and serve immediately.

Serves 4 to 6

BEAN THREAD AND SPINACH SOUP
Bor Choi Fun See Tong

This is truly a soup of the earth. In China, particularly in the south, mung beans grow in profusion, as does spinach, and soups made from them separately and together abound.

1 ounce (½ package) mung bean threads (packages are labeled "bean threads" or "bean thread noodles")

8 cups water

½ teaspoon baking soda

1 tablespoon salt

1 pound fresh spinach, leaves broken in half

5 cups Vegetable Stock (pages 31–32)

2 teaspoons Shao-Hsing wine or sherry

2 teaspoons minced ginger

2 teaspoons minced garlic

2 tablespoons Scallion Oil (page 37)

1. Soak the bean threads in hot water for 30 minutes. Remove from the water, drain, and cut into 4-inch strands. Reserve.

2. In a large pot place the 8 cups water, baking soda, and salt and bring to a boil. Add the spinach. Stir and make certain all the spinach is covered by water. When spinach turns bright green, remove the pot from the heat. Run cold water into the pot, drain, and set the spinach aside.

3. Heat a large pot over high heat and add the stock, wine, ginger, and garlic. Cover the pot and bring to a boil. Lower the heat and allow the broth to simmer for 5 minutes. Raise the heat and add the spinach and bean threads. Bring to a boil, add the Scallion Oil, and mix well. Turn off the heat. Place the soup in a heated tureen and serve immediately.

Serves 4 to 6

LIMA BEAN SOUP WITH SOUR MUSTARD PICKLE
Chom Dau Seun Choi Tong

The usual way of preparing lima beans in China is to allow them to harden, then to deep-fry them and sprinkle them with salt. They are then eaten as a snack. My uncle, I recall, loved these beans with a glass of rice wine. They are also stir-fried, alone or in combination with other vegetables. In this dish they are part of a soup, but in combination with sour mustard pickle, which makes the soup pleasantly tart.

3½ cups Vegetable Stock (pages 31–32)

1½ cups cold water

1½-inch-wide slice fresh ginger, lightly smashed

1 cup sour mustard pickle, cut into ¼-inch dice

1½ cups lima beans, fresh or frozen (if frozen, allow to come to room temperature)

½ teaspoon sugar

4 teaspoons soy sauce

2 tablespoons Szechuan Peppercorn Oil (page 38)

2 cakes fresh bean curd, cut into ⅓-inch cubes

2 tablespoons fresh coriander, chopped

1. In a large pot place the vegetable stock, cold water, ginger, and mustard pickle. Cover and bring to a boil over high heat. Lower the heat to medium and allow to simmer for 7 minutes. Add the lima beans and cook for 5 minutes more. Add the sugar, soy sauce, and Peppercorn Oil and stir well. Return to a boil and add the bean curd. Allow to come to a boil and cook 2 minutes more. Turn off the heat, add the coriander, and stir in. Remove to a heated tureen and serve immediately.

Serves 4 to 6

Hot Mustard Soup
Gai Lot Tong

Mustard not only is used as a dip or an accompaniment to other foods, but is an ingredient in sauces as well. In this preparation all of the other soup ingredients take second place to the taste of the mustard itself.

3½ tablespoons Szechuan Peppercorn Oil (page 38)

1½-inch-wide slice fresh ginger, lightly smashed

¼ teaspoon salt

1 large onion, cut into ¼-inch dice (1 cup)

10 Chinese dried black mushrooms, each 1½ inches in diameter, soaked
   in hot water for 1 hour, stems removed, and caps julienned

4½ cups Vegetable Stock (pages 31–32)

¼ pound snow peas, ends and strings removed, and julienned

3 cakes fresh bean curd, cut into julienne

1½ tablespoons Hot Mustard (page 44)

1. Heat a large pot over high heat for 30 seconds. Add the Szechuan Peppercorn Oil, ginger, and salt. Stir briefly. When a wisp of white smoke appears, add onion. Stir and cook for 1 minute. Add the mushrooms, stir, and cook for 2 minutes. Add the vegetable stock and mix well.

2. Cover the pot and bring to a boil. Lower the heat to medium and boil for 5 minutes. Remove the cover and bring the heat back to high. Add the snow peas, stir, and bring back to a boil. Add the bean curd and bring back to a boil. Cook for 1 minute. Turn off the heat. Add the mustard and stir well to ensure it is well blended. Transfer to a heated tureen and serve immediately.

Serves 4 to 6

ASPARAGUS AND TWO MUSHROOM SOUP
Lo Sun Seung Gu Tong

This is a soup not only of taste but of contrasting, complementary textures—the crispness of the asparagus spears and the softness of the soaked mushrooms. This is a soup for the spring, when asparagus is at its best.

3 tablespoons Scallion Oil (page 37)

1½-inch-wide slice fresh ginger, lightly smashed

2 cloves garlic, peeled

½ teaspoon salt

12 small Chinese dried black mushrooms, soaked in hot water for 1½ hours, water squeezed off, stems discarded, and caps halved

1¼ pounds asparagus, peeled and cut diagonally into ½-inch pieces

6 ounces fresh mushrooms, cut into ¼-inch slices

1 tablespoon Shao-Hsing wine or sherry

4 cups Vegetable Stock (pages 31–32)

1. Heat a large pot over high heat for 40 seconds. Add the oil, ginger, garlic, and salt. Stir until the garlic turns light brown. Add the Chinese mushrooms and stir. Cook for 1 minute. Add the asparagus and stir briefly. Add the fresh mushrooms and stir. Add the wine and mix well. Add the vegetable stock. Cover the pot and bring to a boil over high heat. Lower the heat and cook for 5 minutes. The asparagus should be cooked but still crisp. Turn off the heat, transfer to a heated tureen, and serve immediately.

Serves 4 to 6

TOMATO POTATO SOUP
Fou Keh Siu Jai Tong

People are often surprised to note the presence of both tomatoes and potatoes in the Chinese kitchen, but Asia was only too happy to accept these gifts from the West, and they are now commonplace. When I was a child this was a favorite cool-weather soup.

2½ tablespoons peanut oil

2 teaspoons minced ginger

1 tablespoon minced garlic

2 large onions, cut into ¼-inch dice (1⅔ cups)

6 large tomatoes, cut into ½-inch dice (3 cups)

3 cups potatoes, peeled and cut into ½-inch dice

2 cups Vegetable Stock (pages 31–32)

1½ cups cold water

1¼ teaspoons salt

1¼ teaspoons sugar

2 to 3 scallions, trimmed and finely sliced (½ cup)

1 teaspoon sesame oil

1. Heat a large pot over high heat for 30 seconds, then add the peanut oil. When a wisp of white smoke appears, add ginger and garlic, stir until the garlic turns light brown, and add onions. Stir, lower the heat, and cook for 5 minutes. Return the heat to high, add the tomatoes, stir, add the potatoes, and stir again. Add the stock and cold water and mix well. Add the salt and sugar and stir. Bring to a boil, lower the heat, and cover the pot, leaving a small opening. Allow the soup to cook for 30 minutes, or until the potatoes are softened. Turn off the heat, add the scallions and sesame oil, stir well, transfer to a tureen, and serve.

Serves 4 to 6

PEPPER SOUP
Sam Jiu Tong

This is my "three-pepper" soup, which is the translation of *sam jiu*. It might even be called four-pepper soup, because fresh chilies may be finely chopped and added to it. However, I use my Hot Oil instead, so I must limit the title to three.

3 tablespoons peanut oil

1½ tablespoons minced garlic

½ teaspoon salt, or to taste

1 large onion, cut into ¼-inch dice (1 cup)

2 large red sweet peppers, cut into ½-inch pieces (1½ cups)

2 large yellow sweet peppers, cut into ½-inch pieces (1½ cups)

2 large green peppers, cut into ½-inch pieces (1½ cups)

1 tablespoon Shao-Hsing wine or sherry

5 cups Vegetable Stock (pages 31–32)

2 teaspoons Hot Oil (page 36), or to taste

1. Heat a large pot over high heat for 40 seconds. Add the peanut oil, garlic, and salt and stir briefly. Add the onions and saute until translucent, about 2 minutes. Add all the peppers and stir in well. Cook for 1 minute. Stir in the wine. Add the vegetable stock and mix well. Cover and bring to a boil over high heat. Lower the heat and cook for 3 minutes, or until peppers are tender. Turn off the heat and stir in the Hot Oil, to taste. Transfer to a heated tureen and serve immediately.

Serves 4 to 6

豆

腐

Daufu and the Traditions of Buddha

Vegetarianism in China is as old as Buddha, and for its dedicated adherents there is no vegetable more versatile than the soybean, provider of sauce, flour, paste, milk, and *daufu*, or bean curd, in its many guises. In China the soybean is regarded as having almost the same importance as rice. On a nutritional level it produces more protein than similar yields of other crops or livestock. Because of this, and because of the lack of interest in most of China in dairy products, the soybean is indispensable.

Soybean sprouts are eaten in salads and in vegetable stir-fries. Soybeans boiled and roasted are a common snack. Fermented in the sun, they yield soy sauce, an ingredient essential to Asian cookery in general and Chinese cookery in particular. Milled and sweetened soybeans become hoisin sauce, that sweet puree so integral to many dishes. Boiled soybeans yield a milk. Milled wet, they form a spongy mass that when pressed dry and cooked become those cakes of bean curd, *daufu*.

Daufu itself is eaten fresh, or dried into sheets and sticks that find their way into the kitchen as well. Bean curd skins, a by-product of boiling soybeans, are skimmed and often used, sliced, in such preparations as hot and sour soup. Often *daufu* is dyed, flavored with anise or other spices, pressed into small cakes, and used in preparations as substitutes for other foods. Of infinite variety is *daufu*.

It is so adaptable that it appears in recipes throughout this book—as a supporting ingredient in stir-fried preparations and in soups—in addition to the recipes in this section, where it is the focus. Here you will find *daufu* boiled, stewed, stir-fried, and deep-fried, its inherent faint taste enlivened by sauces and dips.

It is believed that *daufu*, fresh or in processed cakes, was initially made into imitation "chicken" and "duck" and other fowl, as well as into "pork" and "beef," by Buddhist priests and nuns. Buddhists were forbidden to eat meat, and *daufu*, artfully prepared, became a meat substitute. It even became "fish" for those vegetarians who refrained from eating fish as well as meat. The concept of such culinary artifice has come to be known as temple cooking, because it is at its best in the monasteries.

It is in those Buddhist temples, and Taoist temples as well, that the high art of vegetarian cooking thrived, and does so to this day. Outside of Hong Kong proper, in that band of land known as the New Territories, there is a vast, sprawling Taoist temple, Ching Chung Koon, notable for an incredible collection of miniature trees. I have cooked with the monks in the temple's kitchen and have concocted *daufu* "meats" with them. These delicious imitations, many of which I have adapted—I have created many as well—are in this section, and I can say that it is truly amazing how many other foods *daufu* can become.

The concept of food-giving within Buddhist temples goes back well into Chinese history. It was traditional for travelers to be offered food and rest in the temples scattered throughout the countryside. In these temples it was proper for priests and nuns, and travelers, to offer gifts of food to the deities of Buddhism, and often these gifts were imitations of other foods, fashioned from *daufu*, to please the gods.

The popularity of temple food often extended beyond the temple, however, and in various parts of China, so-called temple food is offered in restaurants. A particular center for such cookery is Hangzhou, near Shanghai, where vegetarian banquets of great beauty can be eaten. Hangzhou is a beautiful small city on an attractive body of water, West Lake, and around this lake are many restaurants and pavilions where vegetarian temple foods are served. I recall a marvelous dinner at a small restaurant called Spring Vegetable, a meal that was as much art exhibit as it was food. I ate "beef" that was made from slices of fermented dough, and an entire fish formed from mashed taro roots. I had "meatballs" of minced vegetables, platters of cold "chicken" and "duck" made from *daufu*. My "scallops" were also of fermented dough. All of these were artfully dressed and seasoned, to precede a series of stir-fried vegetable dishes and soups.

I enjoy the artifices of vegetarianism inspired by the Buddhists. As you make these dishes, keep in mind the philosophy behind them. In Western kitchens bean curd is used as a substitute for meat and other foods, but the emphasis is on making the processed bean curd taste like what it appears to be. Not so in China. The Chinese like to fool the eye and surprise the mouth. Often a *daufu* imitation, a vegetable concoction, will resesemble almost perfectly a piece of meat or fish, but when eaten the taste will be original, not at all like what is being imitated. This is always a happy surprise. Occasionally an imitation will taste like what is being imitated, but that will be by design, not accidental. The enjoyment of taste is always based on surprise. I believe you will find that to be the case.

Another aspect of Buddhism with which I concern myself in this section are some special beliefs Buddhists have regarding certain foods. Strictly observant Buddhists will, for example, eat all vegetables but three—chives, shallots, and leeks. Why? Buddhist legend includes this tale:

During the Song dynasty, a thousand years ago, there was a hero named Yue Fei, a patriot who was loyal to his king and beloved by the people. A jealous court official, Qin Guai, persuaded the king that Yue Fei was plotting against him, and the king had Yue Fei executed. The people were outraged. They captured Qin Guai and his wife, burned them to death, and scattered their ashes to the winds. The ashes fell upon a garden of chives, shallots, and leeks, and since that time they have been regarded as unpalatable vegetables.

This was an integral part of some Buddhist observances. My grandmother, Ah Paw, adhered to it, and on the day of the Lunar New Year we were not permitted to have chives, shallots, or leeks at our table. This did not, however, pertain to the remainder of the year.

And though strict Buddhists will eat nothing that has lived, an observance shared by such occasional Buddhists as my grandmother, they do eat mussels, oysters, and clams. Why? There is no legend to explain it, not that I know of, yet I recall my grandmother assuring me, and others, that these three shellfish were permissible to Buddhists. To this day Buddhists, including those who think of themselves as vegetarians, eat mussels, oysters, and clams (as well as oyster sauce, an ingredient basic to the Chinese diet made by boiling oysters down to a thickened essence).

Accordingly, in keeping with Buddhist tradition, I include in this section several recipes each for mussels, oysters, and clams. Ah Paw would approve.

FRIED BEAN CURD
Jah Daufu

This is a simple dish of southern China. Bean curd is boiled, then fried, and eaten with a salt-water dip that the Chinese believe cools the system made hot by eating the bean curd.

6 cups cold water
2 teaspoons salt
1-pound block (4 cakes) fresh bean curd, sliced into pieces 2 inches long
    by ½ inch wide (total of 24 pieces)
3 cups peanut oil
Salt Water Dip (recipe follows)

1. In a large pot place the water and salt. Cover and bring to a boil. Add the bean curd and allow to come back to a boil. Turn off the heat. Remove the bean curd and place in a strainer to drain. Dry the bean curd slices individually with paper towels. They must be completely dry.

2. Heat a wok over high heat for 45 seconds. Add the peanut oil and heat to 350°F. Turn off the heat. Place 6 slices of bean curd in the wok and fry for 30 seconds. Turn the heat on again to medium. The bean curd will rise to the top of the oil. Allow to cook for 1 more minute, until it turns pale gold. Remove from the wok. The slices should have an outer crispness but must be soft inside. Cook all slices, 6 at a time, adjusting heat as necessary to keep the oil at 350°F. Drain on paper towels and serve with Salt Water Dip.

Serves 4 to 6

SALT WATER DIP

3 tablespoons boiling water
¼ teaspoon salt
2 tablespoons chopped chives

1. Mix all ingredients. Dip fried bean curd slices into the liquid and scoop up bits of chives as you do.

   Makes ¼ cup

FRESH BEAN CURD WITH SWEET SCALLION SAUCE
Daufu Tim Chung Yau

This is a deceptively simple dish that depends for its success on the freshness and texture of the *daufu* in combination with my Sweet Scallion Sauce and the crispness of roasted pine nuts. As a youngster I enjoyed bean curd in even a simpler way, with soy sauce poured over the cake. This is better.

3 tablespoons pine nuts
6 cups cold water
4 cakes fresh bean curd
¼ cup Sweet Scallion Sauce (page 37)
½ scallion, green portion only, finely sliced (2 tablespoons)

1. Dry-roast the pine nuts (page 28). Reserve (see note below).
2. Place the water in a large pot. Cover and bring to a boil over high heat. Add the bean curd and boil for 4 minutes. Remove. Drain and place in a heated dish.
3. Cut each cake of bean curd in half. Pour the Sweet Scallion Sauce over them. Sprinkle the pine nuts and scallion on top and serve immediately.

   Serves 4 to 6

Note: Pine nuts may be dry-roasted in advance. In fact, you may dry-roast as much as 1 cup of the nuts and reserve any unused portion. They will keep for 1 week in a tightly closed container, unrefrigerated. They may be frozen for as long as 2 months.

BEAN CURD WITH TOMATOES
Fou Keh Chau Daufu

This is inspired by the Szechuan kitchen, which makes use of bean curd to a great degree and utilizes spicy horse bean sauce widely (see note below). Tomatoes give the dish freshness and life.

Sauce ingredients

4 teaspoons preserved horse beans with chili

2 teaspoons Shao-Hsing wine or sherry

2 teaspoons soy sauce

2 teaspoons mushroom soy sauce

1 teaspoon white vinegar

2 teaspoons sugar

Pinch of white pepper

2 tablespoons cornstarch

1 cup Vegetable Stock (pages 31–32)

1 teaspoon sesame oil

To complete the dish

6 cakes fresh bean curd

2 tablespoons peanut oil

1½ tablespoons minced ginger

1½ teaspoons salt

1 tablespoon minced garlic

1¼ pounds fresh tomatoes, cut into ½-inch cubes

1 tablespoon sugar

1 bunch scallions, trimmed, green and white portions separated and
   diagonally cut into ½-inch pieces

1. Combine the sauce ingredients in a bowl. Reserve. Dry the bean curd with paper towels. Cut into ½-inch dice. Reserve.

2. Heat a wok over high heat for 30 seconds. Add the peanut oil and coat the wok with a spatula. Add the ginger and salt and stir. Add the garlic and stir. When garlic turns light brown, add the tomatoes. Stir and cook until the tomatoes are bubbling, about 2 minutes. Lower the heat, add the sugar, and cook for about 10 minutes, or until the tomatoes are softened.

3. Turn the heat back to high and add the bean curd. Stir until well mixed and coated. Add the scallions and mix. Stir the sauce and add it to the wok. Mix until the sauce is bubbling. Turn off the heat, transfer to a heated serving dish, and serve immediately.

Serves 4 to 6

Note: Preserved horse beans with chili are sold in jars labeled exactly that way. After opening the jar, store in the refrigerator.

BEAN CURD BALLS
Daufu Kai

This is a somewhat fanciful preparation of mine, based on that popular dim sum and Chiu Chow classic, shrimp balls. These balls, of fresh bean curd, look just like the others, but the taste is a fresh surprise.

2 cakes fresh bean curd
2 to 3 fresh water chestnuts, peeled and cut into ⅛-inch dice (¼ cup)
1 large scallion, finely sliced (⅓ cup)
1½ teaspoons minced ginger
¾ teaspoon sugar
¼ teaspoon salt
1½ teaspoons sesame oil
12 Szechuan peppercorns, crushed
Pinch of white pepper
2 tablespoons cornstarch
1 large egg
5 cups peanut oil
2½ tablespoons Chiu Chow Sweet Soy (page 41)

1. Place the bean curd in a large bowl and mash it. Add all other ingredients except peanut oil and Chiu Chow Sweet Soy and mix thoroughly until well blended. Take a small portion of the mixture, about 1½ tablespoons, and form a loose ball, then toss back and forth gently between the palms. This will tend to make the ball firm so it stays together. Repeat to form a total of 12 balls. Reserve.

2. Heat a wok over high heat for 40 seconds. Add the peanut oil and heat to 325°F. Place 6 of the bean curd balls in the oil and fry them, turning them as they cook and regulating heat to maintain proper oil temperature. Fry until golden brown, about 3 minutes. Remove and drain on paper towels. Repeat with remaining 6 balls. Turn off the heat, place the balls in a serving dish, and serve with Chiu Chow Sweet Soy as a dipping sauce.

Serves 4 to 6

怪
味
豆
腐

STRANGE FLAVOR BEAN CURD
Guai Mei Daufu

This "strange flavor" comes from Szechuan, and what makes it strange? Ketchup. In China—where, incidentally, ketchup originated—the condiment is used mainly for color. In this dish it combines with sesame seed paste, Chinese vinegar, and peppercorns to make an exotic and "strange" flavor indeed.

Sauce ingredients

2½ teaspoons sesame seed paste

2½ tablespoons mushroom soy sauce

2 teaspoons Chinese Chekiang vinegar (if unavailable, use red wine vinegar)

2 teaspoons sugar

1½ teaspoons Hot Oil (page 36)

10 whole Szechuan peppercorns, crushed

2 tablespoons minced shallots

2 teaspoons minced garlic

2 teaspoons sesame oil

3 tablespoons ketchup

To complete the dish

6 cups cold water

4 cakes fresh bean curd

½ tablespoon sesame seeds, dry-roasted (page 28)

1. Combine the sauce ingredients in a bowl. Reserve.

2. Place the cold water in a large pot. Cover and bring to a boil over high heat. Add the bean curd, bring back to a boil, and boil for 2 minutes. Turn off the heat, drain off the water, place in a serving dish, and cut each cake into 6 pieces. Stir the sauce and pour over the bean curd. Sprinkle with sesame seeds. Serve immediately.

Serves 4 to 6

BEAN CURD CAKE WITH CHINESE TURNIPS
Daufu Gon Jiu Lor Bok

This is a traditional dish for the elderly, who look upon food not only as nourishment but for what it does for the body's balance. They believe that this dish has purifying powers. I am not certain that this is so, but the dish surely tastes good.

Sauce ingredients

2 teaspoons Shao-Hsing wine or sherry

2 tablespoons oyster sauce

1 teaspoon dark soy sauce

1 teaspoon sugar

Pinch of white pepper

2½ teaspoons cornstarch

⅓ cup Vegetable Stock (pages 31–32)

To complete the dish

3½ tablespoons peanut oil

1½ teaspoons minced garlic

3 soybean cakes (½ package), thinly sliced (see note below)

¼ teaspoon salt

4 cups Chinese turnips, peeled, cut into ¼-inch rounds, and julienned

3½ tablespoons julienned Ginger Pickle (page 295)

3 tablespoons Vegetable Stock (pages 31–32)

3 to 4 scallions, green portions only, cut into 2-inch sections (1 cup)

1. Combine the sauce ingredients in a bowl. Reserve.

2. Heat a wok over high heat for 30 seconds. Add 1 tablespoon peanut oil and coat the wok with a spatula. When a wisp of white smoke appears, add the garlic and stir briefly. Add the bean cake slices and stir-fry for 1½ minutes. Turn off the heat. Transfer to a bowl. Reserve.

3. Raise the heat back to high. Add the remaining peanut oil and salt and stir. When a wisp of white smoke appears, add the turnips and stir-fry for 1 minute. Add Ginger Pickle and stir well. Add 2 tablespoons of vegetable stock and mix well. Cook for 3 minutes, or until the turnips are tender. If the mixture becomes dry, add the remaining stock. Add the bean curd and mix well. Add the scallions and stir-fry together until the scallions turn bright green. Make a well in the center, stir the sauce, and pour it in. When the sauce begins to bubble and turn brown, turn off the heat, transfer to a heated dish, and serve immediately with cooked rice.

Serves 4 to 6

Note: Soybean cakes, basically bean curd dyed with soy sauce, are dark brown. They come in squares, 2 by 2 inches, packed 6 to a package. They are labeled "soybean cake," or they may not be labeled at all except in Chinese, in which case you must ask for "five spice dry bean curd." The cakes are dry and are usually found in refrigerated sections of markets. They may be wrapped and kept in the refrigerator for 1 week, or frozen for as long as 2 months.

LIMA BEANS WITH SOYBEAN CAKE
Chom Dau Chau Daufu Gon

This stir-fried preparation of lima beans is quite familiar in Shanghai, where people eat many dishes containing lima beans. The sweetness of the sauce is also attractive to the Shanghai palate, which in general has a preference for sweeter sauces.

2½ tablespoons peanut oil
1 teaspoon minced garlic
3 soybean cakes (½ package), cut into ¼-inch dice
1½-inch-wide slice fresh ginger, lightly smashed
¼ teaspoon salt
4 to 5 scallions, trimmed and diagonally cut into ½-inch pieces (1 cup)
1¼ cups lima beans, fresh or frozen (see note below)
5 to 6 fresh water chestnuts, peeled and cut into ¼-inch dice (½ cup)
2 teaspoons Shao-Hsing wine or sherry
2 tablespoons Chiu Chow Sweet Soy (page 41)

1. Heat wok over high heat for 30 seconds. Add 1 tablespoon peanut oil. Coat the wok with a spatula. When a wisp of white smoke appears, add the garlic and stir briefly. Add the bean cake and stir-fry for 1 minute. Turn off the heat. Transfer to a bowl. Reserve.

2. Turn the heat back to high. Add remaining peanut oil. Coat the wok with a spatula. When a wisp of white smoke appears, add the ginger and salt and stir briefly. Add scallions and stir-fry for 45 seconds. Add lima beans and stir-fry for 1 minute more. Add the water chestnuts and stir briefly. Add the bean cakes and mix. Add the wine and mix, then add Chiu Chow Sweet Soy and mix well until the sauce is absorbed. Turn off the heat. Transfer to a heated dish and serve immediately.

Serves 4 to 6

Note: If fresh lima beans are used, they should be water-blanched in simmering water for about 1½ minutes, then drained thoroughly and cooled to room temperature. If frozen, allow to come to room temperature before using.

Bean Curd Pan-Fried with Scallions

Chung Jin Daufu

Bean curd is a most versatile food. This is a simple preparation, a most satisfying Buddhist temple food.

Sauce ingredients

2 tablespoons dark soy sauce

1½ tablespoons cornstarch

¼ teaspoon salt

1 teaspoon sugar

1 cup Vegetable Stock (pages 31–32)

To complete the dish

4½ tablespoons peanut oil

6 cakes fresh bean curd, dried with paper towels

¼ teaspoon salt

8 to 10 scallions, trimmed, cut into 1½-inch pieces, and white portions quartered

1. Combine the sauce ingredients in a bowl. Reserve.

2. In a cast-iron frying pan heat 3 tablespoons peanut oil over high heat. When a wisp of white smoke appears, place the bean curd cakes in the pan and fry for 5 to 7 minutes, until they turn light brown. If the heat is too high (if the bean curd begins to burn or there is smoke), lower it. Turn the cakes over and repeat. Remove the cakes from the pan, place in a serving dish, and cut into 1-inch cubes.

3. Heat a wok over high heat. Add the remaining peanut oil and the salt. Coat the wok with a spatula. When a wisp of white smoke appears, add the white scallion portions and stir-fry for 30 seconds. Add the green portions and stir-fry until they become bright green. Remove from the wok and reserve.

4. Stir the sauce and pour it into the wok over low heat. Stir clockwise continuously until the sauce thickens and bubbles. Add the scallions and mix well. Turn off the heat, pour over the bean curd cubes, and serve.

Serves 4 to 6

VEGETARIAN CHICKEN
Chai Gai

The texture of the bean curd with which this "chicken" is made becomes quite like the texture of chicken breasts after the bean curd has been twice-cooked. The aim is to fool the eye and please the taste.

Sauce ingredients

1 teaspoon light soy sauce

1 teaspoon double dark soy sauce

1 teaspoon sugar

1 teaspoon sesame oil

1 teaspoon white vinegar

2 teaspoons Shao-Hsing wine or sherry

2 teaspoons cornstarch

Pinch of white pepper

5 tablespoons Vegetable Stock (pages 31–32)

To complete the dish

½ pound (2 cakes) fresh bean curd

2½ tablespoons Scallion Oil (page 37)

1½ teaspoons minced fresh ginger

1 teaspoon minced garlic

5 Chinese dried black mushrooms, soaked in hot water for 30 minutes, stems removed, caps thinly sliced (⅓ cup)

⅓ cup julienned bamboo shoots

2 scallions, trimmed and julienned (½ cup)

2 to 3 fresh water chestnuts, peeled and julienned (¼ cup)

½ cup julienned carrots

¼ cup julienned sweet red pepper

1½ tablespoons julienned Szechuan mustard pickle

1 tablespoon Vegetable Stock, if needed (pages 31–32)

1. Combine the sauce ingredients in a bowl. Reserve.

2. Bring 4 cups cold water to a boil in a pot. Add the bean curd and cook for 5 minutes. Turn off the heat, run cold water into the pot, drain, and allow to cool. Slice the bean curd into pieces ⅓ by 1 by 2 inches. Dry with paper towels.

3. Heat a wok over high heat for 30 seconds, add 1½ tablespoons Scallion Oil, and coat the wok with a spatula. When a wisp of white smoke appears, add the bean curd slices and fry for 1½ minutes. Turn over and fry another 1½ minutes. The bean curd should be light brown. Turn off the heat. Remove from the wok and reserve.

4. Heat the wok over high heat and add the remaining Scallion Oil. Add the ginger and garlic and stir. When the garlic turns light brown, add all the vegetables and stir-fry for 2 minutes. If the vegetables are too dry, add 1 tablespoon of vegetable stock. Add the bean curd and mix well. Make a well in the center, stir the sauce, and pour it into the well. Mix together. When the sauce begins to bubble and thicken, turn off the heat. Transfer to a heated serving dish and serve immediately.

Serves 4 to 6

Szechuan Mustard Pickle

"CHICKEN" DING WITH WALNUTS
Hop Toh Gai Ding

This, of course, is not chicken. Once again the versatile bean curd stands in for poultry and does so quite well. However, the dish is made in the classic manner. With traditional chicken *ding,* either peanuts, cashews, or walnuts may be used. I chose walnuts for their taste and texture in combination with the bean curd.

12 cups cold water

1½ teaspoons salt

2 cakes fresh bean curd

¾ cup shelled walnuts, in unbroken halves

3 cups peanut oil, for deep-frying

2 tablespoons peanut oil

4 shallots, cut into ¼-inch dice (¼ cup)

½ large sweet red pepper, cut into ½-inch dice (½ cup)

2 ounces string beans, washed, both ends trimmed, and cut into ½-inch pieces (½ cup)

½ cup bamboo shoots, cut into ½-inch dice

3 to 4 fresh water chestnuts, peeled and cut into ¼-inch dice (⅓ cup)

1 tablespoon hoisin sauce

1½ tablespoons oyster sauce

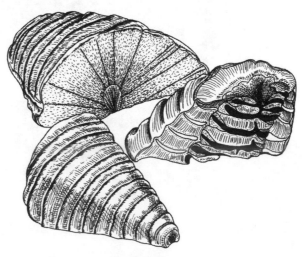

Bamboo Shoots

1. In a pot place 4 cups of the cold water and 1 teaspoon salt. Cover and bring to a boil over high heat. Add the bean curd. Cook for about 5 minutes. Turn off the heat. Drain off the water. Allow to cool and cut into ¾-inch cubes. Reserve.

2. Place 4 cups of the cold water and the walnuts in a pot and bring to a boil. Boil for 5 minutes. Turn off the heat, run cold water into the pot, and drain. Place the walnuts back in the pot, add the remaining 4 cups of water, and bring to a boil again. Boil for 2 minutes. Turn off the heat, run cold water into the pot, and drain. Allow the walnuts to dry completely (see note below).

3. Heat a wok over high heat. Add the 3 cups peanut oil. Heat to 350°F. When a wisp of smoke appears, place the walnuts in a Chinese strainer and lower into the oil. Fry about 4 minutes, or until walnuts have browned. Remove, drain, and reserve (see note below).

4. Heat the wok over high heat for 30 seconds, add 2 tablespoons peanut oil, and coat the wok with a spatula. When a wisp of white smoke appears, add shallots and ½ teaspoon salt and stir-fry for 2 minutes, until shallots soften and release their fragrance. Add peppers, string beans, bamboo shoots, and water chestnuts; mix and stir-fry for 3 minutes. Add reserved bean curd and stir for about 2 minutes, until very hot. Add hoisin sauce and oyster sauce and mix well, making certain all ingredients are coated. Add reserved walnuts and mix well. Turn off the heat, transfer to a heated serving dish, and serve immediately.

Serves 4 to 6

Note: The reason for boiling the walnuts twice is to remove the inherent bitterness from the walnut skins and to ensure that some walnut oil is released. Double-boiling also ensures that the walnuts will be crisp when fried.

The walnuts may be prepared in advance. They will keep, covered, at room temperature for 4 days. They may be frozen for at least 3 months. To use, allow to stand for 10 minutes out of the freezer, then use as above. It is a good idea to make an ample amount of walnuts so as to have them on hand when wanted.

PINEAPPLE STIR-FRIED WITH "CHICKEN"
Bor Law Chau Gai Pin

Here again, *daufu*, bean curd, becomes chicken, and a remarkable substitute it is. In this particular recipe, the slices truly approximate the appearance and texture of chicken. The delightful surprise is in the taste.

4 cups cold water

1½ teaspoons salt

2 cakes fresh bean curd

3 tablespoons peanut oil

5 shallots, chopped (⅓ cup)

1 medium carrot, diagonally cut into ⅛-inch slices (½ cup)

3 to 4 fresh water chestnuts, peeled, washed, dried, and cut into ⅛-inch slices (⅓ cup)

½ large sweet red pepper, cut into 1-inch by ½-inch pieces (½ cup)

½ large sweet green pepper, cut into 1-inch by ½-inch pieces (½ cup)

1½ tablespoons oyster sauce

¼ whole large fresh pineapple, cut into 1-inch by 2-inch pieces (1¼ cups)

1. Bring the cold water and 1 teaspoon of salt to a boil. Add the bean curd and boil for 5 minutes. Turn off the heat, run cold water into the pot, and drain. Allow to cool. Cut bean curd into ¼-inch slices. Place on paper towels to dry thoroughly.

2. As the bean curd dries, heat a wok over high heat for 30 seconds, add 2 tablespoons peanut oil, and coat the wok with a spatula. When a wisp of white smoke appears, turn off the heat and place the slices of bean curd in a single layer in the wok. Turn the heat back to high and fry for 2 minutes. Turn over and fry for another 2 minutes, until crusted and light brown. The slices will resemble slices of chicken breast. Remove and reserve.

3. Heat the wok over high heat for 30 seconds. Add the remaining 1 tablespoon peanut oil and the remaining ½ teaspoon salt and coat the wok with a spatula. When a wisp of white smoke appears, add the shallots. Stir-fry for 2 minutes, until they are soft and release their fragrance. Add the carrots, water chestnuts, and peppers, mix, and stir-fry for 2 minutes. Add the oyster sauce and mix well

to coat all ingredients. Add the reserved bean curd slices and stir. Add the pineapple and mix all the ingredients well, until very hot. Transfer to a heated serving dish and serve immediately.

Serves 4 to 6

"Chicken" Salad with Cantaloupe
Mut Gua Gai Sah Lut

Again bean curd becomes "chicken," and very well. The texture of the bean curd, after frying, is quite like that of roasted chicken breast.

Sauce ingredients

2 teaspoons sesame oil

1 teaspoon sugar

1 tablespoon Chinese Chekiang vinegar (if unavailable, use red wine vinegar)

1 teaspoon Shao-Hsing wine or sherry

¼ teaspoon salt

2 teaspoons soy sauce

To complete the dish

4 cups cold water

2 cakes fresh bean curd

4 cups peanut oil

⅓ whole cantaloupe, peeled and cut into pieces ⅓ inch thick by 2 inches long (1 cup)

½ small cucumber, peeled, washed, dried, and cut into ¼-inch by 2-inch pieces (¾ cup)

½ large green pepper, cut into pieces ¼ inch by 2 inches (½ cup)

4 fresh water chestnuts, peeled, washed, dried, and julienned (⅓ cup)

3 tablespoons shredded Ginger Pickle (page 295)

1. Combine the sauce ingredients in a bowl. Reserve.

2. Place the water in a pot and bring to a boil. Add the bean curd. Return to a boil and cook for 4 minutes. Turn off the heat. Run cold water into pot. Drain. Remove the bean curd and allow to drain thoroughly and cool. Cut each cake into slices ⅓ inch thick, then cut each slice into ⅓-inch strips. Dry thoroughly with paper towels.

3. Heat a wok over high heat for 40 seconds. Add the peanut oil and heat to 350°F. Place the bean curd strips in the oil. Allow to cook for 2 to 3 minutes, or until they become slightly almond colored. Remove. Drain on paper towels. Allow to cool.

4. Place the strips in a large mixing bowl and add all other ingredients. Stir the sauce and pour it in. Mix thoroughly. Serve immediately.

Serves 4 to 6

Note: The sauce in this recipe and that in the Mango "Chicken" Salad (see following recipe) are interchangeable. They are different and impart different tastes, but they blend well in each case.

MANGO "CHICKEN" SALAD
Mong Gua Gai Sah Lut

For this mock chicken I use cooked fresh bean curd, sliced like french fried potatoes, to simulate strips of chicken breast. The illusion works admirably, and the surprises come when the tastes in the salad reach your tongue.

Sauce ingredients

2 teaspoons sesame oil

1 teaspoon sugar

2 teaspoons white vinegar

1 teaspoon Shao-Hsing wine or sherry

¼ teaspoon salt

2 teaspoons soy sauce

To complete the dish

4 cups cold water

2 cakes fresh bean curd

4 cups peanut oil

½ large mango, peeled and cut into ¼-inch by 2-inch matchsticks (¾ cup)

½ medium stalk celery, cut into ¼-inch matchsticks (¼ cup)

½ large sweet red pepper, cut into ¼-inch matchsticks (½ cup)

¼ small jícama, cut into ¼-inch matchsticks (⅓ cup)

3 tablespoons shredded Ginger Pickle (page 295)

1. Combine the sauce ingredients in a bowl. Reserve.

2. Place the water in a pot and bring to a boil. Add the bean curd. Return to a boil and cook for 4 minutes. Turn off the heat, run cold water into the pot, and drain. Remove the bean curd and allow it to drain thoroughly and cool. Cut each cake into slices ⅓ inch thick, then cut each slice into ⅓-inch strips. Dry strips thoroughly with paper towels.

3. Heat a wok over high heat for 40 seconds. Add the peanut oil and heat to 350°F. Place the bean curd strips in the oil. Cook for 2 to 3 minutes, until they are slightly almond colored. Remove. Drain on paper towels. Allow to cool.

4. Place the strips in a large mixing bowl and add all the other ingredients. Stir the sauce and pour it into the mixture. Mix well and serve immediately.

Serves 4 to 6

VEGETARIAN CHICKEN WITH BLACK BEAN SAUCE

Dau See Gai

This dish, which I created, looks exactly like cubes of chicken breast with black beans—a Chinese favorite—and it even has a hint of the taste of chicken.

Sauce ingredients

1 teaspoon light soy sauce

1 teaspoon dark soy sauce

1 teaspoon Shao-Hsing wine or sherry

1 teaspoon sugar

¼ teaspoon salt

Pinch of white pepper

2 teaspoons cornstarch

½ cup Vegetable Stock (pages 31–32)

To complete the dish

1 Fried Bean Curd recipe (page 172)

2 tablespoons peanut oil

1 teaspoon minced ginger

2 tablespoons fermented black beans, washed twice, drained, and mashed with 2 large cloves garlic

2 medium sweet red peppers, cut into ½-inch cubes

2 medium green peppers, cut into ½-inch cubes

1 scallion, both ends trimmed and discarded, cut into ½-inch pieces

3 tablespoons Vegetable Stock (pages 31–32)

1. Combine the sauce ingredients in a bowl. Reserve.

2. Cut the fried bean curd into ¾-inch cubes. Reserve.

3. Heat a wok over high heat for 40 seconds, add the peanut oil, and coat the wok with a spatula. When a wisp of white smoke appears, add the ginger and the black bean/garlic mixture and stir. When the garlic turns light brown, add the bean curd. Stir to mix well and coat. Add all the vegetables and stir-fry together to mix. Add the stock and stir for 2 minutes. Make a well in the center of the mixture, stir the sauce, and pour it into the well. Stir. When sauce thickens and begins to bubble, turn off the heat, transfer to a heated serving dish, and serve.

Serves 4 to 6

"CHICKEN" WITH SESAME PEANUT SAUCE

Mah Jeung Lo Gai See

This is my variation of a Chinese classic, "Pong Pong Chicken," which most people know as hacked chicken. Traditionally chicken is cooked, then pounded with the flat of a cleaver. The pounding is called "pong pong," thus the name of the dish. The shredded chicken is then mixed with sesame seed paste and peanut butter. I have made the recipe with strips of fried fresh bean curd, and it adapts well.

3 cakes fresh bean curd

6 cups cold water

4 cups peanut oil

Sauce ingredients

4½ tablespoons Vegetable Stock (pages 31–32)

1 tablespoon sesame seed paste

1½ tablespoons peanut butter

1½ teaspoons minced garlic

1 teaspoon minced ginger

2 teaspoons sugar

1 tablespoon white vinegar

2 teaspoons Hot Oil (page 36)

1 tablespoon sesame oil

2 teaspoons Shao-Hsing wine or sherry

To complete the dish

1 scallion, finely sliced (¼ cup)

2½ teaspoons mushroom soy sauce

½ cup julienned jícama

½ cup julienned carrots

½ cup julienned cucumber

1. Place the water in a pot, cover, and bring to a boil over high heat. Add the bean curd and boil 4 minutes. Turn off the heat. Run cold water into the pot and drain. Allow to cool. Cut the bean curd into strips ⅓ inch wide. Dry the strips on paper towels.

2. Heat a wok over high heat for 40 seconds. Add the peanut oil and heat to 350°F. Add the bean curd strips and fry for 1 to 1½ minutes, until the strips become firm. Remove from the oil. Drain in a strainer. Reserve.

3. To make the sauce, place the vegetable stock in a small pot and bring to a boil. Put the sesame seed paste, peanut butter, garlic, and ginger in a large bowl and add the boiling stock. Stir until blended and smooth. Add all the other sauce ingredients and mix thoroughly.

4. Add the reserved bean curd strips to the bowl, then the mushroom soy sauce and all the vegetables. Toss well, ensuring that all ingredients are well coated. Serve immediately.

Serves 4 to 6

Note: You might want to make a bed of Fried Noodles (page 253) on a platter and mound this dish on top. The mix of textures is quite fine.

Jicama (Sah Gut)

VEGETARIAN GOOSE
Jai Siu Ngaw

At a formal Chinese banquet there is always fish, fowl, and meat. Among Buddhists it is just as important to have representations of these courses. With vegetarian goose you have bean curd skins cooked so that they resemble the skin of roast goose in texture and color.

Sauce ingredients

4 teaspoons sesame oil

4 teaspoons dark soy sauce

3 teaspoons sugar

Pinch of white pepper

To complete the dish

5 tablespoons peanut oil

7 to 8 Chinese dried black mushrooms, soaked in hot water for 30 minutes, stems removed, and caps julienned (½ cup)

½ cup julienned bamboo shoots

½ cup julienned carrots

1 cup shredded iceberg lettuce

1 large piece bean curd skin (see note below)

1. Combine the sauce ingredients in a bowl. Reserve.

2. In a wok heat 1 tablespoon of the peanut oil until a wisp of white smoke appears. Add the vegetables and stir-fry briskly. Stir the sauce, add it to the wok, and cook, stirring constantly, about 3 minutes. When the vegetables are cooked, place in a dish and reserve.

3. Spread out the bean curd skin flat on a table or work surface. Using kitchen shears, cut the skin into 3 sections, each 6 by 4 inches. (Cover the sections not in use with plastic wrap to ensure pliability.) Dip your fingers in water and wet the skin lightly. Make a ridge of vegetables across the long end of the skin, roll up, and press closed. If your steamer is small, simply make the rolls an appropriate size.

4. Lightly oil a metal pie pan or tempered dish (see page 28). Place the rolls in the pan or dish and sprinkle with a tablespoon of water. Place the pan or dish in a steamer. Pour about 4 cups of water into a wok and bring to a boil. Place the steamer in the wok and steam, covered, for 10 to 15 minutes.

5. Pour the remaining 4 tablespoons of peanut oil into a cast-iron skillet. Pan-fry the steamed rolls until golden and hot, about 4 to 5 minutes.

6. Cut each of the 3 rolls into 4 pieces. Arrange on a bed of lettuce on a platter and serve hot.

Serves 4 to 6

Note: The vegetable filling makes a fine stir-fry dish on its own, to be served with rice.

Bean curd skin can be purchased in any Asian market. Make certain the skin is fresh. If it is hard, it probably is stale and too old for use.

白
鴿
菘

MINCED "SQUAB" WRAPPED IN LETTUCE
Bok Gup Sung

The original of this dish is a Chinese universal. Squab, or pigeon, cooked and minced and wrapped in lettuce leaves, can be found virtually throughout China in some form. Again, soybean cakes stand in for meat.

2½ tablespoons peanut oil

1½ teaspoons minced garlic

3 soybean cakes (½ package), minced

1¼ teaspoons minced ginger

1 teaspoon sugar

⅛ teaspoon salt

½ cup minced carrots

⅓ cup minced jícama

7 to 8 Chinese dried black mushrooms, soaked in hot water for 1 hour, squeezed dry, stems discarded, and caps minced (½ cup)

1 tablespoon oyster sauce

2 teaspoons Shao-Hsing wine or sherry

¾ teaspoon soy sauce

8 large lettuce leaves, iceberg preferred (do not use old green outer leaves)

3 tablespoons hoisin sauce

1. Heat a wok over high heat for 30 seconds. Add 1 tablespoon peanut oil and coat the wok with a spatula. When a wisp of white smoke appears, add the garlic and stir briefly. Add the bean curd and stir for 1½ minutes. Turn off the heat. Remove and reserve.

2. Turn the heat back to high. Add the remaining peanut oil and coat the wok. Add the ginger and stir briefly. Add the sugar and salt and stir. Add all the vegetables and stir-fry for 2 minutes. Add the bean curd and mix well. Add the oyster sauce and stir in. Add the Shao-Hsing wine and mix well. Add the soy sauce and mix until very hot. Turn off the heat and transfer to a heated serving dish.

3. Brush a lettuce leaf with some of the hoisin sauce. Place 2 tablespoons of the filling in the center of the leaf and fold and roll to enclose it. Repeat with all leaves and serve.

Makes 8 bundles, 4 to 6 servings

SPICED "DUCK" SALAD
Op Lot Sah Lut

Once again the supremely versatile bean curd substitutes for another food, this time duck. Dried bean curd, soaked and sliced, becomes, in appearance, sliced duck breast. This salad and the two that follow do indeed fool the eye—and surprise the taste.

8 slices dried bean curd

Sauce ingredients

1 tablespoon peanut butter
½ teaspoon hot pepper flakes (page 36)
1 tablespoon mushroom soy sauce
1½ teaspoons white vinegar
1 teaspoon sugar
⅛ teaspoon salt
1 teaspoon Shao-Hsing wine or sherry
2 teaspoons Scallion Oil (page 37)
1 teaspoon minced garlic

To complete the dish

2 cups Vegetable Stock (pages 31–32)
½ cup julienned sweet red peppers
¾ cup julienned carrots
½ cup julienned celery
2 tablespoons julienned scallions, white portions only

1. Soak bean curd in hot water for 20 minutes, or until the slices soften. Drain and slice into ¼-inch julienne. Reserve.

2. Combine the sauce ingredients in a bowl. Reserve.

3. In a pot bring the vegetable stock to a boil. Add the sliced bean curd. Cook for 45 seconds. Turn off the heat and drain off the stock for future use. Allow the bean curd to cool.

4. Place the bean curd, vegetables, and reserved sauce in a large bowl and toss together thoroughly. Remove to a serving platter and serve immediately.

Serves 4 to 6

"Duck" Salad with Peaches
Op Toh Sah Lut

This is my version of what has become a traditional summer dish of the Cantonese chefs of Hong Kong, where it is made with roast duck. I tasted it in Hong Kong several years ago and was determined to re-create it. I have done so with duck, and also with mock duck. Here is the latter.

8 slices dried bean curd
2 cups Vegetable Stock (pages 31–32)
2 medium-sized fresh peaches, ripe but firm, julienned (¾ cup)
¼ cup julienned celery
⅓ cup julienned carrots
¼ cup julienned sweet yellow pepper
½ teaspoon salt
1 teaspoon sugar
¾ teaspoon soy sauce
2 teaspoons Szechuan Peppercorn Oil (page 38)
1¼ teaspoons white vinegar
1 teaspoon Shao-Hsing wine or sherry
Pinch of white pepper

1. Soak the bean curd in hot water for 20 minutes, or until the slices soften. Drain and slice into ¼-inch julienne.

2. In a pot, bring the vegetable stock to a boil. Add sliced bean curd. Cook for 45 seconds. Turn off the heat and drain off the stock for future use. Allow the bean curd to cool.

3. Place all the ingredients in a large mixing bowl. Mix together thoroughly. Cover and refrigerate for 4 hours. Serve cool, perhaps with orange slices around the edge of the platter.

Serves 4 to 6

"Duck" and Pickle Salad
To Lei Op Sah Lut

This recipe too comes from the Cantonese kitchen, where it is made with roast duck. The bean curd, combined with the tartness of the pickles, is an admirable substitute.

8 slices dried bean curd
2 cups Vegetable Stock (pages 31–32)
1 tablespoon dry-roasted white sesame seeds (page 28)
½ cup Pickled Peaches (page 296), julienned
½ cup Pickled Pears (page 297), julienned
2 tablespoons Ginger Pickle (page 295), julienned
1 cup julienned sweet green peppers
¼ cup julienned celery
1 teaspoon soy sauce
¼ teaspoon salt
¾ teaspoon sugar
1 teaspoon Shao-Hsing wine or sherry
2 teaspoons Green Oil (page 39)

1. Soak the bean curd in hot water for 20 minutes, or until the slices soften. Drain and slice into ¼-inch julienne.

2. In a pot, bring the vegetable stock to a boil. Add sliced bean curd. Cook for 45 seconds. Turn off the heat and drain off the stock for future use. Allow the bean curd to cool.

3. Place all the ingredients in a large mixing bowl. Mix together thoroughly. Cover and refrigerate for 4 hours. Serve cool. Lemons, sliced and cut into half-moons, make a fine garnish around the edges of the serving platter.

Serves 4 to 6

VEGETARIAN MU SHU "PORK"
Jai Muk See Yuk

It is a certainty that almost everyone has eaten *mu shu* pork, wrapped in pancakes, at some time or other. Here is my vegetable version, and I am certain you will not miss the pork, not even a little bit.

Sauce ingredients

1 teaspoon light soy sauce

1 teaspoon sugar

1 teaspoon dark soy sauce

1 tablespoon Shao-Hsing wine or sherry

1½ tablespoons hoisin sauce

Pinch of white pepper

4 teaspoons cornstarch

¼ cup Vegetable Stock (pages 31–32)

1 teaspoon sesame oil

1 teaspoon white vinegar

To complete the dish

3 tablespoons peanut oil

2 teaspoons minced garlic

1½ teaspoons minced ginger

¾ teaspoon salt

½ small head cabbage, cut into 3-inch by ⅛-inch strips (2 cups)

1 medium carrot, peeled and cut into 2-inch julienne (½ cup)

⅓ cup julienned bamboo shoots

2 tablespoons cloud ears, soaked for ½ hour and broken up if larger than
    ¾ inch after soaking

8 Chinese dried black mushrooms, soaked, stems discarded, and caps cut
    into ⅛-inch julienne (⅔ cup)

18 tiger lily buds, soaked in hot water until soft, hard ends cut off, and
    halved

8 slices dried bean curd, soaked in hot water until soft, cut into ⅛-inch strips

2 scallions, trimmed, cut into 1½-inch lengths, and white portions
    quartered

1 to 2 tablespoons Vegetable Stock (pages 31–32)

Pancakes (recipe follows)

1. Prepare the pancakes in advance (see following page). Combine the sauce ingredients in a bowl. Reserve.

2. Heat a wok over high heat for 30 seconds. Add the peanut oil and coat the wok with a spatula. When a wisp of white smoke appears, add the garlic, ginger, and salt. When the garlic turns light brown, add the cabbage and stir. Add the carrot and mix. Add the bamboo shoots and cloud ears and mix well. Add the mushrooms, tiger lily buds, and bean curd and stir-fry all the ingredients together. Add the scallions and mix well. If the mixture is too dry add 1 or 2 tablespoons of vegetable stock, but only if needed. Mix well. Cook for 5 to 6 minutes, or until cabbage softens.

3. Make a well in the center of the mixture. Stir the sauce and pour it in. Cover with vegetables and stir together. When the sauce thickens and begins to bubble, turn off the heat, remove from the wok, and serve folded in pancakes. You will have enough filling for about 15 pancakes.

Serves 4 to 6

Cloud Ears (Mook Yee, *dried and soaked*)

薄
餅
類

PANCAKES
Bok Bang

The pancakes for the above recipe are usually made a day in advance. This makes it easier on the preparer, as you will discover.

3½ cups high-gluten flour
1½ cups boiling water
1 cup flour, for dusting
3 tablespoons sesame oil

1. Place the 3½ cups flour in a mixing bowl and add the boiling water. Mix with chopsticks or a wooden spoon in one direction, continuously. When the flour absorbs the water and cools, place on a work surface dusted with flour. Knead until the dough is thoroughly mixed, about 2 minutes. Place in a mixing bowl, cover with plastic wrap, and allow to sit for 30 minutes.

2. Divide the dough into 2 equal parts. Roll 1 part into a 12-inch sausage. Divide into 12 equal pieces. Dust the work surface again with flour and flatten each piece with the palm of the hand. Use more flour to dust if dough sticks. As you work, use plastic wrap to cover unused dough. Repeat with second half so that you have 24 pieces.

3. Working with 2 pieces at a time, wipe the top of 1 piece gently with sesame oil and place the other flattened piece on top. Dust with flour, if necessary, and roll into a circle 7 inches in diameter. The result will be a 2-layer pancake. Repeat with remaining pieces.

4. Heat a wok over medium-low heat for about 1 minute. Place a pancake into the hot, dry wok and cook for 1 minute, or until pancake begins to bubble up. Turn over and cook for about another minute. When the pancake is cooked a few brown spots will be visible. (Heat in the dry wok must be carefully controlled. If too high, pancakes will burn.) When done, remove from the wok and separate the two layers. You will have 2 pancakes, each browned lightly on one side. Reserve. Repeat until finished. This will yield 24 pancakes.

5. When ready to use, steam the pancakes for 5 to 7 minutes, and serve.

6. To serve with *mu shu* filling, place 3 to 4 tablespoons of filling in the center of a pancake. Fold up the bottom, fold the two sides, fold top down to cover, and eat with the fingers.

Yield: 14 to 16 filled pancakes

Note: The *mu shu* "pork" recipe will fill 14 to 16 pancakes. I have deliberately formulated this pancake recipe to make more, so you can freeze the remaining pancakes for future use. Wrapped in plastic wrap and refrigerated, they will keep for 1 week. They may also be wrapped doubly in plastic wrap, then in foil, and frozen for 6 weeks. This is a true time-saver, so that if you fancy *mu shu* "pork" again some evening, your pancakes need only be defrosted, brought to room temperature, and then steamed.

Shredded "Pork" with Garlic Sauce
Yue Heung Yuk See

This is another interpretation of a classic dish from China's west. Usually the dish is made with shredded pork. In its stead I use a variety of soybean cake flavored slightly with chilies.

Sauce ingredients

2½ teaspoons white vinegar

1 teaspoon minced garlic

2 tablespoons ketchup

⅛ teaspoon freshly ground Szechuan peppercorns

2 teaspoons minced ginger

1 tablespoon sugar

1 teaspoon sesame oil

2 teaspoons Shao-Hsing wine or sherry

1 tablespoon preserved horse beans with chili

1½ teaspoons cornstarch

¼ cup Vegetable Stock (pages 31–32)

To complete the dish

2½ tablespoons peanut oil

1 teaspoon minced garlic

4 ounces small soybean cakes (see note below), thinly sliced

⅛ teaspoon salt

½ cup peeled and julienned carrots

⅓ cup julienned jícama

4 scallions, trimmed, cut into 2-inch lengths, and white portions quartered

1. Combine the sauce ingredients in a bowl. Reserve.

2. Heat a wok over high heat for 30 seconds. Add 1 tablespoon peanut oil and coat the wok with a spatula. When a wisp of white smoke appears, add the garlic and stir briefly. Add the bean curd cake and stir-fry for 1½ minutes. Turn off the heat. Transfer to a bowl. Reserve.

3. Raise heat back to high. Add remaining peanut oil and salt and coat the wok. When a wisp of white smoke appears, add all the vegetables and stir-fry for 1½ minutes, until very hot. Add the bean curd and mix well. Cook for 1 minute. Make a well in the center of the mixture, stir the sauce, and pour it in. Mix thoroughly. When the sauce begins to bubble and thicken, turn off the heat. Transfer to a heated dish and serve immediately with cooked rice.

Serves 4 to 6

Note: There are several variations of these soybean cakes. Most are simply dyed brown with soy sauce and flavored lightly with spices. The bean cakes used in this recipe come not 6 in a tight package but loosely packed, more than 25 in a plastic bag, and the bags usually weigh 8 ounces. They are flavored with chilies. They should be asked for specifically.

SOUR MUSTARD PICKLE WITH "PORK"

Seun Choi Chau Yuk See

Yuk see translates as "shredded pork." In this dish, which has variations in both the Hakka and Chiu Chow kitchens and in the Cantonese repertoire as well, the ubiquitous soybean cake becomes the "pork."

Sauce ingredients

2 teaspoons dark soy sauce

2 tablespoons oyster sauce

2 teaspoons Shao-Hsing wine or sherry

2 teaspoons sugar

1 teaspoon sesame oil

Pinch of white pepper

1 tablespoon cornstarch

½ cup Vegetable Stock (pages 31–32)

To complete the dish

3 tablespoons peanut oil

2 teaspoons minced garlic

3 soybean cakes (½ package), thinly sliced

1½ tablespoons shredded young ginger

1 cup sour mustard pickle, squeezed dry and diagonally sliced into ⅛-inch pieces

4 to 5 fresh water chestnuts, peeled and julienned (⅓ cup)

½ large red sweet pepper, julienned (½ cup)

½ large cucumber, peeled, halved lengthwise, seeded, and cut into 2-inch-long julienne (1 cup)

1. Combine the sauce ingredients in a bowl. Reserve.

2. Heat a wok over high heat for 30 seconds. Add 1½ tablespoons peanut oil. Coat the wok with a spatula. When a wisp of white smoke appears, add the garlic. Stir briefly. Add the bean cake and stir-fry for 2 minutes. Turn off the heat. Transfer to a bowl. Reserve.

3. Turn heat back to high. Add the remaining peanut oil and ginger and stir for 30 seconds. Add the sour mustard pickle and stir-fry for 1 minute. Add the water chestnuts and stir well. Add the red pepper and cucumber and stir-fry until the mixture is very hot. Add the reserved bean cake and stir-fry for 1 minute. Make a well in the center of the mixture, stir the sauce, and pour it in. When the sauce begins to bubble and turn brown, turn off the heat. Transfer to a heated dish and serve with cooked rice, which I recommend because of the direct flavors in the stir-fry.

Serves 4 to 6

Sour Mustard Pickle

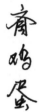

VEGETARIAN "EGGS"
Jai Gai Dan

This is a popular dish among religious Buddhists. When cooked, these imitations look quite like eggs that have been cooked in soy sauce, but as with other dishes of this sort, the happy surprise comes with the first bite.

2 baking potatoes, Idaho preferred, unpeeled (1¼ pound)

6 cups cold water

½ cup wheat starch

7 ounces water

1¾ teaspoons sugar

1 teaspoon salt

1 teaspoon five-spice powder

3 tablespoons peanut oil

1 cup cornstarch, for dusting

6 cups peanut oil, for deep-frying

Hot Mustard (page 44) mixed with an equal amount of chili sauce, for
    serving

1. Place the potatoes in a pot with the 6 cups water and bring to a boil. Lower the heat to medium-high and cook for 45 minutes. Turn off the heat, let cool, peel, mash, and reserve.

2. Place the wheat starch in a bowl. Bring 7 ounces of water to a boil and pour into the bowl. Mix quickly with a wooden spoon to blend. Add the mashed potatoes, then add the sugar, salt, five-spice powder, and 3 tablespoons peanut oil and mix into a smooth dough.

3. Divide into 12 equal portions. Roll each into an egg shape. Dust with cornstarch.

4. Heat a wok over high heat for 40 seconds. Add the 6 cups peanut oil. When a wisp of white smoke appears, place 3 of the "eggs" into a Chinese strainer and lower into the oil. Fry for 3 to 4 minutes, turning, until golden brown. Drain and reserve, keeping warm in the oven. Repeat until all 12 are cooked. Serve immediately with the Hot Mustard mixed with an equal amount of chili sauce, or to taste.

Serves 4 to 6

BEAN CAKE DING
Daufu Gon Ding

苙
三腐
乾
丁

The word *ding* in the Chinese kitchen means "small squares"; accordingly, all of the ingredients in this dish are diced. Again, soybean cake stands in for roast pork. I have altered the classic recipe so that the roasted peanuts are served on top of the vegetables, not mixed with them.

2½ tablespoons peanut oil

1½ teaspoons minced garlic

3 soybean cakes (½ package), cut into ¼-inch dice

One ½-inch-wide slice fresh ginger, peeled and lightly smashed

⅛ teaspoon salt

3 to 4 ounces string beans, both ends discarded, cut into ⅓-inch pieces (¾ cup)

1 medium stalk celery, cut into ⅓-inch dice (½ cup)

4 to 5 ounces lotus root, peeled and cut into ⅓-inch dice (½ cup)

2 teaspoons Shao-Hsing wine or sherry

1½ tablespoons oyster sauce

¾ cup raw peanuts, dry-roasted (page 28)

1. Heat a wok over high heat for 30 seconds. Add 1 tablespoon peanut oil and coat the wok with a spatula. When a wisp of white smoke appears, add the garlic and stir briefly. Add the diced bean cake and cook for 1 minute. Transfer to a bowl. Reserve.

2. Return the wok to high heat. Add the remaining peanut oil and coat the wok. When a wisp of white smoke appears, add the ginger, stir, and cook for 40 seconds. Add the salt, string beans, celery, and lotus root. Stir-fry for 1 minute. Add the wine and mix well. Add the oyster sauce and stir thoroughly into mixture. Add the bean curd and stir-fry for 1½ minutes. Turn off the heat and transfer to a heated dish. Serve immediately with roasted peanuts sprinkled on top.

Serves 4 to 6

Note: The dry-roasted nuts may be prepared up to 1 week in advance. Once roasted, they should be allowed to come to room temperature, then placed in a closed container. They need not be refrigerated.

VEGETARIAN SWEET AND SOUR "PORK"
Jai Woo Lo Yuk

This is another of the artifices of the Chinese kitchen. Everyone is familiar with sweet and sour pork, but when you bite into this dish, you find the "pork" is a walnut.

Sauce ingredients

4½ tablespoons red wine vinegar

4½ tablespoons sugar

3 tablespoons tomato sauce

1 tablespoon cornstarch mixed with 1 tablespoon cold water

1 teaspoon dark soy sauce

3 ounces cold water

To continue

4 cups water

20 walnut halves, unbroken

Batter ingredients

¾ cup bleached all-purpose (high-gluten) flour

1 teaspoon baking powder

5 ounces cold water

1 teaspoon peanut oil

To complete the dish

4 cups peanut oil

¼ large sweet red pepper, cut into ¾-inch cubes (¼ cup)

¼ large fresh green pepper, cut into ¾-inch cubes (¼ cup)

2 tablespoons carrot, peeled and cut into ⅛-inch by ¾-inch pieces

1¼ canned pineapple rings, cut into ¾-inch squares

1. Combine the sauce ingredients in a bowl. Reserve.

2. In a wok, heat 2 cups of the water to boiling. Add the walnuts and cook for 5 minutes, to remove the bitter taste. Remove from the water, drain, and run cold water over them. Drain again, then place back in the wok with another 2 cups of water. Bring to a boil, cook for another 5 minutes, and repeat the draining process. Set aside and allow to dry completely.

3. To make the batter, place the flour in a bowl, add the baking powder, and mix. Add the water slowly while stirring. Add the peanut oil and blend thoroughly until batter is smooth. Set aside.

4. Heat a wok over high heat for 45 seconds to 1 minute. Add the 4 cups peanut oil. When white smoke appears, place the walnuts in a flat strainer and lower them into the oil. Deep-fry for about 5 minutes. Remove and set aside to cool.

5. Strain peanut oil from wok to remove any walnut particles. Return oil to wok over high heat and heat oil to 350°F. Using tongs or chopsticks, dip the walnuts into the batter and place in the oil. Cook for 2 to 3 minutes on each side, until golden brown. Cook 4 to 5 walnuts at a time. Repeat until all the walnuts are fried. Place in a serving dish.

6. Heat the sauce ingredients over medium heat, stirring constantly. When sauce starts to darken and thicken and begins to bubble, add the vegetables and pineapple, stir together, and mix until the sauce starts to bubble again. Pour the mixture into a sauceboat and serve with the sweet and sour "pork" walnuts.

Serves 4 to 6

"BEEF" WITH BROCCOLI
Jai Ngau Chau Sai Lou

Again the ubiquitous bean curd serves as a perfect alternative to another food, this time in a classical Cantonese stir-fried preparation, beef with broccoli. I believe its taste may be finer than that of the meat version.

Sauce ingredients

2 tablespoons oyster sauce

2 teaspoons dark soy sauce

2 teaspoons Shao-Hsing wine or sherry

½ teaspoon sesame oil

1¼ teaspoons sugar

1 tablespoon cornstarch

Pinch of white pepper

½ cup Vegetable Stock (pages 31–32)

To complete the dish

8 cups cold water

One ½-inch thick slice fresh ginger, lightly smashed

½ teaspoon baking soda, optional (see note below)

1 pound broccoli flowerets (from 2-pound bunch broccoli)

3 tablespoons peanut oil

2 teaspoons minced garlic

1 package soybean cakes (see note below), each cake cut into ⅛-inch slices

⅛ teaspoon salt

2 tablespoons shredded young ginger (see note below)

1. Combine the sauce ingredients in a bowl. Reserve.

2. Place cold water, ginger, and baking soda in a large pot. Bring to a boil. Add the broccoli and blanch for 5 seconds, until the flowerets become bright green. Turn off the heat, run cold water into the pot, and drain. Reserve.

3. Heat a wok over high heat for 30 seconds, add 1½ tablespoons of peanut oil, and coat the wok with a spatula. Add the garlic and stir. When garlic turns light brown, add the sliced bean curd and stir-fry for 2 minutes. Turn off the heat, transfer to a dish, and reserve.

4. Turn the heat back to high and add the remaining peanut oil, salt, and ginger. Stir for 45 seconds, then add the broccoli and stir-fry for 2 minutes, until very hot. Add the bean curd and stir-fry together for 1½ minutes, making certain all ingredients are very hot. Make a well in the center of the mixture, stir the sauce, and pour it in. Mix well, and when sauce begins to bubble and turn brown, turn off the heat. Transfer to a heated dish and serve immediately. I recommend that this be served with cooked rice because of the intense flavor of the sauce.

Serves 4 to 6

Note: Baking soda is used in water-blanching to keep vegetables bright green. Use it if you wish.

Note: Young ginger is preferred for its mildness and crispness. If unavailable, use half the specified amount of regular ginger.

SZECHUAN "BEEF"
Sei Chun Chau Ngau Yuk

In this dish, soybean cake stands in for the beef of a traditional dish of Szechuan province, to the west of Canton. And again the result is successful. My younger son, the severest of critics, considers this to be as good as any other Szechuan preparation I have ever made.

Sauce ingredients

1 tablespoon preserved horse beans with chili

2 tablespoons oyster sauce

1 teaspoon dark soy sauce

1 teaspoon sesame oil

2 teaspoons Shao-Hsing wine or sherry

1 teaspoon white vinegar

1¼ teaspoons sugar

Pinch of white pepper

1 tablespoon cornstarch

½ cup Vegetable Stock (pages 31–32)

To complete the dish

3 tablespoons peanut oil

2 teaspoons minced garlic

3 soybean cakes (½ package), julienned

2 tablespoons shredded young ginger

2 medium carrots, peeled and julienned (1 cup)

2 medium stalks celery, julienned (1 cup)

3 scallions, trimmed, cut into 2-inch sections, and white portions quartered

3 tablespoons Szechuan mustard pickle, julienned

1. Combine the sauce ingredients in a bowl. Reserve.

2. Heat wok over high heat for 30 seconds. Add 1½ tablespoons peanut oil and coat the wok with a spatula. When a wisp of white smoke appears, add the garlic. Stir briefly, add the soybean cake, and stir-fry for 2 minutes. Turn off the heat. Transfer to a bowl. Reserve.

3. Turn the heat back to high. Add the remaining peanut oil and the ginger and stir for 30 seconds. Add all the remaining ingredients and stir-fry for 1 minute. If the mixture is dry, sprinkle water into the wok. This will create steam, which will cook the vegetables. Add the bean cake and stir into the mixture. Make a well in the center, stir the sauce, and pour it in. Mix thoroughly. When sauce bubbles and turns brown, turn off the heat. Transfer to a heated serving dish and serve immediately with cooked rice. I recommend the rice because of the strong tastes in this dish.

Serves 4 to 6

PEPPER "STEAK"
See Jiu Chau Naau

This is another Cantonese classic reinterpreted—beef stir-fried with black beans and green peppers, which becomes a different dish with the use of that marvelous soybean cake. The texture of the cake feels like meat to the teeth, and the taste of the black beans and the five-spice powder, with which the bean curd is slightly flavored, satisfies the palate.

Sauce ingredients

2 teaspoons dark soy sauce

2 teaspoons Shao-Hsing wine or sherry

2 tablespoons oyster sauce

1 teaspoon sesame oil

1¼ teaspoons sugar

1 tablespoon cornstarch

Pinch of white pepper

½ cup Vegetable Stock (pages 31–32)

To complete the dish

2 tablespoons Chinese fermented black beans, washed 3 times to remove salt and drained

2 cloves garlic

3 tablespoons peanut oil

1 tablespoon shredded young ginger

3 large green peppers, cut into ¼-inch slices (3 cups)

6 soybean cakes (1 package), each cut into ⅛-inch slices

1. Combine the sauce ingredients in a bowl. Reserve.

2. Mash together the black beans and garlic with the heel of a Chinese cleaver handle, to make a paste. Reserve.

3. Heat a wok over high heat for 30 seconds. Add 1 tablespoon peanut oil and coat the wok with a spatula. When a wisp of white smoke appears, add ginger and stir for 5 seconds. Add the green peppers and mix well. The liquid in the peppers should be released with the heat to create steam, which will cook them. However, if the preparation is too dry, add a tablespoon of vegetable stock. Cook until the peppers are bright green, about 1 minute. Turn off the heat. Transfer to a dish and reserve. Wipe the wok and spatula with paper towels.

4. Heat the wok over high heat for 20 seconds. Add the remaining 2 tablespoons peanut oil and coat the wok. When a wisp of white smoke appears, add the black bean paste. Break it up with a spatula until the aroma is released. Add the bean cake slices and stir-fry until they are well coated. Add the reserved peppers and mix together until very hot. Make a well in the center of the mixture, stir the sauce, and pour it in. Mix thoroughly. When sauce begins to bubble and turn brown, turn off the heat. Transfer to a heated dish and serve immediately. I recommend serving this dish with cooked rice because of its strong flavors.

Serves 4 to 6

BEAN CURD CAKE WITH ORANGE FLAVOR
Chong Pei Daufu

The basics for this recipe I have borrowed from the Hunan and Szechuan kitchens. This sweet and tangy dish is customarily based on beef, and the orange peel that is used is always aged and called *chun pei*, or "old skin." In my version I use soybean cake and fresh orange peel, *chong pei*. The old peel is not eaten, but the new peel, cut small, is eaten. What emerges is a new interpretation of an old classic.

Sauce ingredients

2 teaspoons Shao-Hsing wine or sherry

2½ teaspoons white vinegar

4 teaspoons sugar

1 tablespoon dark soy sauce

1½ teaspoons sesame oil

Pinch of white pepper

¼ cup Vegetable Stock (pages 31–32)

1 teaspoon cornstarch

To complete the dish

3 tablespoons peanut oil

2 teaspoons minced garlic

6 soybean cakes (1 package), thinly sliced

10 small chili peppers

2 teaspoons minced ginger

2½ tablespoons orange peel, pith carefully trimmed away, cut into shreds
    (see note below)

3 to 4 scallions, trimmed and diagonally cut into ½-inch pieces (1⅓ cups)

½ large sweet red pepper, julienned (½ cup)

6 orange slices cut into half-moons, for garnish

1. Combine the sauce ingredients in a bowl. Reserve.

2. Heat a wok over high heat for 30 seconds. Add 1 tablespoon of peanut oil and coat the wok with a spatula. When a wisp of white smoke appears, add 1 teaspoon minced garlic and stir briefly. Add bean curd cake slices and stir-fry for 2 minutes. Turn off the heat. Transfer to a bowl. Reserve.

3. Raise the heat back to high, add the remaining peanut oil, and coat the wok. When a wisp of white smoke appears, add the chilies. Stir and turn until chilies become dark brown, about 1 to 1½ minutes. Add the ginger and remaining garlic and stir briefly. Add the orange peel and stir briefly. Add the scallions and red pepper and stir-fry until the scallions turn bright green. Add the bean curd and stir-fry until well mixed and hot. Make a well in the center, stir the sauce, and pour it in. Mix thoroughly. When sauce begins to bubble and turn brown, turn off the heat. Transfer to a heated serving dish, garnish the edges with orange slices, and serve immediately, with cooked rice.

Serves 4 to 6

Note: Removing as much as possible of the pith—the soft, white inside of the orange peel—is necessary so that more orange flavor will be imparted from the peel.

CHINESE TURNIPS BUDDHIST STYLE
Lor Bok Jai

This dish is traditional among Buddhist monks and nuns. The use of the word *jai* in its name indicates a dish of vegetarian nature for Buddhists. The sweetness of the turnip, combined with bean curd and bean threads, creates a dish that the Chinese say has such a fine taste that you have to eat it even if you are not hungry.

Sauce ingredients

1½ tablespoons oyster sauce

2 teaspoons Shao-Hsing wine or sherry

1 teaspoon soy sauce

1½ teaspoons sesame oil

1 teaspoon sugar

1 tablespoon cornstarch

¼ cup Vegetable Stock (pages 31–32)

To complete the dish

3½ tablespoons peanut oil

One ½-inch thick slice fresh ginger, lightly smashed

5 scallions, trimmed, cut into 2-inch sections, and white portions quartered lengthwise

1 pound Chinese turnips, peeled, sliced into ¼-inch-thick rounds, then cut into ¼-inch julienne

6 slices dried bean curd (see note below), soaked in hot water for ½ hour, drained, and cut crosswise into ¼-inch pieces

6 tablespoons Vegetable Stock (pages 31–32)

⅛ teaspoon salt

⅛ teaspoon freshly ground Szechuan peppercorns

1 ounce bean threads, soaked in hot water for ½ hour, drained, and cut into 4-inch sections

1. Combine the sauce ingredients in a bowl. Reserve.

2. Heat a wok over high heat for 30 seconds. Add the peanut oil and coat the wok with a spatula. When a wisp of white smoke appears, add the ginger. Cook for 20 seconds. Add the scallions and stir for 45 seconds. Add the turnips and stir

together. Add the bean curd and mix well. Add the vegetable stock and stir thoroughly. Add the salt and ground Szechuan peppercorns and stir well.

3. Cover the wok. Lower the heat to medium. Cook for 7 to 10 minutes, until turnips are tender. Remove the cover. Raise the heat to high, add the bean threads, and stir well into the mixture. Make a well in the center of the mixture, stir the sauce, and pour it in. Mix thoroughly, and when sauce thickens and bubbles, turn off the heat. Remove to a heated serving dish and serve immediately.

Serves 4 to 6

WALNUT AND MUSHROOM SALAD
Hop Toh Dong Su Sah Lut

Walnuts are eaten extensively by Buddhist priests and nuns, who believe that these nuts are quite beneficial to the lungs and stomach, and that they help to keep the skin clear. I just like the tastes of this Buddhist-inspired dish.

4 cups water
1 cup shelled walnuts
16 Chinese dried black mushrooms, each 1½ inches in diameter, steamed for 45 minutes, cooled to room temperature, and steaming liquid reserved
4 cups peanut oil

1. Place the water in a pot and bring to a boil. Add the walnuts, return to a boil, and allow to boil for 4 minutes. Turn off the heat and run cold water into the pot. Drain. Repeat the rinsing and draining process twice more. Allow the walnuts to dry and cool.

2. Heat a wok over high heat for 40 seconds. Add the peanut oil and heat to 350°F. Add the walnuts and turn off the heat. Let cook for 1 minute, then turn the heat back on. Regulate the heat so as not to burn the walnuts. Cook for 3 to 4 minutes, or until nuts have browned. Turn off the heat. Remove and drain.

3. When the walnuts are cool and crisp, place in a bowl and add the mushrooms. Toss together. The tastes should blend quite well. If you desire a stronger taste, add 1 to 2 tablespoons of the mushroom steaming liquid. Serve immediately as a salad course.

Serves 4 to 6

VEGETARIAN "SEA BASS"
Jai See Bah

Again, the intent is to surprise. This looks like a fish, but the tastes and textures are all vegetable. It is a happy deception practiced both in Hangzhou, where I had this fish for the first time, and in Canton.

1¼ pounds taro root
½ teaspoon five-spice powder
½ teaspoon salt
1 teaspoon sugar
Pinch of white pepper
1 cup plain bread crumbs
½ cup wheat starch
⅞ cup boiling water
6 tablespoons peanut oil
⅓ cup sliced almonds
1 black olive
5 cups peanut oil
Sprigs of parsley, for garnish

1. Cut the taro root into quarters or 2-inch slices and place in a steamer. Add 4 to 5 cups of water to a wok, bring to a boil, and steam the taro for 1 to 1½ hours. Keep additional water on hand to replenish that which evaporates. To test the taro for doneness, insert a chopstick into a piece of root; if it goes in easily, the taro is done. Remove from wok and allow to cool.

2. Peel the skin off the taro and discard. Mash the root and discard any hard pieces (they will not cook properly). There should be 2½ cups mashed taro. Place mashed root in a large bowl and add five-spice powder, salt, sugar, white pepper, and bread crumbs. Mix together.

3. In another bowl, place the wheat starch and add the boiling water, stirring constantly with a wooden spoon until the mixture thickens. Add to the taro blend and mix well. Add the 6 tablespoons peanut oil to the mixture and knead until a dough is formed. If the dough is dry, add 1 to 2 more tablespoons of peanut oil. Refrigerate, uncovered, for 4 hours, or covered, overnight.

4. Place the dough on a large sheet of waxed paper. Mold into a fish shape, adding sliced almonds as scales, working from tail end to head. Cut olive into an eye shape and place on fish's head. Use a pizza cutter or a fork to make fin lines on tail and fins.

5. Heat a wok for 45 seconds to 1 minute and add 5 cups peanut oil. Heat to 350°F. Put the fish into the oil by means of a flat strainer and cook for 5 to 7 minutes, until it is brown. Serve immediately, garnished with sprigs of parsley.

Serves 4 to 6

"SHARK FIN" SOUP
Yue Chee Tong

Shark fin soup is a must at virtually every banquet, every seasonal feast, every meal of importance. So highly regarded is the dorsal fin of the shark that great emphasis is placed on its quality and grade—there are many grades, with prices that correspond. When a shark fin is repeatedly boiled in preparation for a soup, it becomes strandlike. In this adaptation, strands of bean threads take the place of the shark fin.

1 ounce bean threads
2⅔ cups Vegetable Stock (pages 31–32)
1¼ cups cold water
¼ teaspoon salt, or to taste
½ cup julienned shiitake mushrooms
1 cake fresh bean curd, julienned
3½ ounces snow peas, washed, both ends and strings removed, and julienned (1 cup)
1 tablespoon Shao-Hsing wine or sherry
2½ tablespoons Szechuan Peppercorn Oil (page 38)

Snow Pea Shoots

1. Soak bean threads in hot water for 30 minutes. Drain and cut into 2-inch strands. Reserve.

2. In a pot place the stock, water, and salt and bring to a boil. Add the mushrooms, bring back to a boil, and allow to cook for 2 minutes. Add the bean curd, mix, and bring back to a boil. Add the reserved bean threads, stir, and bring back to a boil. Add the snow peas and bring back to a boil again. Add the wine and oil and mix well into the soup. Turn off the heat, transfer to a heated tureen, and serve immediately.

Serves 4 to 6

Note: As an added touch, I sometimes add 6 fried and crushed walnuts to this soup, after the soup has been placed in the tureen. (See instructions for fried walnuts in recipe for "Chicken" Ding, pages 184–85.) They should be sprinkled atop the soup precisely at serving time.

VEGETARIAN "OYSTERS"

Jai Tio See

The monks at the Taoist monastery, Ching Chung Koon, in Hong Kong taught me this recipe. In China, the best vegetarian cookery comes from temples, both Buddhist and Taoist. With this dish the surprise is in the taste, for the dish should only look like a fried oyster.

2 small Chinese eggplants

Batter ingredients

1½ cups high-gluten flour
2 teaspoons baking powder
10 ounces cold water
2 tablespoons peanut oil

To complete the dish

3 tablespoons shredded Ginger Pickle (page 295)
¼ medium onion, thinly sliced
4 cups peanut oil
Szechuan Peppercorn Salt (page 38), for serving

1. Slice the eggplants diagonally at ⅛-inch intervals, cutting the first slice all the way through (discard the first slice), then the next about three-quarters of the way through and the next all the way through. The result will be a slice with a pocket. Repeat until both eggplants are sliced. There should be 20 pockets.

2. To make the batter, place the flour in a bowl, add baking powder, then add water gradually, stirring until smooth. Add the peanut oil and blend in until batter is even and smooth. Set aside.

3. Into each eggplant pocket put 5 to 6 pieces of shredded Ginger Pickle and an equal amount of sliced onion. Repeat until all the eggplant pockets are filled.

4. In a wok heat the peanut oil to 350°F. Dip each "oyster" into the batter, holding tightly with chopsticks or tongs. Coat well. Place 4 to 5 "oysters" at a time into the hot oil. As soon as you place the "oysters" in oil, turn off the heat. When they brown on one side, turn them over. Turn the heat on again to bring the temperature of the oil up. The oil should be a constant 325°F to 350°F, but no hotter. This will ensure that the eggplant pockets will fry to a golden brown. Remove and serve immediately with Szechuan Peppercorn Salt.

Serves 4 to 6

MUSSELS IN BROWN BEAN SAUCE
Dau See Chau Hak Hin

In China the mussel is *hak hin*, the "black clam." It is one of the three creatures of the sea that vegetarian Buddhists may eat, the others being clams and oysters. Mussels come either fresh in the shell, or dried and shelled. The dried oysters must be reconstituted in warm water before being used in stir-fry dishes or in soups. Fresh mussels are, of course, preferred.

Sauce ingredients

1½ teaspoons dark soy sauce

1½ tablespoons oyster sauce

1 teaspoon sesame oil

1½ teaspoons sugar

2 teaspoons Shao-Hsing wine or sherry

Pinch of white pepper

1½ tablespoons cornstarch

1 cup Vegetable Stock (pages 31–32)

To complete the dish

2 pounds mussels in shell

10 cups water

One 1-inch-wide slice fresh ginger, lightly smashed

2 teaspoons white vinegar

1 tablespoon salt

2 tablespoons peanut oil

1 tablespoon shredded ginger

1 tablespoon brown bean sauce

3 scallions, trimmed, cut into 1½-inch sections, and white sections
    quartered

1. Combine the sauce ingredients in a bowl. Reserve.

2. Scrub the mussels well with a hard brush to remove sand and beards. Wash at least 4 times, until thoroughly clean.

3. In a large pot place the water, ginger, vinegar, and salt. Cover and bring to a boil over high heat. Allow to boil for 1 minute, then add the mussels and stir. As the mussels open, remove from water and transfer to a bowl. Reserve.

4. Heat a wok over high heat for 30 seconds. Add the peanut oil and coat the wok with a spatula. When a wisp of white smoke appears, add the ginger and stir briefly. Add the brown bean sauce and stir into mixture. Stir the sauce and pour into mixture. Stir continuously in one direction until sauce turns dark brown and begins to bubble. Add the scallions and mix well. Add the mussels and toss, making certain the mussels are well coated. Turn off the heat, transfer to a heated dish, and serve immediately.

Serves 4 to 6

MUSSEL AND NOODLE SOUP
Hok Hin Mai Fun Tong

Traditionally the mussels used in soups are dried. These mussels, which are sold in Chinese and Asian groceries, do have a deep, intense flavor when reconstituted, but they tend to be quite tough. Fresh mussels are preferable and these days easily obtainable. Also, soups made with mussels generally do not contain noodles. I believe their addition makes for an unusual dish that adds to tradition.

1½ pounds mussels in shell

16 cups water

One 1-inch-wide slice fresh ginger, lightly smashed

1 teaspoon salt

1 teaspoon white vinegar

½ pound rice noodles (like linguine, about ¼ inch wide)

3 cups Vegetable Stock (pages 31–32) diluted with 1½ cups water

¼ teaspoon salt, or to taste

1 tablespoon soy sauce

1 tablespoon Shao-Hsing wine or sherry

2 teaspoons Green Oil (page 39)

¼ pound snow peas, halved on the diagonal

3 tablespoons thinly sliced scallion, white portions only

2 tablespoons fresh coriander, chopped

1. Scrub the mussels well with a hard brush to remove sand and beards. Wash at least 4 times, until thoroughly clean. In a large pot, place 10 cups water, ginger, 1 teaspoon salt, and vinegar. Cover and bring to a boil over high heat. Boil for 1 minute, then add the mussels. As they open, remove them from water to a bowl. Reserve.

2. Into a pot place remaining 6 cups water. Cover and bring to a boil over high heat. Add the noodles and cook about 45 seconds, until just pliable. Turn off the heat. Run cold water into the pot and drain. Repeat twice more. Drain well.

3. Place the vegetable stock in a large pot. Add the ¼ teaspoon salt, soy sauce, wine, and Green Oil. Cover and bring to a boil over high heat. Add the snow peas and scallions and return to a boil. Add the noodles and return to a boil. Turn off the heat, add the mussels, and stir well. Transfer to individual soup plates, sprinkle each with chopped fresh coriander, and serve immediately.

Serves 4 to 6

BATTER-FRIED OYSTERS
Jah Sahng Ho

Oysters, one of the fruits of the sea permissible to Buddhists, are a favorite all along the coast of China. Cooking them with a batter is customary, whether in Shanghai or Canton or points in between.

Batter ingredients

1½ cups bleached all-purpose (high-gluten) flour

10 ounces cold water

2 tablespoons baking powder

2 tablespoons peanut oil

To complete the dish

5 cups peanut oil

20 medium-sized oysters, opened (have your fishmonger open them) and removed from shell

Szechuan Peppercorn Salt (page 38), for serving

1. Combine the batter ingredients in a bowl. Reserve.

2. Heat a wok for 1 minute. Pour in the 5 cups peanut oil. When a wisp of white smoke appears, you can cook the oysters; dip each oyster into the batter until well coated and lower into oil. Deep-fry 5 at a time until light brown, about 3 minutes. Remove the oysters, place in a strainer, and allow to drain over a bowl.

3. Deep-fry the last batch to a golden brown, about 4 minutes. Then place the others back in the oil for about 2 minutes more so they can also become golden brown. Serve all immediately, with Szechuan Peppercorn Salt.

Serves 4 to 6

FRIED OYSTERS
Jah Sahng Ho

Oysters are, of course, best when fresh from the water. The word *sahng* actually means "to be still alive." In this instance it means that the oyster has just been opened and is at its freshest. Here is an alternative method of batter-frying them.

Batter ingredients

¾ cup bleached all-purpose (high-gluten) flour

¾ cup cornstarch

1½ tablespoons baking powder

10 ounces cold water

2 tablespoons peanut oil

To complete the dish

12 medium-sized oysters, opened (have your fishmonger open them) and
    removed from shell

5 cups peanut oil

Sweet and Sour Sauce (page 41), for serving

1. Combine the batter ingredients in a bowl and stir until mixture is smooth and even, resembling a pancake batter. If too thick, add more water.

2. Dust each oyster with a bit of cornstarch to absorb its moisture. Reserve.

3. Heat a wok over high heat for 1 minute. Add the peanut oil and heat to 350°F. As the oil heats, dip each oyster into the batter to completely coat it. Turn off the heat, then with chopsticks or tongs lower the oysters into the oil, 4 at a time. Keep turning the oysters so they will brown evenly. Regulate the heat as you cook. They should cook perfectly in 2½ to 3 minutes. Remove from oil. Drain on paper towels and serve immediately with Sweet and Sour Sauce.

Serves 4 to 6

BAKED OYSTERS WITH SHIITAKE MUSHROOMS
Sok Sin Ho

The fact that these oysters are baked in an oven makes them unusual to the traditional Chinese kitchen. Historically the Chinese have cooked *on* wood-burning stoves, not *in* them. But Western influences have come to the East.

Sauce ingredients

½ cup Vegetable Stock (pages 31–32)
1½ teaspoons white vinegar
1 tablespoon minced garlic
1 tablespoon Shao-Hsing wine or sherry
2 teaspoons soy sauce
2 teaspoons Scallion Oil (page 37)
½ teaspoon sugar
Pinch of white pepper

To complete the dish

12 shiitake mushrooms, each large enough to hold an oyster in its cap,
     stems removed
Twelve 7-inch squares of aluminum foil
12 large fresh oysters, opened (have your fishmonger open them) and
     removed from shell

1. Combine the sauce ingredients in a bowl. Place the shiitake mushrooms in the bowl with the sauce and mix, making certain the mushrooms are well coated.

2. Place a mushroom in the center of a foil square, cup side up. Place an oyster in the cup. Lift the ends of the foil square slightly so that no sauce will run out.

3. Divide the sauce among all the mushrooms and oysters, then close each foil square and squeeze the top so as to completely seal the package. Each package should look like a small bag with a stem like a mushroom stem.

4. Preheat oven to 450°F. Place all on a baking sheet. Bake for 7 minutes. The oysters should be cooked perfectly, the mushrooms slightly softened, and the sauce should permeate both. Caution: Do not overbake or oysters will become tough and chewy. Serve immediately.

Serves 4 to 6

CLAMS STEAMED WITH GINGER AND SCALLIONS
Geung Chung Jing Hin

Clams are permitted to observant Buddhist vegetarians. They are also significant creatures in Chinese traditions. Clams denote prosperity and are always a part of the festive New Year meal. I cannot remember a meal of any importance in my family that did not include clams.

Sauce ingredients

2 teaspoons minced ginger

3 tablespoons trimmed and finely sliced scallions

1 tablespoon soy sauce

1 tablespoon Shao-Hsing wine or sherry

1½ teaspoons sugar

1½ teaspoons white vinegar

1 tablespoon Scallion Oil (page 37)

3 tablespoons Vegetable Stock (pages 31–32)

Pinch of white pepper

To complete the dish

12 clams, large cherrystones preferred, on the half-shell, opened (have your fishmonger open them)

6 sprigs fresh coriander

1. Combine the sauce ingredients in a bowl. Place the clams in a heatproof dish. Stir the sauce, pour over clams, and steam for 1½ to 2 minutes (page 231). Do not oversteam or the clams will become tough. Turn off the heat. Remove the dish from the steamer, garnish clams with sprigs of fresh coriander, and serve immediately. Serve with cooked rice.

Serves 4 to 6

STEAMED CLAMS WITH BLACK BEANS

Dau See Jing Heen

This classic Cantonese recipe, in which clams are steamed with fermented black beans, is a perennial favorite not only of observant Buddhists but of everyone else as well.

Sauce ingredients

1 tablespoon fermented black beans, washed and drained
1 tablespoon Scallion Oil (page 37)
2 tablespoons soy sauce
2½ tablespoons Vegetable Stock (pages 31–32)
2 tablespoons Shao-Hsing wine or sherry
2 teaspoons sugar
2 teaspoons white vinegar
1 tablespoon sesame oil
Pinch of white pepper

To complete the dish

18 clams, such as cherrystones, on the half-shell, opened (have your fishmonger open them)

1. Combine the sauce ingredients in a bowl. Place the opened clams in a heatproof dish and divide the sauce mixture evenly among them, spooning some atop each clam.

2. Steam for 2 to 3 minutes. Avoid oversteaming, because the clams will become tough if steamed too long. Turn off the heat and serve the clams in the dish in which they were steamed. They are delicious with cooked rice.

Serves 4 to 6

CLAMS IN HUNAN PEPPER SAUCE
Hunan Lot Hiu

I prefer smaller clams for this dish. They take the heat better and absorb the flavor of the spices better than would larger clams.

Sauce ingredients

1 teaspoon Hot Pepper Flakes (page 36; see note below)

1½ tablespoons oyster sauce

3 tablespoons ketchup

1½ teaspoons sugar

1 teaspoon white vinegar

1 tablespoon Shao-Hsing wine or sherry

1½ tablespoons cornstarch

1 cup Vegetable Stock (pages 31–32)

To complete the dish

30 clams in shell, littleneck preferred

8 cups cold water

1¾-inch-wide slice fresh ginger, lightly smashed

1½ teaspoons white vinegar

1 teaspoon salt

2 tablespoons peanut oil

1 tablespoon minced ginger

2 teaspoons minced garlic

2 scallions, white portions cut into ¼-inch slices and green portions
finely sliced

1. Combine the sauce ingredients in a bowl. Reserve.

2. Prepare the clams. Wash thoroughly and brush to remove sand. In a large pot place the water, slice of ginger, vinegar, and salt and bring to a boil over high heat. Boil for 1 minute, then add clams and boil. As the clams open, remove from the water and reserve.

3. Heat a wok over high heat for 30 seconds. Add the peanut oil and coat the wok with a spatula. When a wisp of white smoke appears, add the minced ginger and stir briefly. Add the minced garlic and stir briefly. Add the white scallion portions and cook until the aroma is released. Stir the sauce and pour into the wok. Stir well in one direction. When sauce bubbles and thickens, add the clams and toss until well coated.

4. Turn off the heat. Sprinkle the green scallion portions over the clams, transfer to a heated dish, and serve immediately with cooked rice.

Serves 4 to 6

Note: If you wish the sauce to be a bit more hot and spicy, add an additional ¼ teaspoon hot pepper flakes to the sauce mixture.

類 *Yue*

The Occasional Fish

Much attention in China, even among those who consider themselves vegetarians, is accorded fish. It is not at all uncommon for observant Buddhists to occasionally eat small amounts of fish, though Buddhist priests and nuns would never eat it, limiting themselves to the three permissible shellfish—oysters, clams, and mussels. Even in the West, avowed vegetarians who refrain from meat eat fish every now and then. I expect that in the case of the Chinese, the close acquaintance with hundreds of varieties of fresh fish, particularly in the south, accounts for this interest.

It is said that the first fish in the world ever to be farmed was a species of carp, in China. And it is the carp that is revered in Buddhism, particularly the *koi* variety, a type of carp related to the goldfish. Buddhist legend has it that at some point in Buddha's life, when he was in great danger, the *koi* led Buddha to safety. Because of this the *koi* is never eaten by Buddhists, though other carp are.

My grandmother, Ah Paw, would never eat the *koi* carp. Instead we might have grass carp, particularly from West Lake in Hangzhou, or any other variety of that freshwater fish, which abounds in China.

According to another legend, all of the fish in a vast river volunteered their scales to make a straw basket into a watertight boat, enabling the diety Kwan Yin, the goddess of mercy, to cross the river. The one fish that refused to give its scales was the snakehead, and for its greed its head became forever completely covered with scales. It is, by the way, a most difficult fish to clean.

Because of their great numbers, fish are regarded as representations of plenty. Even in parts of China where fish are scarce or rarely eaten, often a wooden carved fish is placed upon a platter in the center of the dining table, to be "eaten" symbolically.

CRISP SOLE
Choi Pei Loong Lei

In China, sole is referred to as loong lei, or "dragon's tongue." The way this dish is made is unusual. The fish is fried thoroughly, so crisp that even the small fin bones are cooked and edible. It is not at all greasy.

1 sole (1½ pounds), scales, gills, and intestines removed

Marinade ingredients

1½ tablespoons white wine
1¼ teaspoons salt
1½ teaspoons white vinegar
⅛ teaspoon white pepper

To complete the dish

6 cups peanut oil
1 extra-large egg, beaten
¾ cup flour
2 tablespoons finely sliced scallions, green portions only
2 tablespoons finely chopped fresh coriander

1. Wash the fish and remove the membranes. Dry thoroughly with paper towels. Place in a large dish, combine the marinade ingredients, and pour the marinade over the fish. Rub in the marinade with your hands, coating the fish well. Allow to rest for 15 minutes.

2. Dry fish thoroughly with paper towels. Heat a wok over high heat for 1 minute. Add the peanut oil. As oil heats, coat the fish with the beaten egg. Spread the flour on a sheet of waxed paper and place the fish on it. Coat the fish thoroughly with flour and shake off the excess.

3. The oil should be heated to 375°F. Place the fish in a Chinese strainer and lower it into the oil. Deep-fry for 3 minutes. Reduce the heat and allow the oil temperature to lower to 350°F. Fry the fish for another 4 to 6 minutes, until it turns light brown. (Note: If oil temperature is regulated carefully, the fish will not burn.) Turn off the heat, place the fish in a strainer over a bowl, and allow the oil to drain away and the fish to cool to room temperature, about ½ hour.

4. Reheat the oil to 350°F. Place the fish in the strainer, lower into the oil, and deep-fry for another 5 to 7 minutes, or until the fish is golden brown and very crisp. Turn off the heat. Place the strainer over a bowl and allow the fish to drain for 1 minute. Transfer to a heated platter, sprinkle scallions on top, then fresh coriander, and serve immediately.

Serves 4 to 6

Note: The technique used to cook the sole is quite like that used for making the best *pommes frites*. The Chinese and the French have a few things in common.

SOLE WITH BLACK BEANS
Jing Loong Lei

This is "steamed dragon's tongue" to the Chinese. It is the same fish as in the preceding recipe, but cooked in quite a different way.

Marinade ingredients

2 large cloves garlic, peeled

1½ tablespoons black beans, washed and drained

2 tablespoons white wine

1 tablespoon soy sauce

1½ tablespoons Scallion Oil (page 37)

3 tablespoons trimmed and finely sliced scallions

1 teaspoon sesame oil

1 teaspoon white vinegar

⅛ teaspoon salt

¾ teaspoon sugar

Pinch of white pepper

To complete the dish

Two ½-pound fillets of sole

1½ tablespoons Scallion Oil (page 37)

2 tablespoons finely chopped fresh coriander, for garnish

1. To make the marinade, place the garlic in a bowl with the black beans and mash into a paste. Add all the other marinade ingredients, combine well, and reserve.

2. Place the sole fillets in a heatproof dish. Pour the marinade over the fish. Place the dish in a steamer and steam for 8 minutes, or until the fish turns white and firm. If you use a metal dish to hold the fish, the steaming time will be about 4 minutes.

3. When fish is done, remove from heat, pour Scallion Oil over the fillets, sprinkle with fresh coriander, and serve immediately.

Serves 4 to 6

清
蒸
石
班

STEAMED SEA BASS
Ching Jing Sek Bou

This is a classic fish preparation, an illustration of the Cantonese kitchen at its best. Steaming preserves the flesh of a fresh fish, retaining its flavor and even its shape. A steamed fish is virtually always part of an important banquet, always served to an important guest, always part of the New Year celebration. Sea bass is particularly suited to steaming because it is meaty and has fewer bones than other fish. Often it is accompanied by shredded black mushrooms, black beans, ginger, and scallions. This is my original, with my Scallion Oil in the marinade and as a finish. It imparts an unusual aroma and taste.

One 2-pound whole fresh sea bass, scales, gills, and intestines removed

Marinade ingredients

2 tablespoons Scallion Oil (page 37)
2 tablespoons soy sauce
2 tablespoons white wine
1½ teaspoons sesame oil
1½ teaspoons white vinegar
½ teaspoon salt
⅛ teaspoon white pepper

To complete the dish

1 tablespoon Scallion Oil (page 37)
2 scallions, trimmed and finely sliced
1 tablespoon finely chopped fresh coriander

1. Clean the fish well. Remove the membranes, and wash inside and out. Make 3 cuts with a sharp knife into the side of the fish, to (but not through) the bone. Repeat on the other side. Dry the fish well with paper towels and place in a heatproof dish.

2. Combine the marinade ingredients in a bowl. Pour the marinade over fish and rub in with your hands. Be certain to rub well into the cuts. Allow it to stand for 10 to 15 minutes.

3. Place dish in a steamer and steam for about 30 minutes, or until the flesh seen in the cuts turns white and is firm. Turn off the heat. Pour Scallion Oil over the fish. Sprinkle with the scallions and fresh coriander and serve immediately.

Serves 4 to 6

BEAN CURD FISH ROLLS
Woo Jook Bau Yue

Once made in this manner only in Shanghai, this preparation, like many preparations in China, has become a staple in Canton and other places south as well.

¾-pound fish fillets (sea bass, flounder, or sole); 3 fillets, each ¼ pound

Marinade ingredients

1 tablespoon white vinegar

1 tablespoon white wine

1½ teaspoons soy sauce

¾ teaspoon sugar

1 teaspoon shredded fresh ginger

Pinch of white pepper

1 teaspoon sesame oil

¼ teaspoon salt

To complete the dish

2 tablespoons cornstarch

Three 6-inch-square bean curd pieces, cut from fresh bean curd (see note below)

3 to 4 cups peanut oil

1. Cut each fish fillet into 3 equal portions. Combine the marinade ingredients in a bowl and soak the fish in marinade for 10 minutes. Remove from marinade, then dust each piece with cornstarch and wrap in bean curd.

2. Heat a wok over high heat for 1 minute. Add peanut oil and heat to 350°F. Holding each roll with chopsticks or tongs, lower into oil. Continue to hold until the bean curd seals. The fish is ready when the bean curd turns golden brown, in about 3 to 4 minutes. Remove, cut each roll in half, and serve immediately.

Serves 4 to 6

Note: Fresh bean curd sheets come two to a package. They are found in refrigerated sections of Chinese markets and are usually round, twenty-four inches in diameter, and pliable. Refrigerated, they will keep about ten days. The packages are not labeled and must be requested from a store employee.

FISH CONGEE
Yue Jook

There is no end to what the Cantonese add to their breakfast rice porridge. Vegetables, eggs, fish—all are proper with congee.

1 Congee recipe (page 135)
One 3-pound fresh fish (sea bass, sole, flounder, or carp; 3 pounds will
    yield 1½ pounds when prepared)

Marinade ingredients

1 teaspoon white vinegar
2 tablespoons white wine
2 teaspoons soy sauce
2 teaspoons sesame oil
2 tablespoons peanut oil
1 teaspoon salt
Pinch of white pepper
4 slices fresh ginger; paper thin, peeled, and julienned
2 scallions, trimmed and cut into 1½-inch pieces

To complete the dish

1 tablespoon Scallion Oil (page 37)
⅛ teaspoon white pepper
1 teaspoon soy sauce
3 scallions, trimmed and finely sliced, for garnish
1 tablespoon chopped fresh coriander, for garnish (optional)

1. While the congee is cooking, place the fish in a heatproof dish. Combine the marinade ingredients well and pour over the fish. Place the pieces of ginger and scallions from the marinade beneath fish, in the body cavity, and on top.

2. Steam the fish for 25 minutes. Remove from the steamer and allow to cool to room temperature. Discard the skin, bones, ginger, and scallions and break the fish flesh into very small pieces.

3. Place the fish pieces in a bowl. Add the Scallion Oil, white pepper, and soy sauce. Mix lightly with fish. When the congee is cooked, add the fish to it. Mix

together and allow the congee to come to a boil. Turn off the heat, pour the congee into a serving tureen, sprinkle the finely sliced scallions on top (and fresh coriander, if desired), and serve immediately.

Serves 4 to 6

ASPARAGUS ROLLED IN CARP
Wan Yue Yung Lo Sun

Carp is a very popular fish in China. It is also versatile and is steamed, stewed, and often minced to use as a stuffing or wrapping.

¾ pound skinless carp fillets

2½ tablespoons cornstarch

1½ teaspoons grated ginger

1½ teaspoons white wine

½ teaspoon soy sauce

1½ teaspoons sesame oil

1 tablespoon oyster sauce

1 teaspoon sugar

1½ tablespoons lightly beaten egg white

Pinch of white pepper

5 scallions, white portions only, minced

3 cups cold water

½ teaspoon baking soda (optional)

12 asparagus spears, cut 6 inches from tip

3½ tablespoons peanut oil

Orange slices, halved, for garnish

1. Dry the carp well with paper towels. Using a cleaver or sharp knife, cut the fish into thin slices and then chop into a paste. Transfer the fish to a bowl and add the cornstarch, ginger, white wine, soy sauce, sesame oil, oyster sauce, sugar, egg white, white pepper, and scallions. With a wooden spoon, beat until thoroughly blended and very stiff. Refrigerate for at least 3 hours.

2. In a large pot bring the water and baking soda to a boil. Add the asparagus and water-blanch until they turn bright green, about 30 seconds. Drain and refresh under cold water. Set aside to drain on paper towels. (The recipe, to this point, can be prepared a day ahead. Cover and refrigerate the fish paste and asparagus separately.)

3. When the fish paste cools, divide it into 12 equal portions. Flatten each portion into an oval about 4 inches long and wide enough to enclose an asparagus spear. Center a spear along the oval length, with the ends protruding, and with the help of a small knife scoop up the fish paste oval and fold around the asparagus spear to enclose it snugly. Repeat with remaining fish paste and asparagus spears.

4. Heat a cast-iron skillet over high heat for 45 seconds. Add 2 tablespoons peanut oil, or just enough to cover the bottom of the pan. When a wisp of white smoke appears, place 6 of the asparagus rolls in the pan and fry until golden brown, about 1½ minutes on each of the 4 sides of each roll. Remove to paper towels to drain. Transfer the rolls to a serving plate and place near the stovetop to keep warm. (Do not place in the oven, or they will become soggy.) Fry the remaining 6 rolls, adding the remaining peanut oil if necessary. When all are fried and drained, place on a platter, garnish with the orange slices, and serve hot.

Serves 4 to 6

Note: These may be steamed as well as fried. If you opt for steaming, the rolls should be steamed for 8 to 10 minutes. Brush the dish holding the rolls with a bit of peanut oil to prevent sticking.

STEAMED SHRIMP
Jing Har

It is the sauce that makes this shrimp preparation. Throughout coastal China, where shrimp abound, there are regional variations of sauces to dress steamed shrimp.

Sauce ingredients

2 tablespoons peanut oil

3 tablespoons Vegetable Stock (pages 31–32)

1 tablespoon soy sauce

1 tablespoon oyster sauce

1 teaspoon sugar

1 tablespoon Shao-Hsing wine or sherry

1 teaspoon Tientsin preserved vegetable

1 tablespoon minced garlic

¼ cup minced scallions, white portions only

To complete the dish

½ pound medium shrimp (about 18), unshelled

1. Combine all the sauce ingredients and allow to stand for at least 30 minutes.

2. Wash the shrimp but leave the shells on. With pointed kitchen shears cut along back of shrimp, along the vein line, to the tail. Devein the shrimp. Place the shrimp on a chopping board. With a sharp knife cut along the open vein line and butterfly the shrimp. Do not cut through tail.

3. Arrange the shrimp in a heatproof dish. Stir the sauce and pour over shrimp evenly. Allow to marinate in the sauce for 45 minutes. Place the dish in a steamer and steam for 4 to 5 minutes, or until the shrimp turn pink. Turn off the heat and serve immediately.

Serves 4 to 6

DRUNKEN SHRIMP
Joy Har

This traditional dish is found in some form all along China's eastern coast. Usually it is made with live shrimp, marinated and then flambéed in rice liquor. Here is a version that is less visually stimulating but equally tasty.

Dipping sauce ingredients

2 tablespoons Vegetable Stock (pages 31–32)

1 scallion, thinly sliced, green portion only

3 small chili peppers, minced

1½ tablespoons soy sauce

2 teaspoons white vinegar

2 teaspoons sesame oil

½ teaspoon sugar

To complete the dish

24 medium shrimp (about ¾ pound), unshelled

3 tablespoons Cognac or other brandy

3 cups Vegetable Stock (pages 31–32)

2 scallions, trimmed and halved crosswise

1 piece fresh ginger, 1½ by ½ inch, peeled and smashed

1. Combine the dipping sauce ingredients in a bowl. Reserve.

2. Using kitchen shears, cut through the shrimp shells along the back from the heads to just before the tails; leave the shells on. Remove the veins. Rinse the shrimp in cold water, drain, and pat dry with paper towels. In a bowl toss the shrimp with Cognac until thoroughly coated. Cover and marinate in refrigerator for 2 hours.

3. In a saucepan, combine the 3 cups vegetable stock with the scallions and ginger. Cover and bring to a boil over high heat. Reduce heat to moderately low and simmer for 2 minutes. Return the heat to high and bring to a boil. Add the shrimp and the Cognac marinade and stir to immerse shrimp completely. When the liquid returns to a boil, remove the pan from the heat. Cover and set aside until the shrimp are opaque and curled, about 2 minutes.

4. With a slotted spoon transfer the shrimp to 4 to 6 serving plates. Pour the reserved dipping sauce into small dishes and serve alongside shrimp.

Serves 4 to 6

POACHED SHRIMP WITH FRESH CORIANDER
Bok Chuk Har

This dish is quite popular in and around Canton, where it is called "scalded ocean shrimp." Part of the shells are left on, to enhance the flavor after cooking, and they are peeled before eating, as you might do down in Louisiana.

Dipping sauce ingredients

2 tablespoons white wine

2 teaspoons light soy sauce

1 teaspoon white vinegar

3 tablespoons Vegetable Stock (pages 31–32)

½ teaspoon grated ginger

3 tablespoons trimmed and finely sliced scallions

Poaching ingredients

5 cups cold water

Reserved shrimp shells

1 bunch fresh coriander, cut into 3-inch pieces (1 tightly packed cup)

4 scallions, trimmed, each cut into 3 pieces

One 3-inch-wide slice fresh ginger, lightly smashed

¼ teaspoon white peppercorns

1 teaspoon white vinegar

1 teaspoon salt

2 teaspoons sugar

¼ cup white wine

To complete the dish

1 pound medium shrimp (36 to 40), unshelled

1. Shell shrimps, leaving on end portion of shell with tail. Devein, wash, and drain. Reserve shells.

2. Combine the dipping sauce ingredients in a bowl. Reserve.

3. Combine the water and all other poaching ingredients in a large pot. Cover. Over high heat bring to a boil. Lower the heat and simmer for 30 minutes. Turn off the heat, strain off the coriander, scallions, and shrimp shells, and discard. Retain the ginger in the liquid.

4. Bring the liquid back to a boil over high heat. Add the shrimp. Cook, stirring, for 1 minute, or until the shrimp turn pink and curl. Turn off the heat and strain off the liquid. Remove the ginger. Serve the shrimp with the dipping sauce.

Serves 4 to 6

STEAMED SCALLOPS
Dai Ji Ching Jing

This preparation is prized for both its lightness and its whiteness. As with rice, the Chinese like white—for its purity—on their plates.

12 scallops (each 1 inch thick by 1½ inches wide)

Sauce ingredients

1 tablespoon white wine
1 tablespoon soy sauce
1 tablespoon Scallion Oil (page 37)
¾ teaspoon sugar
2 teaspoons minced ginger
1 tablespoon minced scallion whites
½ teaspoon sesame oil
Pinch of white pepper

1. Place the scallops in a heatproof dish. Combine the sauce ingredients well and pour evenly over the scallops. Place the dish in a steamer and steam for 3 to 4 minutes, or until the scallops become white and firm. Do not oversteam, or the scallops will toughen. Remove from heat and serve immediately.

Serves 4 to 6

Note: These scallops are delicious on their own, but often in Hong Kong they are placed in the center of a platter and surrounded by stir-fried broccoli flowerets (page 47). Eaten together, the two dishes complement each other quite well.

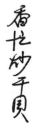

SCALLOPS WITH MANGO
Heung Hong Chau Gon Bui

In southern China, fruits are quite often stir-fried with other ingredients. In the near-tropical south, mangoes are available in the summer and are always eagerly awaited.

1 ripe mango, a bit firm (about 1 pound)

Sauce ingredients

3 tablespoons Vegetable Stock (pages 31–32)
2 teaspoons white wine
1½ teaspoons oyster sauce
1 teaspoon white vinegar
½ teaspoon soy sauce
½ teaspoon sesame oil
1½ teaspoons cornstarch
¼ teaspoon sugar
Pinch of white pepper

To complete the dish

2 cups peanut oil
½ pound sea scallops, halved horizontally
1 teaspoon minced ginger
1 teaspoon minced garlic
3 thin asparagus spears, diagonally sliced into ¼-inch pieces
1 small sweet red pepper, cut into 1-inch by ½-inch pieces
2 scallions, white portions only, diagonally sliced into ¼-inch pieces
6 straw mushrooms, halved lengthwise

1. With a sharp knife, halve the mango lengthwise, cutting around the pit to remove it. Carefully peel the mango, preserving all of the flesh. Cut the fruit into pieces measuring 1½ by 1 by ⅓ inch. Reserve.

2. Combine the sauce ingredients in a bowl. Reserve.

3. Heat a wok over high heat for 30 seconds. Add the peanut oil and heat until oil reaches 350°F, about 5 minutes. Add the scallops and oil-blanch until they turn white, 15 to 20 seconds. With a slotted spoon transfer scallops to paper towels to drain.

4. Pour off all but 1½ tablespoons of oil from the wok. Heat the remaining oil for 15 seconds. When a wisp of white smoke appears, add the ginger and stir-fry for 30 seconds. Add the garlic and stir-fry until golden, about 30 seconds. Add the asparagus, pepper, scallions, and mushrooms and stir-fry for 1½ minutes. Add the reserved mango and scallops and stir-fry for 45 seconds longer.

5. Make a well in the center of the ingredients. Stir the sauce and pour it into the well. Mix together, stirring, until the sauce bubbles and thickens, about 1 minute. Toss all ingredients together to combine well. Remove the wok from the heat. Transfer contents to a serving dish and serve immediately.

Serves 4 to 6

麵
類 *Mien*
Noodles and
Wrappings

What is as familiar, or as comforting, as a bowl of noodles? Noodles, or some form thereof, are as universal in China as elsewhere in the world, and the Chinese have been noodle makers since the Han dynasty, two centuries before Christ, when the milling of flour became an art.

Whether Marco Polo brought noodles home to Italy from China after his thirteenth-century journeys to the imperial court is an argument that nobody will win, though I might say that if he brought them back from anywhere, it would have had to be China. After all, noodles at that time were a food not only of the court but of street vendors as well.

In China noodles are made from wheat flour (occasionally with a bit of egg added for color), from rice flour, and from mung bean flour. They are of infinite variety and size, from wide, flat noodles to the hair-thin noodles tossed in the air by Beijing chefs to the fine rice noodles used in so many recipes. The Chinese also consider dumpling skins, thin pancakes, and flat cakes to be brothers and sisters of the basic noodle, often referring to them as "noodle food."

Noodles, *mien*, are one of the many representations of long life that exist in Chinese food traditions. This is simply because of their length, and they are offered regularly, fresh, to ancestors at temple altars and at grave sites. Their length also makes them favorites on birthdays, where they symbolize long life. Though the genesis of the noodle was the wheat culture of China's north, it is recognized that the Cantonese, in the south, are the masters of the noodle in China. Noodle shops abound in every city and every village in China, and these

251

cater to those who wish a quick lunch, a fast midmorning or midafternoon snack, or a light evening meal.

Every region of China has its special noodle preparations, its special dough foods, but perhaps the most famed are the *dim sum* created by the Cantonese noodle makers. These small dumplings, steamed, boiled, baked, or fried, have become favorites throughout the world, wherever the Chinese of Canton have immigrated.

The noodle makers in China also make a wide variety of wrappers, often labeled, it seems, to confound the shopper. There are spring roll skins, Shanghai spring roll skins, egg roll skins, bean curd skins, rice paper, won ton skins, water dumpling skins. They are all varieties of the noodle. Yet by wrapping them around different foods and preparing them in different ways, a grand procession of noodles, *dim sum*, dumplings, and rolls is possible.

To make them, to create with whim, is rewarding. In this section I include various noodle dishes from different regions of China, as well as a selection of wrapped preparations. I encourage you to allow your imagination to run and to experiment as you like with noodles and wrappers. You will also find here another Chinese culinary art—minced food wrapped in fresh leaves, usually lettuce. In China the wrapping of food in skins is known as *pei*. Enjoy *pei* and its relations.

FRIED NOODLES
Ja Won Ton Pei

Who has not gone to his or her favorite neighborhood Chinese restaurant and, while waiting for the meal to begin, nibbled on those crisp fried noodles? All of us have. They are a bit too hard for my taste. My version is far lighter. I use won ton wrappers cut into strips and deep-fried. They are crisp and far more delicate than the restaurant version, with just a hint of garlic.

6 cups peanut oil
½ pound won ton wrappers, cut into ⅓-inch strips, divided into 4 equal
    portions
4 cloves garlic, peeled

1. Heat a wok over high heat for 40 seconds. Add the peanut oil. Heat to 350°F. Add 1 clove of garlic to the oil and 1 portion of the won ton strips. Turn and loosen with a wooden spoon or chopsticks to separate. Fry to a golden brown, about 45 seconds to 1 minute. Turn off the heat. Remove from the oil with a Chinese strainer and drain on paper towels.

2. Repeat 3 times until all the strips are fried, adding 1 garlic clove with each portion. Allow the noodles to cool. Place in a large plastic container for storage.

Serves 4 to 6

Note: The noodles will keep for 1 week in a tightly covered container. They can be served as a base beneath any of the salads in this book, if desired. Or they can be added to any of the soups, particularly Hot and Sour Soup (page 152). The noodles are fine just to snack on, as well.

PAN-FRIED NOODLES
Leung Mien Wong

Although noodles in China are a product of the north, of the wheat culture of Peking, these days no part of the country is without its noodle preparations. This dish is a favorite in Canton.

8 cups water

8 ounces fresh noodles (soft noodles, slightly thicker than vermicelli)

Sauce ingredients

2 teaspoons dark soy sauce

1 teaspoon salt

1½ teaspoons sugar

2 teaspoons sesame oil

1 teaspoon white vinegar

1½ teaspoons Shao-Hsing wine or sherry

Pinch of white pepper

1½ teaspoons cornstarch

½ cup Vegetable Stock (pages 31–32)

To complete the dish

5 tablespoons peanut oil

1 teaspoon minced fresh ginger

1 teaspoon minced garlic

¾ cup snow peas, strings and ends removed, diagonally cut into julienne

⅓ cup fresh water chestnuts, peeled and cut into julienne

⅓ cup bamboo shoots, cut into julienne

3 scallions, trimmed and cut into julienne

1. Boil the water in a pot. Add the noodles and cook for 1 minute, until *al dente*. Run cold water into the pot and drain the noodles through a strainer. Place noodles back into pot, add cold water, and drain again. Repeat once again. Allow noodles to drain for 2 hours, turning them occasionally so they will dry completely.

2. Combine the sauce ingredients in a bowl. Reserve.

3. Pour 3 tablespoons of the peanut oil into a cast-iron frying pan over high heat. Heat for 40 seconds. When a wisp of white smoke appears, place noodles in an even layer in the pan, covering the entire bottom. Cook for 2 minutes, moving the pan about on the burner to ensure that the noodles brown evenly. Invert the noodles onto a dish placed over the frying pan, then slide the noodles back into the pan. (Alternately: Slide the noodles onto a large plate. Place another plate over them and invert. Remove the plate, then slide noodles back into frying pan.)

4. Cook the other side of the noodles for 2 minutes. If a bit more oil is needed at this point, pour an additional tablespoon into the pan, but only if it is necessary.

5. As the noodles are cooking, heat a wok over high heat for 40 seconds. Add 2 tablespoons peanut oil and coat the wok with a spatula. When a wisp of white smoke appears, add the ginger and stir. Add the garlic and stir. When the garlic browns, add all the vegetables. Stir together for about 2 minutes. When the vegetables have softened slightly, make a well in the center. Stir the reserved sauce, pour it into the well, and mix together. When the sauce thickens and begins to bubble, turn off the heat.

6. Place the noodles on a serving dish. Pour the contents of the wok atop them and serve immediately.

Serves 4 to 6

SESAME NOODLES
Ji Mah Mien

This noodle preparation is from Szechuan, where the heat from hot peppers and hot oil is present in virtually every meal.

8 cups water
8 ounces fresh noodles (soft noodles, slightly thicker than vermicelli)
1½ tablespoons sesame oil

Sesame sauce ingredients

5 tablespoons Vegetable Stock (pages 31–32)
1 teaspoon sesame seed paste
3 tablespoons peanut butter
2 teaspoons white vinegar
2 tablespoons mushroom soy sauce
1¼ teaspoons soaked red pepper flakes from bottom of jar of Hot Oil
(page 36)
1 tablespoon sugar
Pinch of white pepper
2 tablespoons trimmed and finely sliced scallions

To complete the dish

2 sprigs fresh coriander, broken into pieces

1. Bring the water to a boil. Add the noodles and stir. Cook for 1½ minutes, until *al dente*. Run cold water into the pot and drain the noodles. Run cold water again into the pot and drain the noodles. Repeat for a third time.

2. Place the drained noodles in a mixing bowl and toss with the sesame oil. Refrigerate, uncovered, for 1 hour.

3. To make the sesame sauce, bring the vegetable stock to a boil, so that sesame paste and peanut butter will liquefy. Then add all other ingredients and combine well.

4. When the noodles are cool, toss with sesame sauce, place in a serving dish, garnish with coriander, and serve.

Serves 4 to 6

TWO-SESAME NOODLES
Chi Ma Mien

Like many of the tastes of China, this dish is a pleasurable combination of simple ingredients. One can be as creative as desired, as I have been with this dish.

Sauce ingredients

½ tablespoon dark soy sauce
½ tablespoon light soy sauce
1 teaspoon white vinegar
1 teaspoon sesame oil
½ teaspoon minced garlic
1 teaspoon sugar
Pinch of white pepper

To complete the dish

½ tablespoon black sesame seeds
½ tablespoon white sesame seeds
6 cups water
1 teaspoon salt
1 pound fresh noodles, quite fine, like capellini #11
½ tablespoon Scallion Oil (page 37)

1. Combine the sauce ingredients. Reserve.

2. Dry-roast the two sesame seeds together in a wok over low heat for 1 minute. Reserve.

3. Add water and salt to a large pot and bring to a boil. Add noodles and cook for 45 seconds, or until *al dente*, stirring and loosening with chopsticks or a fork as they cook. Turn off the heat, run cold tap water into the pot, and drain the noodles immediately through a strainer. Place the noodles back in the pot and fill with cold water. Mix with your hands and drain the noodles again through a strainer. Repeat once more, until the noodles are cool. Allow to drain for 3 minutes, loosening with chopsticks to assist the draining.

4. Place the noodles in a bowl. Add the Scallion Oil and mix thoroughly. Add the reserved sauce to the noodles and mix well. Add the roasted sesame seeds and toss well. Serve immediately.

Serves 4 to 6

FRESH RICE NOODLES WITH BLACK BEANS
See Jiu Chau Hor Fun

Fresh rice noodles are usually sold in Asian storefront "factories" in neighborhoods with Chinese and Asian food shops. They are soft, come in sheets, and are made fresh daily. These noodles, which can be combined with just about anything, are a staple in Canton. The Cantonese translate their name, *sah hor fun,* as "sand river noodles."

Sauce ingredients

1½ tablespoons oyster sauce

1 teaspoon mushroom soy sauce

½ teaspoon sugar

½ teaspoon sesame oil

Pinch of white pepper

To complete the dish

2 tablespoons peanut oil

1 cup onions, thinly sliced

⅛ teaspoon salt

1 cup green bell peppers, thinly sliced

2 tablespoons fermented black beans, rinsed twice and mashed with
    3 cloves garlic into a paste

¾ pound fresh rice noodle sheets, cut into ½-inch-wide strips

1. Combine the sauce ingredients in a bowl and reserve.

2. Heat a wok over high heat for 30 seconds. Add 1 tablespoon peanut oil and coat the wok with a spatula. When a wisp of white smoke appears, add the onions and salt, stir, and cook for 45 seconds. Add the peppers and stir-fry until peppers turn bright green, about 1 minute. Turn off the heat, move the ingredients to a bowl, and reserve.

3. Wipe the wok and spatula with paper towels. Heat over high heat for 30 seconds. Add the remaining 1 tablespoon peanut oil and coat the wok again. When a wisp of white smoke appears, add the black bean and garlic paste. Break up with a spatula and cook for 45 seconds, until the beans release their aroma. Add the sliced noodles and stir-fry together for 2 minutes. Stir the reserved sauce, pour into the wok, and mix well, making certain the noodles are well coated.

4. Add the reserved onions and peppers and stir-fry together until coated and very hot. Turn off the heat, transfer to a heated serving dish, and serve immediately.

Serves 4 to 6

Note: Rice noodles may be kept, refrigerated, for up to 3 days. They become hard when refrigerated, so allow them to stand for 30 minutes before using. They may also be frozen for 4 to 6 weeks. Before using frozen rice noodles, however, allow them to come to room temperature. Then slice and cook.

SPICY RICE NOODLES
Chau Jai Mai Fun

Rice noodles are familiar to the people of Canton and Fukien, as well as the inhabitants of Southeast Asia. But they are rare in China's west. However, there is no reason not to combine the rice noodle with the flavors of Szechuan. The result is a delight.

6 ounces dry rice noodles (usually sold in 1-pound packages labeled "rice noodles" or "rice vermicelli")

6 cups water

3½ tablespoons Scallion Oil (page 37)

1 tablespoon minced fresh ginger

1 teaspoon salt

3 tablespoons Szechuan mustard pickle, julienned

1 large hot red pepper, minced

¾ cup sweet red peppers, julienned

½ cup snow peas, strings and both ends removed, cut diagonally into julienne

3 scallions, trimmed and julienned

1 teaspoon sesame oil

Snow Peas

1. At least 2½ hours before preparing this dish, boil the noodles in 6 cups water for about 1 minute. Separate the noodles as they boil and cook until barely *al dente*. Run cold water into the pot and drain through a strainer. Add cold water again and drain. Repeat a third time. Reserve. While the noodles are resting, separate and turn them 3 times to ensure that all water has drained.

2. Heat a wok over high heat for 40 seconds. Add 1½ tablespoons Scallion Oil and use a spatula to coat the wok. When a wisp of white smoke appears, add the ginger and ½ teaspoon salt. Cook until the ginger browns. Add all the vegetables. Stir-fry for about 1½ minutes, until the vegetables are slightly softened. Remove and drain over a strainer. Reserve.

3. Wash and dry the wok and spatula and place the wok back over high heat for 1 minute. Add the remaining Scallion Oil and coat the wok. Add the remaining salt and wait until wok becomes quite hot and smoky. Add rice noodles to wok by allowing them to slide over the spatula into the wok. This avoids spattering the hot oil. Separate the noodles as they fry, turning with spatula and chopsticks. If the noodles stick or burn, add an additional 1 tablespoon Scallion Oil, but only if needed. After 2 minutes, lower the heat to medium and stir-fry until noodles are hot, about 5 minutes. Raise the heat back to high and add the vegetables. Stir together until well mixed and hot. Turn off the heat. Add the sesame oil and toss to give the noodles a nutty aroma. Transfer to a serving dish and serve immediately.

Serves 4 to 6

SWEET SOY NOODLES
Tim See Mien

These distinctive noodles are from the Chiu Chow kitchen. Though they are faintly sweet, they are not thought of as a dessert, but they do appear toward the latter part of a meal. They are made with a special soy sauce, sweet soy, which is available to the Chiu Chow people in bottles but is not available in the United States. However, I have re-created this dish using double dark soy and sugar in my sauce mixture, and the taste is identical.

8 cups cold water

1 teaspoon salt

9 ounces fresh noodles (or fettucine)

½ tablespoon black sesame seeds (if unavailable, use white sesame seeds)

Sauce ingredients

1½ teaspoons double dark soy sauce

2½ teaspoons sugar

1½ teaspoons light soy sauce

2 teaspoons Shao-Hsing wine or sherry

2 teaspoons sesame oil

1 tablespoon oyster sauce

¼ cup Vegetable Stock (pages 31–32)

To complete the dish

3 tablespoons peanut oil

⅓ cup trimmed and finely sliced scallions, plus 2 tablespoons for garnish

2 teaspoons minced garlic

2 teaspoons Tientsin preserved vegetable

1. Place the water and salt in a large pot. Cover and bring to a boil over high heat. Add the noodles. As they cook, stir with chopsticks or a fork to separate. Cook for 1 minute, or until *al dente*. Turn off the heat. Run cold water into the pot and drain. Place the noodles back in the pot and run cold water in again. Drain for 30 minutes, loosening the noodles to ensure that they are dry throughout.

2. As noodles drain, dry-roast the sesame seeds and reserve. As sesame seeds cool, combine the sauce ingredients and reserve.

3. Heat a wok over high heat for 45 seconds. Add the peanut oil and coat the wok with a spatula. When a wisp of white smoke appears, add ⅓ cup scallions, garlic, and Tientsin preserved vegetable and stir together for 1 minute. Stir the sauce, pour it into the wok, and mix well. When sauce begins to bubble, add the noodles, stir, and use chopsticks to separate the noodles. Cook until all the sauce is absorbed. Turn off the heat, add sesame seeds, and toss well. Transfer to a heated dish, sprinkle with scallion garnish, and serve immediately.

Serves 4 to 6

LEMON NOODLES WITH MUSH-ROOMS
Ling Mung Mien

In China noodle dishes abound, but not many with the taste of fresh lemon. This is my design, and combining the lemon's tartness with the pungency of the cooked mushrooms is, I believe, exciting as well as unusual.

2 quarts water
2 teaspoons salt
½ pound dry rice noodles (thin, like capellini #11)
3 tablespoons Scallion Oil (page 37)
1½ teaspoons minced garlic
¾ teaspoon salt
1 teaspoon sugar
½ cup steamed black mushrooms (page 95), julienned
1 teaspoon grated lemon rind
1 tablespoon fresh lemon juice
4 teaspoons hot red pepper sauce
1 teaspoon sesame oil
2 tablespoons trimmed and finely sliced scallions

1. Place the water and 2 teaspoons salt in a large pot and bring to a boil. Add the noodles and cook for 1 minute, loosening them with chopsticks as they cook. Cook until *al dente*, then remove from heat, run cold water into the pot, and drain noodles through a strainer. Place the noodles back in the pot, run cold water in, and strain again. Repeat once more, then reserve.

2. Place a large pot over high heat. Add the Scallion Oil, garlic, ¾ teaspoon salt, and sugar. Stir. When the garlic turns light brown, add the mushrooms. Stir for 30 seconds, then add the lemon rind and the reserved noodles. Lower the heat to medium and mix thoroughly.

3. Add the lemon juice and toss. Add the hot red pepper sauce and toss. When the noodles are well coated, add the sesame oil and toss again. When the noodles are well mixed, turn off the heat, add sliced scallions, mix well, and serve immediately on a heated platter.

Serves 4 to 6

GINGER NOODLES
Geung Chung Mien

This noodle dish represents the Cantonese kitchen, with its respect for an individual vegetable, ginger root, at its finest. It contains the taste of fresh ginger, particularly the young ginger of spring and summer and, even lately, of fall. The taste is subtle and less hot than that of older ginger root.

8 cups cold water
2 teaspoons salt
½ pound fresh flat noodles, like linguine

Sauce ingredients

1 tablespoon soy sauce
1 teaspoon sugar
⅓ cup Vegetable Stock (pages 31–32)
1 teaspoon sesame oil
Pinch of white pepper

To complete the dish

2 tablespoons peanut oil

4 tablespoons fresh young ginger, shredded (if unavailable, use
   3 tablespoons regular ginger)

1¼ cup scallions, trimmed, cut into 1½-inch pieces, and white portions
   quartered lengthwise

1. Place the water and salt in a large pot and bring to a boil. Add the noodles and cook for 30 seconds, until *al dente*, stirring and loosening them with chopsticks or a fork as they cook. Turn off the heat, run cold tap water into pot, and drain the noodles immediately through a strainer. Place the noodles back in the pot and fill with cold water. Mix with your hands and drain the noodles again through strainer. Repeat once more, until the noodles are cool. Allow to drain for 10 or 15 minutes, loosening with chopsticks to assist draining. Reserve.

2. Combine the sauce ingredients and reserve.

3. Heat a wok over high heat for 45 seconds. Add the peanut oil and coat the wok with a spatula. When a wisp of white smoke appears, add the ginger and stir-fry for 30 seconds. Add the noodles and mix well with the ginger until noodles become very hot.

4. Add the scallions, mix well, and cook for 1 minute. Make a well in the center of the mixture, stir the reserved sauce, and pour it into the well. Cook for 1 minute, mixing well, making certain the noodles are coated. Turn off the heat, transfer to a heated serving dish, and serve immediately.

Serves 4 to 6

CURRIED RICE NOODLES
Gah Lee Chau Mai Fun

This dish originated in Singapore and was first brought into Canton by immigrants as "Singapore noodles." Cooking rice noodles with curry has become a tradition in the Cantonese kitchen. Here is one adaptation, my own.

8 ounces dry rice noodles

3 quarts warm water

Curry mixture

1 tablespoon peanut oil

2 teaspoons minced ginger

1½ teaspoons minced garlic

2 tablespoons minced fresh coriander

1½ tablespoons curry powder mixed with 1½ tablespoons Vegetable Stock (pages 31–32)

3 tablespoons Vegetable Stock (pages 31–32)

2½ tablespoons oyster sauce combined with 1 tablespoon double dark soy sauce

To complete the dish

3½ tablespoons peanut oil

1¼-inch-thick slice fresh ginger

¼ teaspoon salt

1¼ cups snow peas, julienned diagonally

6 scallions, cut into 1½-inch slices, white portions quartered

1 medium sweet red pepper, julienned (1 cup)

1. Soak the noodles in warm water until moderately softened, 15 to 20 minutes. Drain well, tossing occasionally to assist the draining process. Allow to stand at least an hour.

2. As the noodles drain, prepare curry mixture. In a saucepan, heat the peanut oil over high heat. Add ginger, garlic, and coriander and stir. When the garlic turns light brown, add the curry powder–stock mixture. Stir and allow to cook for 1 minute. Add the vegetable stock, stir and simmer for 10 minutes, covered, over lower heat. Add the oyster sauce–soy sauce mixture and stir in well. Cook for 5 more minutes, stirring 3 or 4 times until smooth and blended. Reserve.

3. Heat a wok over high heat, add 1½ tablespoons peanut oil, and coat the wok with a spatula. When a wisp of white smoke appears, add the slice of ginger and salt. Cook for about 30 seconds, until the ginger turns light brown. Add all vegetables and stir-fry for 1½ minutes, or until the snow peas turn bright green. Turn off the heat, drain, and set aside in a bowl.

4. Heat the wok over high heat for 45 seconds and add the remaining peanut oil to coat the wok. When a wisp of white smoke appears, add the noodles, allowing them to slide over the spatula into the wok to avoid spattering the oil. Loosen the noodles with chopsticks. If the noodles begin to burn, lower the heat. Cook for 5 minutes, until the noodles are very hot, then add the curry mixture and combine well with the noodles. Add the reserved vegetables and stir thoroughly. Turn off the heat, transfer to a heated serving dish, and serve immediately.

Serves 4 to 6

MUNG BEAN NOODLE SOUP
Leung Hau Mien Fou Tong

These very special noodles, made with the starch of ground mung beans and water, have a fine, chewy texture. The Chinese call them "dragon mouth" noodles. They are added to soups, tossed with other foods, and used in stir-fried dishes. They can be used, in short, just as any other noodle. The only difference is in their inherent elasticity. In this recipe I have combined the noodles with some special ingredients from the Chiu Chow kitchen that make it unique.

4 bundles of mung bean noodles (see note below)

2 tablespoons peanut oil

1½-inch-thick slice ginger, lightly smashed

1 teaspoon minced garlic

1 cup onions, cut into ¼-inch dice

2 soybean cakes (⅓ package), thinly sliced

2 cups Tientsin bok choy, washed, dried, and cut crosswise into ¼-inch pieces

2 tablespoons Tientsin preserved vegetable, minced

¾ cup quartered straw mushrooms

3½ cups Vegetable Stock (pages 31–32)

¼ teaspoon salt

5 tablespoons Chiu Chow Sweet Soy (page 41)

1 cup trimmed scallions, diagonally cut into ¼-inch slices

3 tablespoons minced fresh coriander

1. Place the noodles in a large bowl of hot water and allow to soak for 15 minutes, or until they soften. Drain and cut with kitchen shears to 5-inch lengths. Reserve.

2. Heat a wok over high heat for 30 seconds. Add the peanut oil and ginger and stir. Cook for 20 seconds. Add the garlic and stir briefly. Add the onions, stir, and cook until they soften, about 3 minutes. Add the bean cake slices, stir, and cook for 1 minute. Add the bok choy and stir. Add the preserved vegetable and mix. Add the mushrooms and mix. Add the vegetable stock and salt and stir well. Add the Chiu Chow Sweet Soy and mix. Cover the wok and bring to a boil over high heat. Lower the heat to medium and cook for 3 minutes, or until the bok choy softens.

3. Return the heat back to high, add the scallions, and stir. Add mung bean noodles, mix, and bring back to a boil. Turn off the heat. Stir in the coriander. Serve the soup and noodles in individual bowls.

Serves 4 to 6

Note: Mung bean noodles come rolled together in bundles in large, plastic-wrapped bags, usually 8 bundles to a package. They may be kept indefinitely, in a dry place, until used.

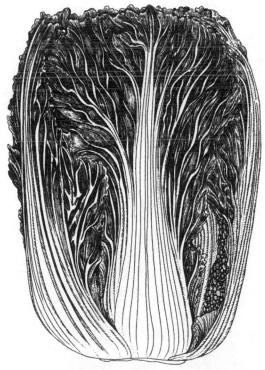

Tientsin Bok Choy

MUNG BEAN NOODLES WITH TIENTSIN BOK CHOY
Leung Hau Mien Tientsin Bok Choy

The delightful chewiness of the mung bean noodles, these "dragon mouth" noodles, contrasts with the crispness of the bok choy and the water chestnuts in this dish. It begins as a traditional stir-fry, but the noodles, in effect, replace the cooked rice that would be eaten with it.

4 bundles of mung bean noodles (see note below)

Sauce ingredients

1 teaspoon dark soy sauce

1 teaspoon light soy sauce

1½ tablespoons oyster sauce

1½ teaspoons sugar

1½ teaspoons sesame oil

1 tablespoon Shao-Hsing wine or sherry

1½ tablespoons cornstarch

Pinch of white pepper

1 cup Vegetable Stock (pages 31–32)

To complete the dish

2½ tablespoons peanut oil

1½-inch-thick slice ginger, lightly smashed

2 teaspoons minced garlic

½ teaspoon salt

8 small Chinese dried black mushrooms, soaked in hot water for 1½ hours, drained, stems removed, and caps julienned

½ pound Tientsin bok choy, leaves and stalks separated and cut crosswise into ¼-inch pieces

⅓ cup bamboo shoots, julienned

⅓ cup fresh water chestnuts, peeled and julienned

½ cup sweet yellow peppers, julienned

2 tablespoons Vegetable Stock (pages 31–32)

1. Place the noodles in a large bowl of hot water and allow to soak for 15 minutes, or until they soften. Drain, dry, and cut into 5-inch lengths with kitchen shears. Reserve.

2. Combine the sauce ingredients and reserve.

3. Heat a wok over high heat for 30 seconds. Add the peanut oil, ginger, garlic, and salt. Stir briefly. Add the mushrooms, stir, and cook for 30 seconds. Add the bok choy stalks, mix, and cook for 1 minute. Add the bamboo shoots and water chestnuts, stir, and cook for 30 seconds. Add the peppers and stir. Add the bok choy leaves and stir. Add the vegetable stock. Stir-fry and cook for 3 minutes, or until bok choy stalks are tender. Make a well in the center of the mixture. Stir the sauce and pour it in. Mix thoroughly. When the sauce begins to bubble and turn brown, add the reserved noodles and toss thoroughly, making certain the noodles are well coated and hot. Turn off the heat, place on a heated serving platter, and serve immediately.

Serves 4 to 6

Note: Mung bean noodles come rolled together in bundles in large plastic bags, usually 8 bundles to a package. They may be kept indefinitely, in a dry place, until use.

VEGETARIAN SPRING ROLLS
Jai Chun Geun

This is a delicate preparation, quite different indeed from the so-called egg roll that evolved from it. In Sha nghai and Canton it is traditionally made with vegetables combined with pork or shrimp. This all-vegetable roll has a fresh and different taste.

Sauce ingredients

1½ teaspoons mushroom soy sauce

1½ tablespoons oyster sauce

1 teaspoon Shao-Hsing wine or sherry

1 teaspoon white vinegar

1 teaspoon sesame oil

1 teaspoon sugar

½ teaspoon salt

Pinch of white pepper

1 tablespoon cornstarch mixed with 1½ tablespoons water

To complete the dish

5 cups peanut oil

10 Chinese dried black mushrooms, soaked in hot water for 30 minutes, rinsed, squeezed dry, stems discarded, and caps thinly sliced

1 bunch scallions, trimmed, cut into 1½-inch pieces, and white portions quartered lengthwise

1 large Tientsin cabbage (about 1½ pounds), stalks quartered lengthwise and cut into ¼-inch slices

18 spring roll skins (sold in plastic bags)

Sweet and Sour Sauce, for dipping (page 41)

Chili Soy Sauce, for dipping (page 42)

1. In a small bowl stir together the sauce ingredients. Mix well and reserve.

2. Heat a wok over high heat for 30 seconds. Add 2½ tablespoons of the peanut oil and coat the wok with a spatula. When a wisp of white smoke appears, add the mushrooms and scallions and stir-fry for 45 seconds. Add the cabbage and stir-fry until wilted, about 2 minutes. Make a well in the center of the

vegetables, stir the sauce, and pour it into the well. Stir to combine all the ingredients and cook until the sauce bubbles and thickens, about 1 minute. Remove from the heat and transfer to a shallow dish. Let cool to room temperature, then cover and refrigerate for at least 8 hours, or overnight.

3. Lay a spring roll skin on a flat surface with a corner facing you. Place 2 tablespoons of the filling across the bottom third of the wrapper. Brush water around the edges of the entire wrapper. Fold up the bottom corner and roll once. Then fold in both sides and roll up all the way. Press the end to seal. Repeat with remaining wrappers and filling.

4. In a large saucepan or deep-fryer, or a wok, heat the remaining peanut oil to 350°F. Deep-fry the spring rolls in batches, without crowding them, turning frequently, until golden brown, about 3 to 5 minutes. Drain on paper towels and serve with Sweet and Sour Sauce or Chili Soy Sauce, or both.

Serves 4 to 6

Note: These rolls can be frozen after they have been lightly browned. To cook, defrost, allow to come to room temperature, and dry off moisture with paper towels. Deep-fry until golden brown.

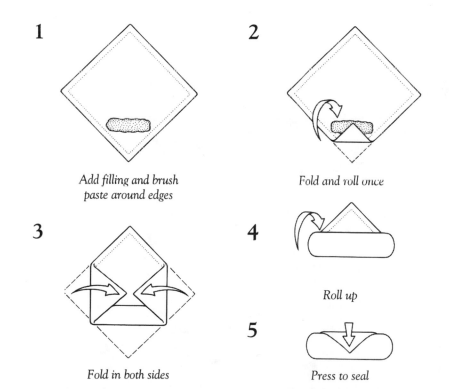

1 Add filling and brush paste around edges

2 Fold and roll once

3 Fold in both sides

4 Roll up

5 Press to seal

BEAN SPROUT SPRING ROLLS
Nga Choy Chun Geun

Here is another vegetable combination enclosed in a wrapper. The key to these preparations is choosing compatible vegetables while remaining true to the tradition of the spring roll.

1 pound bean sprouts
6 cups cold water

Paste ingredients

1½ tablespoons cornstarch
1½ tablespoons cold water
¾ cup boiling water

To complete the dish

1½ tablespoons peanut oil, plus 5 cups for deep-frying
¾ cup peeled and julienned carrots
2½ tablespoons julienned Szechuan mustard pickle
1½ tablespoons shredded fresh ginger (young ginger preferred)
½ teaspoon salt
1 teaspoon sugar
16 square Shanghai spring roll skins (see note below)
Sweet Scallion Sauce (page 37)
Hot Mustard (page 44)

1. Place the cold water in a pot and bring to a boil over high heat. Add the bean sprouts and make certain they are completely submerged. Cook for 10 seconds. Turn off the heat. Run cold water into the pot and drain. Repeat. Make certain the sprouts are drained thoroughly.

2. To make the paste, mix the cornstarch and cold water until well blended. Add the boiling water and stir to make a smooth, thick paste. Reserve.

3. Heat a wok over high heat for 30 seconds. Add 1½ tablespoons peanut oil and coat the wok with a spatula. When a wisp of white smoke appears, add the carrots, Szechuan mustard pickle, ginger, salt, and sugar. Stir-fry for 1 minute. Add the bean sprouts and stir-fry for 1 minute more. Turn off the heat. Transfer the bean sprout mixture to a strainer and drain.

4. The skins tend to stick together. Allow them to stand for an hour before use. Separate the 16 skins to be used and cover with plastic wrap. Use one at a time. Place 2 tablespoons of bean sprout mixture in a 3-inch length diagonally across a corner of a skin. Brush the corner with the cornstarch paste. Fold and roll tightly. Brush the edges of the skin with paste and fold in as you roll to create a tight, sealed cylinder. Repeat with remaining skins.

5. Heat a wok over high heat for 40 seconds. Add the 6 cups peanut oil. Heat to 350°F. Place 4 rolls at a time in the oil and allow to cook 2 to 3 minutes, until they brown. Keep turning to ensure they brown evenly. Repeat until all 16 are done. Serve with Sweet Scallion Sauce as a dip, or with Hot Mustard, or both.

Serves 4 to 6

Note: Shanghai spring roll skins, white in color, are kept in either the refrigerated or frozen sections of markets. They are round or square and are sold by weight or by number of slices. Ask for them by name. They may be kept refrigerated for 4 to 5 days. Wrapped in plastic and frozen, they will keep for 2 months.

"PORK" EGG ROLLS
Jiu Yuk Dan Geun

The egg roll does not exist in China. It is a Western invention, patterned after the far more delicate spring roll. Nevertheless, the egg roll has become, over the years, an expected entry on the typical Chinese-American restaurant menu. Usually there is no egg inside an egg roll. It is called "egg" because it is wrapped in a skin that is often made with egg. Instead of the pork that is customarily in an egg roll, I have used soybean cakes. The result is a happy combination, even if it is not genuinely Chinese.

8 cups water

One 1-inch-wide slice fresh ginger, lightly smashed

2 teaspoons salt

2-pound head of green cabbage, tough outer leaves removed, halved,
    corded, and finely chopped

1 medium onion, cut into ¼-inch dice

2 celery stalks, cut into ¼-inch dice

Paste ingredients

2 tablespoons cornstarch

2 tablespoons cold water

1 cup boiling water

To finish the dish

3 soybean cakes (½ package), cut into ¼-inch dice

1 teaspoon sesame oil

¾ teaspoon sugar

⅛ teaspoon salt

12 egg roll wrappers

5 cups peanut oil

Hot Mustard, for dipping (page 44)

1. In a pot place the water, ginger, and 2 teaspoons salt. Cover and bring to a boil over high heat. Place the cabbage, onions, and celery in the water and blanch until cabbage turns bright green, about 1½ minutes. Turn off the heat, run cold water into the pot, and drain. Discard the ginger. Allow the vegetables to cool, place in a towel, and squeeze out excess water. Place in a large bowl and reserve.

2. To make the paste, combine the cornstarch and cold water until well blended. Add the boiling water and stir to a smooth consistency. Reserve.

3. To the bowl of vegetables add the diced bean curd, sesame oil, sugar, and ⅛ teaspoon salt and mix thoroughly. Divide mixture into 12 equal portions.

4. As you use an egg roll wrapper, keep the others under a damp cloth. Place a portion of the filling in a line diagonally across one corner of the wrapper. Brush some of the cornstarch paste on the corner, fold to cover the filling, then roll. Brush the edges of the wrapper with the paste. Fold in the ends and roll tightly to make a sealed cylinder. Repeat with remaining wrappers.

5. Heat a wok over high heat for 40 seconds. Add peanut oil and heat to 350°F. Slide the egg rolls into the oil, 4 at a time. Cook, turning the rolls, to ensure that they brown evenly, about 4 to 5 minutes. Remove and drain on paper towels. As you cook, regulate the heat so the rolls will not burn. Cook until all egg rolls are done. Serve immediately with Hot Mustard.

Serves 4 to 6

FRESH BEAN CURD SKIN
VEGETABLE ROLLS I

Sin Zhu Pei Guen

Rolling foods into wrappings of various kinds has become most popular of late in the West, although in Asia the practice has been common for centuries. The use of bean curd wrappings, egg roll skins, rice paper, won ton wraps, Shanghai spring roll skins, and various vegetable leaves has become widespread. Here is a recipe for an unusual roll, one that is commonly served in dim sum restaurants and on special occasions in the home. It requires some time, but the result is surely worth the effort.

½ cup steamed and julienned Chinese dried black mushrooms (page 95)
½ cup finely julienned carrots
¾ cup trimmed and finely shredded scallions

Paste ingredients

1 tablespoon cornstarch
1 tablespoon cold water
½ cup boiling water

To complete the dish

2 sheets fresh bean curd skin (see note below)
5 cups peanut oil
2 tablespoons Sweet Scallion Sauce (page 37)

1. Prepare the steamed mushrooms. Allow to cool and reserve.

2. To make the paste, combine the cornstarch and cold water. Add the boiling water. Stir into a smooth paste and reserve.

3. To prepare the bean curd skins, cut the sheets into ten 6-inch squares. Cover the squares with plastic wrap to retain their softness. Before using each square, dampen it to help it remain pliable.

4. Toss the mushrooms, carrots, and scallions together, then divide them into 10 equal portions. Place a portion diagonally across one corner of a bean curd skin and shape it into a 2½-inch length. Brush the square with a bit of the cornstarch paste, fold the corner over the vegetables, and roll tightly. Brush the edges of the sheet with paste as you roll, sufficient to seal and create a cylinder. Repeat the process to make 10 rolls.

5. Heat a wok over high heat for 40 seconds. Add the peanut oil and heat to 350°F. When a wisp of white smoke appears, place 3 of the rolls in a Chinese strainer and lower into oil. Deep-fry until they turn brown and become crisp, about 3 to 4 minutes. Keep turning to allow all sides to brown evenly. Remove. Allow to drain on paper towels. Repeat until all 10 rolls are fried. Serve immediately with Sweet Scallion Sauce, as a dip, in individual soy dishes.

Serves 4 to 6

Note: Fresh bean curd skin sheets come frozen in packages. They are large, yellow-brown circles 24 inches in diameter and come 8 to a 1-pound package. They are folded in half in the package so that they resemble large half-moons. Often the packages read "spring roll pastry," but they should not be confused with spring roll skins. Request them by name from the Chinese or Asian grocer; ask for *sin wu pei*, which translates as "fresh bean curd skin."

When frozen they are brittle, but out of the freezer they will defrost almost immediately and become soft and pliable. Refrigerated and wrapped in plastic, they will keep for about 3 weeks.

If these skins are unavailable, use Shanghai spring roll skins in their place (see page 279).

FRESH BEAN CURD SKIN VEGETABLE ROLLS II

Sin Wu Pei Geun Yee

This recipe is made in the same manner as the previous fresh bean curd skin rolls, but I have made these rolls with an entirely different, fresh filling. They become totally new with these flavors, the only common denominator being the skins themselves. The word *yee* added to their name simply means "two."

½ cup sun-dried tomatoes, soaked in hot water until softened, and julienned
¾ cup julienned jícama, tossed with ⅛ teaspoon salt
¾ cup finely sliced onion, tossed with ⅛ teaspoon salt

Paste ingredients

1 tablespoon cornstarch
1 tablespoon cold water
½ cup boiling water

To complete the dish

2 sheets fresh bean curd skin (to yield 10 squares)
5 cups peanut oil
Hot Mustard, for dipping (page 44)
Chinese chili sauce (available in jars, Tabasco sauce may be subtituted)

1. Mix the vegetables together in a bowl. Reserve.
2. To make the paste, combine the cornstarch with the cold water. Add the boiling water. Stir into a smooth paste. Reserve.
3. To prepare the bean curd skins, cut from the sheets ten 6-inch squares. Cover the squares with plastic wrap to retain their softness. Before using each square, dampen it to help it remain pliable.
4. Divide the mixed vegetables into 10 equal portions. Place a portion diagonally across one corner of a bean curd skin and shape it into a 2½-inch length. Brush the square with a bit of the cornstarch paste, fold the corner over the vegetables, and roll tightly. Brush the edges of the square with paste as you roll, sufficient to seal and create a cylinder. Repeat the process to make 10 rolls.

5. Heat a wok over high heat for 40 seconds. Add the peanut oil and heat to 350°F. When a wisp of white smoke appears, place 3 of the rolls in a Chinese strainer and lower into the oil. Deep-fry until they turn brown and become crisp, about 3 to 4 minutes. Keep turning to allow all sides to brown evenly. Remove. Allow to drain on paper towels. Repeat until all 10 rolls are fried. Serve immediately with 1 tablespoon Hot Mustard (page 44) mixed with 1½ teaspoons Chinese chili sauce.

Serves 4 to 6

RICE PAPER VEGETABLE ROLLS
Mai Jee Saw Choi Geun

Rice paper is the ideal wrapper for fresh, raw vegetables. These wrappers have a neutral taste and fulfill their function of holding the vegetables and seasonings without interfering.

2 ounces fine rice noodles

Sauce ingredients

1 tablespoon white vinegar
2 tablespoons soy sauce
2 teaspoons sugar
2 tablespoons Vegetable Stock (pages 31–32)
Pinch of white pepper
1½ tablespoons minced fresh red chilies
1 teaspoon minced garlic

To complete the dish

1½ tablespoons peanut oil
1½ teaspoons minced garlic
1 soybean cake, thinly sliced
1¼ cups shredded carrots
½ cup julienned jícama (or fresh water chestnuts)
1¼ cups fresh bean sprouts
12 sprigs fresh mint
24 rice paper wrappers (see note below)

1. Place the rice noodles in a bowl of hot water and soak for 45 minutes. Remove, drain well. Cut into 4-inch lengths and reserve.

2. Combine the sauce ingredients in a bowl. Reserve.

3. Heat a wok over high heat for 30 seconds. Add the peanut oil and coat the wok with a spatula. When a wisp of white smoke appears, add the garlic and stir briefly. Add the bean cake slices and stir-fry for 1½ minutes. Turn off the heat. Remove to a small bowl. Reserve.

4. Mound the rice noodles in the center of a platter. Around the noodles arrange the carrots, jícama (or water chestnuts), bean sprouts, bean cake slices, and fresh mint. Have the sauce and rice papers at hand, along with a shallow plate of cool water.

5. Wet each sheet of rice paper by passing it through the water, then stack the papers. They will soften but will not stick together, and you will be able to remove each wrapper individually. To eat, place a wrapper on your plate and mound on it items from the platter, to your taste. Place a bit of the sauce, to taste, on top. Then roll the wrapper tightly around the mixture, fold in the ends, and roll into a cigar-shaped bundle. Eat as wrapped or with a further dip into the accompanying sauce. Or serve with Crystal Sauce as a dip (page 43).

Serves 4 to 6

Note: Rice paper wrappers come in 1-pound packages usually labeled "rice paper." Most of them are from Thailand and are either round or triangular. Usually the rounds are 7 inches in diameter, but occasionally they are larger. Each package contains at least 50 wrappers. Wrapped in plastic and stored in a cool, dry place, they will keep indefinitely.

RICE PAPER SPRING ROLL
Mai Jee Chun Geun

Rice paper makes an admirable fried spring roll. One would not think so, to look at a moist rice paper wrapper in its translucent state. But these have good tensile strength; when fried they emerge crisp and do not at all lose their shape. This filling, by the way, is equally good as a stir-fry served with cooked rice.

½ cup Chinese dried black mushrooms
1 package bean thread noodles
¾ pound Tientsin bok choy

Sauce ingredients

½ cup Vegetable Stock (pages 31–32)
1 tablespoon oyster sauce
1½ teaspoons sugar
¼ teaspoon salt
Pinch of white pepper
1½ tablespoons cornstarch

To complete the dish

2 tablespoons peanut oil
2 tablespoons shredded fresh ginger
¼ teaspoon salt
⅓ cup fresh water chestnuts, peeled and julienned
2 tablespoons Vegetable Stock, if needed (pages 31–32)
20 round rice paper wrappers, 7 inches in diameter
5 cups peanut oil
Crystal Sauce, for dipping (page 43)

Soak the mushrooms in hot water to cover for 1½ hours. Wash, squeeze dry, discard stems, and slice the caps finely. Reserve. Soak the bean thread noodles in hot water to cover for ½ hour. Drain and cut into 5-inch strands. Reserve. Wash the bok choy, dry, and cut crosswise into thin slices. Separate the stalks and leaves. Reserve.

2. Combine the sauce ingredients and reserve.

3. Heat a wok over high heat for 30 seconds. Add the peanut oil and coat the wok with a spatula. When a wisp of white smoke appears, add the ginger and salt and stir briefly. Add the mushrooms, stir, and cook for 1 minute. Add the bok choy stalks, stir, and cook for 2 minutes. Add the water chestnuts and bok choy leaves and stir-fry for 2 minutes. If the mixture is too dry, add 1 tablespoon of vegetable stock. Continue to stir. If still dry, add remaining vegetable stock. Make a well in the center of the mixture, stir the sauce, and pour it in. Mix well. When sauce begins to bubble and turn brown, turn off the heat. Add the bean thread noodles and mix well. Remove to a bowl and allow to cool. For best results, refrigerate uncovered for 4 hours.

4. Moisten each rice paper sheet by passing it through a shallow pan of cold water. Lay it flat and it will soften as you work. Place 2 tablespoons of the filling, in a 3-inch line, at one end of the wrapper. Fold tightly and roll, then fold in the sides and continue to roll to create a tight, cigar-shaped bundle. Repeat with remaining wrappers.

5. Heat a wok over high heat for 40 seconds. Add the peanut oil and heat to 350°F. Turn off the heat. Slide 5 spring rolls into the oil, one at a time, waiting 20 seconds between each addition. Fry them, regulating the heat and removing each spring roll as it turns golden brown (2 to 3 minutes). Drain on paper towels. Repeat with 3 more batches, until all 20 spring rolls are done. Serve with Crystal Sauce as a dip.

Serves 4 to 6

Note: For convenience, these spring rolls may be prepared and half fried (about 1½ to 2 minutes) in advance on the day they are to be served. Allow to cool to room temperature. Then cover with plastic wrap. At serving time, fry again until golden brown, about 1 to 1½ minutes. I have tried both ways of preparing them several times and I actually prefer half-cooking them in advance, since when they are cooked the final time the wrappers are more crisp.

A caution: Test the rice paper wrappers. Different brands come in different thicknesses. Some may therefore require more moistening than others. If you moisten too much, the rice paper can become a formless mass. If you moisten too little, they remain brittle and will snap. It may require a couple of tests before you come to know your batch, but you have plenty with which to test.

SURPRISE PACKAGE
But Jee Lai Mut

百奇
奇乱
粉

This is my surprise. My inspiration was the poppers that are often part of young childrens' birthday parties. This wrapped surprise, this *but jee*, is a true discovery, filled with Chinese ingredients.

1 cake fresh bean curd
5 cups peanut oil, for deep-frying
½ cup steamed Chinese dried black mushrooms (page 95), shredded
2½ tablespoons Pickled Peaches (page 296)
8 sun-dried tomatoes, washed in hot water and shredded
⅓ cup scallions, white portions only, cut into 2-inch pieces and shredded
2 large, fresh water chestnuts, peeled and cut into ⅛-inch-thick julienne
16 won ton skins
Hot Mustard, for dipping (page 44)
Sweet and Sour Sauce, for dipping (page 41)

1. Place the bean curd in 4 cups of boiling water and boil for 5 minutes. Remove from the heat. Run cold water into the pot to cool. Drain. Repeat. Allow to cool. Cut into 16 equal strips and pat dry with paper towels. Heat 3 cups of the peanut oil in a wok over high heat to 350°F. Deep-fry the sliced bean curd for 3 to 4 minutes, until light brown. Remove from the oil and drain. Allow to cool. Reserve. Leave deep-frying oil in wok.

2. Steam and prepare mushrooms. Prepare all other ingredients and divide each into 16 equal portions.

3. Place a won ton skin, floured side down, on a dry plate. (Keep the remaining skins covered at all times with a damp towel.) Dip your fingers in water and wet the edges of the won ton skin. Place 1 portion of the filling in the center of the skin. Fold in half and squeeze along the wet edge to create an envelope. Twist both ends to seal. Repeat. (See page 290 for diagram.)

4. Add the remaining 2 cups peanut oil to the wok and heat over high heat. When a wisp of white smoke appears, slide a package down the side of the wok into the oil. Fry 3 or 4 packages at a time, turning constantly to ensure that the packages brown evenly. Fry for 2 minutes, or until golden brown. Remove, place in a strainer, and drain over a bowl. Repeat with all packages. Serve immediately with Hot Mustard or with Sweet and Sour Sauce.

Serves 4 to 6

MUSHROOM LETTUCE ROLLS
Sahng Choi Bau

The word *bau* translates as "wrapping" or "bundle," in this recipe the wrapping of iceberg lettuce around a stir-fried vegetable mix. This is my variation of a combination quite popular in China. In Canton in particular food is wrapped in lettuce bundles, with the filling varying by the season, so that the *bau* is often a surprise. (For me, the ideal season was summer, since the lettuce was so sweet then.) As with several other wrapper fillings, this may be served unwrapped as a stir-fry, with cooked rice.

¾ cup Chinese dried black mushrooms, soaked in hot water for 1½ hours
6 cups cold water
½ pound bean sprouts
2 tablespoons peanut oil
½ teaspoon salt
3 tablespoons minced fresh coriander
⅓ cup shredded Ginger Pickle (page 295)
1 cup finely julienned sweet red peppers
1 teaspoon sugar
1½ tablespoons oyster sauce
10 large iceberg lettuce leaves

1. Wash and squeeze dry the mushrooms. Discard the stems and finely slice the caps. Reserve.

2. Place the 6 cups cold water in a large pot. Cover and bring to a boil over high heat. Add the bean sprouts and water-blanch for 20 seconds. Remove from the heat. Run cold water into pot and drain. Repeat. Allow to dry. Reserve.

3. Heat a wok over high heat for 30 seconds. Add the peanut oil and coat the wok with a spatula. When a wisp of white smoke appears, add the salt and coriander and stir briefly. Add the mushrooms and stir-fry for 1½ minutes. Add the Ginger Pickle and stir. Add the peppers and stir briefly. Add the sugar and oyster sauce and mix well, to ensure that all the ingredients are well coated. Add the bean sprouts and toss to mix. Turn off the heat. Remove to a serving bowl.

4. Serve or allow self-service on individual lettuce leaves. Place a mound of filling, about 2 tablespoons, in the center of each leaf and fold the leaf around the filling to make a cylinder. Serve.

Serves 4 to 6

MUSHROOM WON TONS
Seung Gu Won Ton

This preparation, familiar to most of us, is usually made with pork and shrimp as its base. I have replaced these with fresh and dried mushrooms to give contrast and complementary tastes, and so we have "two-mushroom won tons."

Sauce ingredients

1 teaspoon sesame oil

1 teaspoon soy sauce

1 teaspoon Shao-Hsing wine or sherry

1¼ teaspoons sugar

Pinch of white pepper

1 tablespoon cornstarch

4 tablespoons Vegetable Stock (pages 31–32)

To complete the dish

2 tablespoons peanut oil

1½ teaspoons minced garlic

1½ teaspoons minced fresh ginger

½ teaspoon salt

3 large fresh water chestnuts, peeled and cut into ¼-inch dice

5 ounces fresh white mushrooms, cut into ¼-inch pieces

⅔ cup Chinese dried black mushrooms, soaked in hot water for 30 minutes, squeezed dry, stems removed, and caps cut into ¼-inch pieces

1 cup onions, chopped into ¼-inch pieces and tightly packed

24 won ton skins

½ tablespoon salt

1 tablespoon peanut oil

1. Combine the sauce ingredients in a bowl. Reserve.

2. Heat a wok over high heat for 40 seconds, add 2 tablespoons peanut oil, and coat the wok with a spatula. When a wisp of white smoke appears, add the garlic, ginger, and ½ teaspoon salt. Mix together. When the garlic turns light brown, add the fresh mushrooms, onions, and water chestnuts and stir-fry for 3 minutes, or until onions change color. Make a well in the center of the mixture, stir the sauce, and pour it in. Stir well to ensure that all ingredients are mixed thoroughly. Turn off the heat, transfer to a shallow dish, and allow to cool. Refrigerate at least 4 hours, or overnight.

3. Won ton skins should be kept in plastic wrap at room temperature. Twenty minutes before fashioning the won tons, peel off the plastic wrap and cover the skins with a wet towel. When working with one skin, be sure to keep the remainder under the towel.

4. Keep a bowl of water at hand so that the 4 edges of the won ton can be wetted. Place about 1 tablespoon of the mixture on the non-floured side of the skin. Wet the edges of the won ton, then fold the skin in half over the mixture and press the sides together to seal.

5. Once folded and sealed, wet the 2 corners of the folded side, then draw them together and squeeze with the fingers to create a bowlike dumpling. (It will look like a tortellini.) As each won ton is made, place it on a floured cookie sheet so that it will not stick.

6. Add ½ tablespoon salt and 1 tablespoon oil to 2 quarts of water and bring to a boil over high heat. Cook the won tons for 5 to 7 minutes, or until translucent. Stir with a wooden spoon while cooking.

7. Remove the won tons from the heat and run cold water into the pot. Drain. Run more cold water in. Drain again. Place on waxed paper and allow to dry.

Serves 4 to 6

Note: The above instructions are for making won tons that will be reserved and eaten later. They may, however, be eaten, boiled, as they come out of the water, or they may be added to a soup. For a soup, bring 3 cups of vegetable stock to a boil, add won tons, 3 for each person, and return to a boil. Add 4 cups of iceberg lettuce and bring back to a boil again. Turn off heat and serve immediately.

Note: Leftover won ton skins can be frozen. Double-wrap them in plastic wrap and aluminum foil. Be certain they are thoroughly dry before wrapping. Completely defrost before using.

POTATO AND MUSHROOM ROLLS
Sooh Gai Dong Gu Geun

This is an unusual role for the potato to play, but there is no reason at all why it should not be rolled in a wrapping, as other vegetables are. My combination of the sweet tartness of the ginger, the steamed potato, and the intensity of the mushrooms is a union of which I am proud.

2 medium-sized Idaho potatoes
6 cups cold water
¼ teaspoon salt, or to taste
2 cups steamed and shredded Chinese dried black mushrooms (page 95)
2 tablespoons shredded young fresh ginger
12 square won ton skins
5 cups peanut oil
Chiu Chow Sweet Soy, for dipping (page 41)

1. Wash the potatoes. Place the cold water and potatoes in a large pot. Cover and bring to a boil over high heat. Lower the heat to medium and cook for 50 minutes. Turn off the heat, remove the potatoes, and allow to cool. Peel off the skin. Cut the potatoes into pieces 2 inches by ⅓ inch, the shape of french fried potatoes. You should have 24 pieces. Sprinkle salt to taste over the potatoes.

2. Mix the mushrooms and ginger and divide into 12 equal portions.

3. Place a won ton skin on the work surface. Spread a half portion of the mushroom-ginger mixture in the center of the skin. Place 2 pieces of potato on top, then the remaining half of the mixture on top of them (see note below). Use your fingers to wet the edges of the skin. Pick up two sides and fold up over the filling. Press to seal. Also seal the other sides by squeezing. Fold the sealed end down like a flap to create a tight roll. Twist the sides of the skin so that the shape resembles a child's birthday noisemaker. Repeat until all rolls are made.

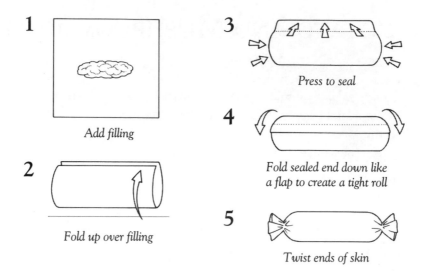

1 Add filling

2 Fold up over filling

3 Press to seal

4 Fold sealed end down like a flap to create a tight roll

5 Twist ends of skin

4. Heat a wok over high heat for 40 seconds. Add the peanut oil and heat to 350°F. Place 4 of the rolls in a Chinese strainer and lower into the oil. Cook until the rolls brown, about 2 minutes, turning them to ensure that they brown evenly. Remove and drain on paper towels. Repeat process until all rolls are done. Serve with Chiu Chow Sweet Soy as a dip.

Serves 4 to 6

Note: The reason why the mushroom-ginger mixture and the potatoes must be arranged in the skin so carefully is to maintain a balance as they deep-fry. If they are weighted to one side they will roll about and will not cook evenly.

Note: These dumpling skins, as all dumpling skins and wrappings, may be frozen. They will keep for 8 weeks. If you wish to keep them for earlier use, they may be refrigerated, but not for more than 3 days.

POTATO WATER DUMPLINGS
Sooh Jai Soi Gau

This is a unique version of a classical teahouse dumpling. A water dumpling is usually made with a filling of shrimp, pork, and chives, and there are other water dumplings as well. But never will you find, I believe, this dumpling in a restaurant, because the use of potatoes in vegetable dim sum is rare.

¾ pound Idaho potatoes (2 potatoes; see note below)

6 cups cold water

¾ cup onions, chopped into ¼-inch dice

1½ tablespoons peanut oil

2 scallions, trimmed and finely sliced

4 fresh water chestnuts, peeled and cut into ⅛-inch dice (⅓ cup)

½ teaspoon salt

½ teaspoon sugar

1½ tablespoons oyster sauce

2 teaspoons sesame oil

24 round water dumpling skins, 3½ inches in diameter (see note below)

8 cups water

1½ teaspoons salt

1 tablespoon peanut oil

1 tablespoon Hot Mustard (page 44) mixed with 1½ teaspoons Chinese chili sauce for serving

1. Wash the potatoes, place in a pot along with the 6 cups cold water, and bring to a boil, covered, over high heat. Lower the heat and cook for 50 minutes. Turn off the heat, remove the potatoes, and allow to cool. Peel and mash them coarsely. Reserve.

2. As the potatoes cool, saute the onions in 1½ tablespoons peanut oil for 3 to 4 minutes, or until they soften and become translucent. Turn off the heat. Place the onions in a mixing bowl, add the mashed potatoes, scallions, water chestnuts, ½ teaspoon salt, sugar, oyster sauce, and sesame oil, and combine thoroughly.

3. Remove the skins from the refrigerator at least 30 minutes before use. Keep the skins at hand, covered with a damp cloth. Use one at a time, keeping the others covered. Place 1 tablespoon of filling in the center. Wet the entire border of the round skin and fold in half to create a half-moon shape. With thumb and index finger squeeze the edges, crimping them to seal. The border seal should be about ½ inch wide. Repeat until 12 dumplings are made.

4. In a large pot place the 8 cups water, 1½ teaspoons salt, and 1 tablespoon peanut oil. Cover and bring to a boil over high heat. Add the dumplings, stir, return to a boil, and cook for 1½ minutes. Turn off the heat. Run cold water into the pot to stop the cooking process. Drain and serve immediately with the Hot Mustard–chili sauce mixture.

Serves 4 to 6

Note: I suggest using 2 potatoes because they will cook more quickly than will 1 large potato.

Note: These skins are usually labeled "water dumpling skins." Occasionally they are not, so simply ask for them, or for round dumpling skins. They come in various sizes, from 3½ to 4 inches in diameter. If unable to find them, use won ton skins and cut them into rounds. See page 288 for storage instructions.

酸

頹 *Seun*

Pickles and Salads

Among the treats of the table I remember vividly from the time I was growing up in China were pickles, or *seun*—sour, tart, and salty vegetables and fruits with perhaps a little leavening sweetness, foods that I and my cousins would plead for. And we would laugh, for when we had our pickles and enjoyed them we would shout "*ho seun,*" which we knew had two meanings. *Ho seun* translates as "very sour," but it also sounds precisely like the words that mean "very good grandchild." So we would eat our pickles and shout, for the benefit of the ears of Ah Paw, our grandmother, how good we were.

Pickles were important in our house. In summer there were always vegetables and fruit in excess of what we needed for our daily table, and so we pickled bok choy, mustard greens, turnips, cucumbers, jícama (which we called *sah gut*), ginger, cabbage, cauliflower, peaches, pears, baby green mangoes, and watermelon rind. We would place them in white vinegar, add salt and sugar—with some we also added garlic—and let them soak and absorb the flavors. I remember Ah Paw telling everybody precisely how much of each ingredient to add. She would say how many catties of vegetables or fruit were to be pickled (a catty is 1 pound 4 ounces); then she would quickly dictate the amount of vinegar, salt, and sugar to be added, or whether garlic was necessary. I do not know how she was able to do it so quickly, but she was. And she did not even go out to the kitchen of her house; it would come from her as she sat on the couch in her salon.

Pickling is an old art in China. From discovered remains and from writings of the many dynasties, it has been learned that vast numbers of foods were pickled, not only for preservation but for taste and variety. As far back as the Chou dynasty, which stretched from one thousand to two hundred years before Christ, the imperial court had on its culinary staff an official pickler, a position that also existed during the Tang dynasty of A.D. 618 to 907, and presumably in the years in between.

Through history, the Chinese have pickled chestnuts, hazelnuts, bamboo shoots, and the red dates known as jujubes. The Tangs pickled soybeans and red and white garlic; and the Sungs the growing tips of melon plants, perhaps our zucchini blossoms. Under the Ch'ings, the last dynasty, which ended in 1912, Chinese cabbage was put in brine, cucumbers were pickled in soy and vinegar, and eggplant too was pickled.

Pickles were, and are, eaten as snacks or as condiments accompanying meals. It is customary in many of today's Chinese restaurants to place small dishes of pickled cabbage, cucumbers, carrots, or chilies on the table. Many pickles are used as bases for, or ingredients in, salads. I grew up with all kinds of salads at our meals, many of which are to be found in this section.

Fruits too are *seun*—sour, tart, but balanced by the innate sweetness of the fruit, or occasionally by a touch of sugar. To this day, no week goes by, particularly in summer, when I do not make at least two or three of the salads I recall from my girlhood.

GINGER PICKLE
Wor Mei Dzi Geung

This should be made only with young ginger which absorbs the pickling flavors much more easily than does older ginger. You can find pickled ginger in jars in food markets, and it is creditable, but it's better to make it yourself. It adds so much to other foods.

4 cups water
½ teaspoon baking soda
¾ pound fresh, young ginger, peeled and thinly sliced

Marinade ingredients

¾ teaspoon salt
⅓ cup white vinegar
½ cup sugar

1. In a large pot bring water and baking soda to a boil. Add the ginger and boil for 30 seconds to 1 minute. Remove from the heat. Run cold water into the pot to reduce the temperature. Drain. Add cold water a second time and drain. Repeat a third time. Drain well, then place the ginger in a bowl.

2. Combine the marinade ingredients in a bowl. Add the marinade to the ginger. Mix thoroughly. Cover and refrigerate for at least 24 hours before serving.

   Note: Ginger pickles placed in a tightly closed jar will keep, refrigerated, for at least 3 months. Young ginger is occasionally difficult to obtain. It is usually available only twice each year, in late spring and late fall.

PICKLED PEACHES

Soon Tim Toh

Pickled peaches are a favorite preparation in Canton, and peaches are pickled as soon as they become available, usually in May or June. Peaches are symbolic of long life and are traditionally served on birthdays; in the months when peaches are not available, peach-shaped steamed buns, *sao bau* ("long-life buns"), are served on birthdays instead.

I use these pickles either separately or in conjunction with other pickles that appear in these pages. They are ideal tossed in cool salads or in stir-fries.

2 pounds fresh peaches, very hard, but with color indicating that they are
ripening (about 8 peaches)
2 cups white vinegar
3¾ cups cold water
⅔ cup sugar (see note below)
2¼ teaspoons salt

1. Wash the peaches well. Dry thoroughly. Do not slice or peel. Reserve.

2. In an oversized glass jar sufficiently large to hold all the peaches plus the pickling ingredients, place the vinegar, water, sugar, and salt. Mix well with a wooden spoon until sugar and salt are completely dissolved.

3. Add the peaches and stir well. Cover tightly. (A jar with a plastic screw top is preferred. If unavailable, place a piece of plastic wrap over the mouth of the jar before putting the lid on.) Refrigerate for 3 days, untouched, before serving. The peaches will keep, refrigerated in the covered jar, for 3 to 4 months.

Note: These peaches have a pleasing sweet and sour taste, which in Chinese is called *war mei,* or "even taste." If you prefer a sweeter taste, you can add 2 additional teaspoons of sugar to the pickling mixture, but this must be done at preparation time. Sugar should not be added later, for its sweetness will not penetrate the peaches once they have been pickled.

PICKLED PEARS
Soon Tim Sah Leh

China is home to many varieties of pear. For these pickled pears I recommend the Bosc, for it is closest to the pear we refer to in China as *sah leh*, or "sand pear," which is round, almost apple-shaped, and crisp.

2 pounds Bosc pears, very hard, barely ripe (5 or 6 pears)
1⅓ cups white vinegar
1⅓ cups cold water
½ cup sugar
2 teaspoons salt

1. Peel, wash, and dry the pears, and reserve.

2. In an oversized glass jar large enough to hold all of the pears and the pickling ingredients, place the vinegar, water, sugar, and salt. Mix with a wooden spoon until the sugar and salt are completely dissolved.

3. Place the pears in the jar, mix thoroughly, then close the jar. (A jar with a plastic screw top is preferred. If unavailable, place a piece of plastic wrap over the mouth of the jar before putting the lid on.) Allow to stand in the refrigerator for at least 3 days, untouched, to ensure that the pears absorb the pickling ingredients. Covered and refrigerated, they will keep 3 to 4 months. Serve cold.

MY SUMMER SALAD
Hah Tin Sah Lut

This is a favorite salad of mine, one that I make often for my family. It is quite refreshing, best in summer, and best, I think, when eaten cold directly out of the refrigerator. Though it may be eaten immediately after preparation, I think it improves in flavor when left to marinate overnight in the refrigerator. The sweetness and sourness come through equally and pleasantly.

1 cup julienned cucumbers
¾ cup shredded carrots
¾ cup julienned celery
¼ cup scallions, white portions only, julienned
¼ cup Pickled Peaches (page 296)
4 tablespoons Crystal Sauce (page 43)

1. Place all the vegetables in a bowl with the pickled peaches and toss together well. Add the Crystal Sauce and mix until all ingredients are coated and well mixed. Taste before serving; you may wish to add a bit more sauce.

Serves 4 to 6

Note: As noted, this salad may be served at room temperature or cold. It also can be made in advance. It will keep, and even improve, over the course of a week. This versatile salad may also be wrapped in moistened rice papers and eaten as a salad roll, a delightful variation.

PICKLED PEAR SALAD
Wor Mei Lei Sah Lut

This is a perfect summer dish, refreshing and cold, with the tastes of vegetables just out of the ground mixed with the sweet tartness of the pickled pears. Each of the recommended garnishes enhances this salad.

½ cup Pickled Pears (page 297), julienned

1 cup julienned jícama

1 cup julienned sweet red peppers

3 tablespoons scallions, white portions only, julienned

2 teaspoons white vinegar

1 teaspoon sugar

½ teaspoon salt

1 tablespoon Scallion Oil (page 37)

1. Combine all ingredients in a bowl and toss thoroughly until well mixed. Refrigerate for at least 3 hours before serving. Serve either on a bed of Fried Noodles (page 253) or sprinkled with 3 tablespoons Cinnamon-Roasted Soybeans (page 311).

Serves 4 to 6

SOUR TURNIPS WITH GINGER
Soon Law Bak

This is a special salad of the Cantonese. It is served on special occasions such as weddings and the birthdays of one's grandparents. Children regard it fondly, and I recall looking forward to eating it at family gatherings.

2 pounds Chinese white turnips, both ends trimmed, peeled and cut in
    half lengthwise

1 teaspoon salt

1 tablespoon julienned fresh ginger

2 tablespoons sugar

3½ tablespoons white vinegar

½ teaspoon white pepper

1. Partially cut each length of turnip at ⅛-inch intervals along the length, but do not cut all the way through. After doing this, cut each sliced half into 2-inch segments.

2. Place the turnips in a bowl with the salt and allow to stand for an hour, to let excess water drain out. Remove the water and add the ginger, sugar, white vinegar, and white pepper. Mix thoroughly and place in refrigerator, covered with plastic wrap, for 4 hours. Serve cold with Hot Mustard (page 44), as the Chinese do.

Serves 4 to 6

PEPPER CABBAGE
Lot Yeh Choi

In Canton, where I grew up, there were miles and miles of cabbage fields, and we ate that vegetable in soups and stir-fries because of its sweetness. It was in America that I learned that cabbage could become coleslaw. What I have done with this dish is use the flavors of western China, of Szechuan and Hunan, to create a hot coleslaw-like salad.

2 pounds cabbage, cut into 1-inch-square pieces
1¼ teaspoons salt
½ sweet red pepper, cut into ¼-inch slices
2 tablespoons sugar
4½ tablespoons white vinegar
Pinch of white pepper
2 teaspoons Hot Oil (page 36)
2½ tablespoons peanut oil
10 small hot peppers

1. In a large bowl mix the cabbage with the salt and allow to sit for 2 hours. Drain off all liquid.

2. Add the red pepper, sugar, vinegar, white pepper, and Hot Oil and mix.

3. Heat a wok over high heat for 30 seconds. Add the peanut oil. When a wisp of white smoke appears, add the hot peppers. Stir-fry until peppers turn dark brown or black. Add to the cabbage mixture and mix well.

4. Refrigerate for 24 hours before serving.

   Serves 4 to 6

POTATO SALAD
Fou Sui Sah Lut

Traditionally, sweet potatoes are an integral part of the diet of Buddhist monks. Not only do the monks eat them, but they raise them as well. This is my variation of a salad eaten in Canton and made with this special vegetable.

1¼ pounds sweet potatoes or yams

3 tablespoons white vinegar

1 teaspoon sesame oil

1½ tablespoons sugar

1 teaspoon salt

1 teaspoon chopped fresh coriander

1. Peel, wash, and dry the sweet potatoes. Cut into ¼-inch by 2-inch julienne. Place in a bowl and add the vinegar, sesame oil, sugar, and salt. Mix together thoroughly, then cover and refrigerate overnight. Sprinkle on the chopped fresh coriander and mix. Serve cool.

Serves 4 to 6

PICKLED CAULIFLOWER
War Mei Yeh Choi Far

8 cups water

3 cloves garlic, peeled

1 slice fresh ginger, at least 1 inch wide

2 pounds fresh cauliflower, cut into 1½-inch flowerets

1 cup sugar

1 cup white vinegar

3 cups cold water

¼ teaspoon salt

1. In a large pot, bring water to a boil with garlic and ginger. Add the cauliflower and water-blanch for 30 to 45 seconds. Do not overcook. Turn off the heat, remove from heat, and run cold water into pot until cauliflower cools. Drain.

2. Place the sugar, vinegar, cold water, and salt in an oversized glass jar. (A jar with a plastic screw top is preferred.) Stir with a wooden spoon to ensure that the sugar and salt are completely dissolved. Add the cauliflower, ginger, and garlic and stir. Cover and refrigerate for 24 hours before serving. Serve cold. This will keep, covered and refrigerated, for 2 to 3 months.

SPICY CAULIFLOWER SALAD
Yeh Choi Far Sah Lut

Here is another variation on the theme of cauliflower. It is from Hong Kong, where many of the food traditions of Asia meet. This salad is of Indonesian origin, and the yellowness provided by the turmeric reminds the Chinese of gold.

1 head cauliflower (about 1½ pounds)

8 cups water

1 teaspoon fresh or frozen turmeric, minced (see note below)

1 teaspoon minced ginger

2 cloves garlic, minced

1 cup white vinegar

½ cup sugar

1 teaspoon salt

1½ cups water

1. Cut the flowerets from the cauliflower into pieces 2½ inches long by 1½ inches wide. Wash and drain them.

2. Place 8 cups of water in a large pot. Bring the water to a boil, add the cauliflower, and cook for 10 to 15 seconds, until the flowerets whiten slightly. Remove from the heat and run cold water into the pot. Drain the cauliflower, put back in the pot, and run cold water over it again. Drain. Put cauliflower in a bowl and reserve.

3. Place all other ingredients in the pot and bring to a boil. Stir to dissolve the sugar. Turn off the heat, pour the mixture over the cauliflower, and mix well so that the flowerets are covered and turn bright yellow. Place the bowl, covered, in the refrigerator for at least 12 hours, or overnight. Serve cold. Leftovers may be kept in a jar, refrigerated, for 4 to 6 weeks.

Serves 4 to 6

Note: Fresh or frozen turmeric can be found in Indian, Thai, and Mexican markets.

JÍCAMA AND CARROT SALAD
Sah Gut Gum Sun Sah Lut

Jícama, that favorite of American Southwest cooking, is known as *sah gut* in China. This root is most popular in Canton, where it is eaten in stir-fries, soups, and salads. Often the Chinese just peel its outer skin and eat it as is, because of its sweetness. Carrots in China are *gum sun*, or "golden shoots."

6 cups cold water
1 teaspoon salt
1 pound carrots, trimmed, peeled, and cut into 2-inch by ¼-inch sticks
¾ pound jícama, peeled and cut into 2-inch by ¼-inch sticks
3 tablespoons white vinegar
3 tablespoons sugar (see note below)
1¼ teaspoons salt

1. In a pot over high heat, place the 6 cups cold water and 1 teaspoon salt. Bring to a boil, add the carrot sticks, and blanch for 20 seconds. Turn off the heat and run cold water into the pot to cool. Repeat. Drain off the water and allow the carrots to cool. (Water-blanching the carrots allows them to absorb the seasonings.)

2. In a large bowl place the carrots, jícama, vinegar, sugar, and 1¼ teaspoons salt. Mix well together. Refrigerate, covered, for at least 4 hours or overnight. Serve cold.

Serves 4 to 6

Note: This salad is quite sweet, which is the way it is served in China. If you wish it less sweet, reduce the amount of sugar, to taste.

Lotus Root Salad
Lin Ngau Sah Lut

Lotus root is a must at Chinese New Year, because its name, *lin ngau*, when said quickly, sounds like the word for plentiful, *lin yau*, reminding the Chinese that every year is plentiful. It is therefore a vegetable of exceedingly good luck.

1 pound lotus root, washed, peeled, and cut into ¼-inch-thick round
    slices
2 tablespoons sugar
2 tablespoons white vinegar
1 teaspoon salt

1. Mix all ingredients in a bowl. Cover and refrigerate at least 4 hours, or overnight. This salad will keep for 3 to 4 days.

    Serves 4 to 6

Bean Sprout Salad
Nga Choi Sah Lut

In Canton, bean sprout salad is a dish for all seasons, for bean sprouts are available the year round, as are scallions. I have made this a summer salad with the addition of red peppers. In China sweet red peppers are rare, except in the summer months.

1 tablespoon peanut oil
1 pound bean sprouts
1 medium-sized sweet red pepper, thinly sliced
3 scallions, trimmed, cut into 1½-inch sections, and white portions
    quartered lengthwise
2 tablespoons white vinegar
4 teaspoons sugar
½ tablespoon salt
1 teaspoon sesame oil

1. Heat a wok over high heat for 1 minute. Add the peanut oil and coat the wok with a spatula. When a wisp of white smoke appears, add the bean sprouts. Stir-fry for 30 to 45 seconds. Add the peppers and stir. Add the scallions and stir. Remove the vegetables, place in a strainer, and allow the liquid to drain off.

2. Place the vegetables in a large bowl. Add vinegar, sugar, salt, and sesame oil and mix well. Refrigerate overnight before serving.

   Serves 4 to 6

PEPPER AND CUCUMBER SALAD
Lot Jiu Ching Gua Sah Lut

Cucumbers have been known in China from as early as the fifth century, but sweet peppers came later from the West, as did tomatoes. No matter. The Chinese kitchen, particularly in the south, is adaptable. Thus this salad.

2 large cucumbers, about 2 pounds
1 teaspoon salt
2½ teaspoons sugar
1½ tablespoons white vinegar
1½ teaspoons sesame oil
½ cup julienned sweet red peppers

1. Peel, wash, and dry cucumbers. Cut in half lengthwise and remove seeds with a spoon or grapefruit knife. Slice into ¼-inch pieces.

2. In a bowl, thoroughly mix the cucumber slices with the salt and allow to rest for 1 hour. This will remove excess water from the cucumbers. Drain off the water and add the sugar, white vinegar, and sesame oil. Mix well. Add the julienned peppers and toss together. Allow to marinate, covered and refrigerated, overnight. Serve cold.

   Serves 4 to 6

Spiced Tientsin Bok Choy Salad

Tientsin Lot Bok Choy

This combination of Tientsin bok choy and fresh chilies is a recipe found in Shanghai and farther north as far as Beijing. The chilies provide a subtle hotness to the dish, rather than overpowering it.

2 pounds Tientsin bok choy, white portions only (10 cups tightly packed)
1½ teaspoons salt
½ large sweet yellow pepper, cut into ¼-inch julienne (½ cup)
3 tablespoons white vinegar
2 tablespoons sugar
1½ teaspoons sesame oil
½ teaspoon Hot Oil (page 36)
2 tablespoons peanut oil
10 small hot chili peppers

1. Cut the bok choy stalks diagonally in ¼-inch slices. Place in a large bowl. Sprinkle with salt and mix well with hands. Cover and refrigerate overnight.

2. Drain off the liquid. Add the yellow peppers, vinegar, sugar, sesame oil, and Hot Oil. Toss together. Reserve.

3. Heat a wok over high heat for 30 seconds. Add the peanut oil and heat until hot, about 30 seconds. Add the chilies and stir until they turn quite dark. Turn off the heat. Pour the contents of the wok into the bowl and mix well. Cover and refrigerate for 8 hours, or overnight.

Serves 4 to 6

Note: This salad will keep refrigerated for 1 week.

Guor

Fruits and Nuts,
Sweets and Snacks

Customarily the Chinese do not eat sweet desserts at the end of their meal. Fresh fruit is the refreshment of choice, and tart green apples, hard sweet pears, oranges, and tangerines are favored. In Canton, where I grew up, the tropical climate gave us pineapples, papayas, mangoes, and melons as well. Never would we eat *bang*, the sweet cakes of the teahouse.

We ate nuts, seeds, and beans, sweetened or salted, as snacks. Often we preserved sweet fruits in honey. And we had sweet steamed cakes and pastries, even the cake of the Lunar New Year, made of "eight precious rice" (glutinous rice) steamed into a cake, inside of which were lotus seeds, almonds, red dates, sweet bean paste, several kinds of candied fruit, and sugarcane syrup. But never as dessert.

These days we see all manner of Chinese "desserts," complicated efforts such as sweetened custards and spongy cakes, designed to duplicate European cakes. Most of these were born in Shanghai, that most Western of Chinese cities, created by chefs as oversweet imitations of what they saw Westerners liked. On a recent visit to Shanghai I recall signs offering "ice cream sodas," which turned out to be scoops of vanilla ice cream dropped into black coffee. Coffee shops abound in Shanghai, in Hong Kong, and in Chinese enclaves of Western cities, and they are pleasant, but their tradition is not Chinese.

There are, to be sure, fine traditional sweets in China—steamed sweet cakes, sweet nut soups, buns meant to be enjoyed in coffee houses and in tea shops. Occasionally you will see them on the carts of the dim sum restaurants. Never are they served as desserts.

In this section you will find a selection of authentic Chinese sweets—a sweet cake and a variation, sweet and salted nuts and beans, sweet soups, and sweetened fruit preparations. Make them, enjoy them (as I believe you will), have them as snacks or with coffee or tea. But do not consider them to be desserts.

Unless you would rather. In which case, enjoy them as such.

WATER CHESTNUT CAKE
Sang Maw Mah Tai Goh

The Chinese esteem this sweet vegetarian preparation highly. Not only is it tasty, but it is a most versatile food that can be enjoyed in three distinctive ways. My grandmother loved this combination of water chestnuts and sugar very much and would feed it to me and to my brother constantly. It was, she used to say, good for purifying one's system, good for combating measles, good for just about anything.

Water Chestnut Cake can be eaten as is, or it can be pan-fried or batter-fried. In the latter two cases, the cake must be made (steamed) a day in advance and then refrigerated. The recipes for these variations follow.

Water Chestnut Cake can be frozen, either whole or in slices. To reheat, allow the cake to return to room temperature, then steam for 15 to 20 minutes, or until heated through. The cake can also be pan-fried or batter-fried after defrosting.

1¼-pound can water chestnuts (see note below)

1¾ cups sugar

3¾ cups boiling water

½ pound water chestnut powder

1 cup cold water

1. Drain the water chestnuts and dice finely. Reserve. Dissolve the sugar in boiling water. Reserve.

2. In a mixing bowl combine the water chestnut powder with the 1 cup cold water. Add the sugar water and the diced water chestnuts and mix well. Then pour this mixture into a wok and heat over medium heat. Using a metal spatula, stir continuously in one direction for 5 to 7 minutes, until it is very thick and pasty.

3. Grease a 9-inch-square cake pan with peanut oil. Pour the chestnut mixture into the pan and place it in a steamer. Steam the cake for 30 to 45 minutes, until it is firmly set and translucent. Remove from the heat and allow to settle and cool slightly. Slice as you would a cake and serve.

Serves 10 to 12

Note: To make this cake, canned water chestnuts are as good as fresh water chestnuts. Moreover, the use of the canned variety will save you about an hour of peeling time.

Since this recipe will make 10 to 12 servings, it may be cut into sections for freezing. Once frozen and defrosted, it may not be refrozen. However, a section, once defrosted, will keep refrigerated for 8 to 10 days, as will a fresh unfrozen cake.

PAN-FRIED WATER CHESTNUT CAKE
Jin Mah Tai Goh

½ Water Chestnut Cake (page 308)
2 to 3 tablespoons peanut oil

1. Prepare the Water Chestnut Cake, 1 day ahead of the intended day of use. Refrigerate, unsliced.

2. Cut the chilled cake into pieces 2½ inches by ¼ inch. Pour 2 to 3 tablespoons peanut oil into a 9-inch cast-iron skillet. Heat over high heat until a wisp of white smoke appears. Pan-fry the cake slices until golden brown. Drain and serve immediately.

Serves 10 to 12

BATTER-FRIED WATER CHESTNUT CAKE

Jah Mah Tai Goh

½ cup flour
½ cup cornstarch
2½ teaspoons baking powder
5 ounces cold water
1 tablespoon peanut oil
½ Water Chestnut Cake (page 308)
4 to 5 cups peanut oil, for deep frying

1. In a large mixing bowl combine the flour, cornstarch, and baking powder. Add the cold water while stirring continuously with chopsticks or a wooden spoon, and keep stirring until batter is well blended. Add 1 tablespoon peanut oil and mix until the oil is blended in smoothly. If the batter seems too thick, add a bit more water.

2. Heat 4 to 5 cups peanut oil in a wok to 350°F to 375°F.

3. Slice the Water Chestnut Cake into pieces 2½ inches by 1 inch. Dip into the batter with tongs or chopsticks. Place slices in the oil, 3 or 4 at a time, and cook, turning, for 2 to 3 minutes, or until the pieces are golden. Drain and serve immediately.

Serves 10 to 12

Eight-Star Anise

CINNAMON-ROASTED SOYBEANS
Gtai Ji Gok Bok Dau

This is a dish I recall enjoying very much as a child. We would be given bowls of these soybeans, freshly picked, steamed, then dried in the sun. They were summertime snacks to which we added a little salt, if we wished, or ate just as they were. They dry-roast quite nicely in an oven, and I expect that if you tried to sun-dry them you would provide a feast for any passing birds. Do not expect the beans to be crisp; they are supposed to be a bit chewy.

1 pound fresh soybeans
1½ teaspoons salt
1 tablespoon Shao-Hsing wine or sherry
1 tablespoon sesame oil
6 pieces star anise
4 cinnamon sticks

1. Place the soybeans in a large bowl. Wash 3 times. Cover with water and soak overnight. Drain the water. Place the beans in a 9-inch-round cake pan with the salt, wine, sesame oil, star anise, and cinnamon sticks and mix well.

2. Steam the soybeans, mixing twice, for 45 minutes (pages 27–28). Remove from the heat. Drain off any liquid. Place on a nonstick baking sheet and roast for 30 minutes in a 350°F oven. Turn beans several times during roasting.

3. Remove from the oven. Serve hot, as a side dish to a salad or as a first course. Or serve as a snack, perhaps with white wine or with cocktails.

Serves approximately 8 to 10

Note: These beans are also delicious as a crisp snack. If you wish them very crisp rather than chewy, allow them to remain in the oven for an additional 10 to 15 minutes. They will become darker, will shrink a bit, and become crisp. They can also be made crisp at a later date simply by roasting for 20 minutes in a 350°F oven.

HONEY WALNUTS
Tim Hop Toh

There are several recipes for these sweetened nuts. This recipe is the classic. Made with care, it is by far the best version of this traditional Shanghai dish.

10 cups water
¾ pound freshly shelled walnuts
⅓ cup water
4 tablespoons sugar
5 cups peanut oil

1. Bring 5 cups water to a boil in a wok. Place the walnuts in boiling water for 5 minutes to remove the bitter taste. Remove from the water, drain, then run cold water over the walnuts. Drain again, then place back in the wok with another 5 cups water. Bring to a boil and cook for another 5 minutes. Repeat the draining process. Set aside and allow to drain.

2. Wash the wok and dry well. Add ⅓ cup water and bring to a boil. Then add the sugar, stirring constantly. Let boil for 1 minute. Add the walnuts. Stir until the walnuts are coated with sugar and the remaining liquid in the wok has evaporated. With a spatula remove the glazed walnuts to a Chinese strainer and allow to strain over a bowl. Reserve.

3. Wash the wok with a brush in extremely hot water to remove sugar. Dry.

4. Heat the wok over high heat for 1 minute. Place the peanut oil in the wok. When a wisp of white smoke appears, lower the strainer with walnuts into the oil. Fry for 4 to 5 minutes, until walnuts turn golden brown. Turn off the heat. Remove the walnuts from the oil and drain over a bowl. Once drained, place the walnuts on a large baking sheet and separate them while warm so they will not stick together. When cool, serve or place in plastic jars for storage.

Serves approximately 8 to 10

Note: Honey walnuts may be frozen for 3 to 4 weeks. Allow to come to room temperature before serving. Surprisingly, they remain quite crisp even after freezing.

SWEET FRIED BANANAS
Ja Heung Jiu

People in Shanghai claim this is another of their sweet inventions, and they may be correct. However, I remember these bananas in my house as a little girl, so perhaps Canton shared in the creation.

Batter ingredients

1 cup flour
2 tablespoons sugar
2 teaspoons baking powder
7 ounces water, at room temperature
1 tablespoon peanut oil

To complete the dish

2 large or 3 medium-sized firm bananas
5 cups peanut oil
20 mint leaves, for garnish

1. Combine the batter ingredients in a bowl. If too dry, add a bit more water. The batter should have the consistency of pancake batter.

2. Break the bananas into 10 equal pieces, each about 1½ inches long. Drop the banana pieces into the batter and coat evenly.

3. Heat a wok over high heat for 1 minute. Add the peanut oil and heat to 350°F or until a wisp of white smoke appears. Deep-fry the bananas for 3 to 4 minutes, 5 pieces at a time, until they turn golden brown and crisp. Turn off the heat, remove from the wok, drain, and serve immediately, garnished with mint leaves.

Serves 5

BANANA SPRING ROLLS
Heung Jiu Chun Geun

This simple but delicious dessert combines the method of the dim sum kitchen with fresh fruit, and the result is most gratifying.

2 small bananas

Paste ingredients

1 tablespoon cornstarch
1 tablespoon cold water
½ cup boiling water

To complete the dish

4 square Shanghai spring roll skins (let stand at room temperature for 1
    hour in advance)
5 cups peanut oil

1. Peel the bananas and cut off both ends. Cut each into 2-inch sections. Cut each section into quarters, lengthwise.

2. To make the paste, stir the cornstarch and cold water together. Add the boiling water and stir into a smooth, thick paste.

3. Separate the spring roll skins and cut each into 4 equal pieces. Cover with plastic wrap. Use 1 at a time. Place a piece of banana diagonally across the corner of a square. Brush the corner with paste, then fold and roll. Brush the edges of the square with paste and fold the sides inward as you roll to create a tight, sealed cylinder.

4. Heat a wok over high heat for 40 seconds. Add the peanut oil and heat to 350°F. Turn off the heat. Add one-third of the banana rolls, allow to cook for 1 minute, then turn the heat back on. These cook quickly, in no more than 2 minutes. Keep turning the rolls and regulating heat so they will not burn. Remove when done. Repeat until all 16 have been fried. Serve immediately.

Serves 8

STEAMED APPLES
Jing Ping Gua

What is special about this dish, which was created in Shanghai, is the sweet soup that results from condensation as the apples steam.

6 cups cold water
3 tablespoons white vinegar
6 small to medium-sized Macintosh apples, unpeeled
¾ cup sweet red bean paste

1. Place the water and vinegar in a large mixing bowl. Keep at hand.
2. Cut the tops off the apples, about ¼ of the way down. Reserve the tops. Place the apples and the tops immediately in vinegar and water to keep from browning. Scoop out the cores of the apples and a bit of the inner flesh and fill the holes with 1½ to 2 tablespoons of red bean paste.
3. Place each filled apple in a small Chinese rice bowl or soup bowl, arrange in a steamer, place the tops of the apples back on, and steam for 30 minutes.
4. The apples are done when they are slightly soft to the touch and when there is some condensed juice in the bowls. They should be served immediately, hot.

Serves 6

Note: Other fillings may be used instead of the red bean paste, such as lotus seed paste, black bean paste, chestnut puree, or date filling. But red bean paste is the filling of tradition.

WALNUT SOUP
Hop Toh Wu

The word *wu* translates as "thick and smooth." It is used here to differentiate this dish from what the Chinese would call a *tong*, or soup. The word *wu* is always used for sweet foods that are ground or pureed. To make them traditionally, special bowls, *sah poon*, are used. These have a series of interior ridges and are used to grind rice and nuts to powder. Nuts are always fried before being ground in the *sah poon*, probably the first-ever food processor.

¼ cup short- or medium-grain rice

8 cups cold water

1 cup raw walnuts

3 cups peanut oil

3 ounces rock sugar or regular sugar

2 teaspoons finely chopped fresh mint

6 sprigs fresh mint

1. Place the rice in a large bowl. Wash 3 times by rubbing between the hands under running water. Drain. Add 1 cup cold water and allow to soak 6 hours, or overnight.

2. Add 3 cups cold water to a pot. Cover and bring to a boil over high heat. Add the walnuts and stir. Bring back to a boil. Allow to boil for 4 minutes. Turn off the heat. Run cold water into the pot. Drain. Rinse and drain again. Remove the nuts and allow to dry.

3. Heat a wok over high heat for 40 seconds. Add the peanut oil and heat to 350°F. Place the walnuts in a Chinese strainer and lower into the oil. Fry for 3 minutes, or until nuts turn light brown, regulating the heat as they fry. Remove from the oil. Drain. Allow to cool (see note below).

4. Place walnuts in a food processor and process until they are powdered. Reserve.

5. Drain the rice well. Place in the food processor and process to a powder. Place the rice powder and nut powder in a bowl, mix well with 1 cup cold water until smooth, and reserve.

6. Place 3 cups cold water and rock sugar in a pot. Cover and bring to a boil over high heat. Stir until sugar is dissolved. Add the rice-nut mixture to the pot gradually, stirring as you do. This ensures that the soup will not have lumps. Mix well. Lower heat and simmer for 7 minutes, stirring constantly to avoid sticking. Turn off the heat. Transfer to individual bowls, sprinkle with chopped fresh mint, place a sprig of mint in the center of each bowl, and serve.

Serves 4

Note: The walnuts are boiled to remove any trace of bitterness. They may be prepared in advance, up to but not including the step in which they are powdered. The prepared nuts will keep, frozen in a closed container, for at least 2 months.

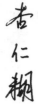

ALMOND SOUP
Hung Yun Wu

This soup, like the previous one, is a favorite sweet snack. It is made in generally the same way. In fact, all manner of nuts may be used for these soups, or *wull*, such as peanuts, pecans, and black or white sesame seeds.

¼ cup short- or medium-grain rice
5 cups cold water
3 cups peanut oil
1 cup raw almonds
3 ounces rock sugar or regular sugar

1. Place the rice in a large bowl. Wash 3 times by rubbing between the hands under running water. Drain. Add 1 cup cold water and allow to soak 6 hours, or overnight.

2. Heat a wok over high heat for 40 seconds. Add the peanut oil. Heat to 325°F. Place the almonds in a Chinese strainer and lower into the oil. Fry for 2½ to 3 minutes, until the nuts turn light brown. Regulate the heat as you fry. Remove from the oil. Drain well. Allow to cool. Place ¾ cup almonds in a food processor, process to a powder, and reserve. Reserve remaining almonds for garnish.

3. Drain the rice well. Place in the food processor and process to a powder. Place the rice powder and nut powder in a bowl and mix well with 1 cup cold water until smooth. Reserve.

4. Place the remaining 3 cups cold water and the rock sugar in a pot. Cover and bring to a boil over high heat. Stir until the sugar is dissolved. Add the rice-nut mixture to the pot gradually, stirring as you do. This ensures that the soup will not have lumps. Mix well. Lower the heat and simmer for 7 minutes, stirring constantly to avoid sticking. Turn off the heat. Transfer to individual bowls and gently place several of the reserved almonds on the surface of each. (The soup will be thick enough to support them.) Serve immediately.

Serves 4

Note: If you use peanuts, you may follow the instructions in this recipe. If you use pecans, follow the steps outlined in the Walnut Soup recipe (page 316). Boiling pecans removes bitterness, as with walnuts.

SUMMER BEAN SOUP
Lok Dau Sah

Here is a soup similar to the previous two. It is made from green mung beans, which are eaten primarily in summer. The Chinese believe that mung beans, with the additional taste and fragrance of rue, help to rid the body of impurities. In fact, it is said by the elderly that this soup relieves prickly heat. Rue, the herb, in its raw form has a bitterness to it that belies its fine fragrance. The aroma is apparent as the soup cooks, and then it vanishes—as does the herb's bitterness when the soup is done.

½ pound Chinese green mung beans (see note below)

7 cups cold water

6 sprigs rue

4½ ounces rock sugar or brown sugar

1. Place the beans in a pot, cover with cold tap water, and wash 3 times between the palms to remove grit. Drain.

2. Place the beans back in a pot, add the 7 cups cold water, turn the heat to high, cover the pot, and bring to a boil. Add the rue, stir together with the beans, lower the heat, and allow to simmer, covered, 1½ to 2 hours, until the beans are tender. Leave a small opening at the edge of the pot cover during the simmering process. Stir occasionally.

3. When the beans are tender and breaking apart, add the sugar. Stir and cook until the sugar dissolves, about 5 to 7 minutes for rock sugar, immediately for brown sugar.

4. Turn off the heat. Pour the bean soup into a bowl. Remove the sprigs of rue. Eat hot or allow the soup to cool to room temperature, then refrigerate, covered, for 8 hours. Serve very cool, from a tureen, in individual bowls.

Serves 6

Note: Green mung beans usually come in 1-pound packages. This recipe will produce a soup that is moderately sweet. It can be made sweeter, to taste, with additional sugar.

RED BEAN SOUP
Hung Dau Sah

This a soup of celebration, a classic served usually during the Lunar New Year period. It is usually eaten hot or warm. But it can be eaten cool, which I prefer, particularly when the weather is warm.

½ pound Chinese red beans (see note below)
7 cups cold water
4½ ounces rock sugar or brown sugar

1. Place the beans in a pot, cover with cold tap water, and rinse 3 times, rubbing between the palms, to remove grit. Drain.

2. Place beans back in pot and add the 7 cups cold water. Turn the heat to high, cover the pot, and bring to a boil. Stir the beans, lower the heat, and allow to simmer 1½ to 2 hours, until the beans are tender. Leave a small opening at the edge of the pot cover during cooking. Stir occasionally.

3. When the beans are tender and coming apart, add the sugar. Cook until sugar dissolves, about 5 minutes for rock sugar, almost immediately for brown sugar.

4. Turn off heat. Eat hot or pour the bean soup into a bowl and allow to cool to room temperature. Refrigerate, covered, for 8 hours. Serve very cool, ladling from a tureen into individual bowls.

Serves 6

Note: These beans come in 1-pound packages. This recipe will produce a bean soup that is moderately sweet. If you prefer, you may add more sugar, to taste.

INDEX